Darrell Kauffman

D1272063

Understanding the Times

PROPHETIC MESSAGES
Delivered at the 2nd International Congress
on Prophecy, New York City

—EDITORS—
DR. WILLIAM CULBERTSON
HERMAN B. CENTZ

PRODUCED FOR
AMERICAN ASSOCIATION FOR JEWISH EVANGELISM
WINONA LAKE, INDIANA, BY

ZONDERVAN PUBLISHING HOUSE
GRAND RAPIDS, MICHIGAN

Two of the three addresses by Dr. Alva J. McClain, President of Grace Theological Seminary, those entitled *Premillennialism as a Philosophy of History* and *The Spirituality of the Millennial Kingdom*, were originally part of a series delivered by him in course of the *W. H. Griffith Thomas Lectureship* at Dallas Theological Seminary in November of 1954 and later published in *Bibliotheca Sacra*, the contents of which are fully copyrighted. Presented by Dr. McClain at the Second International Congress on Prophecy, they are reproduced here with the cordial permission of the editor of *Bibliotheca Sacra*. In expanded form the same material is to appear as part of a volume on *The Greatness of the Kingdom* in a projected set of Dr. McClain's theological works, all rights to which are reserved by the author.

Many of the Bible texts in this book are quoted from the American Standard Edition of the Revised Bible, copyright 1929 by the Division of Christian Education, National Council of Churches, and used by permission.

FOREWORD

Midway in 1955, when Executive Director A. B. Machlin released the information that the American Association for Jewish Evangelism was prepared to sponsor a Second International Congress on Prophecy, the immediate and enthusiastic response to the announcement revealed the fact that men of God in many quarters had been led to feel that the time was again ripe for such a gathering.

World conditions had changed but little since the previous Congress met in 1952, but within the Church, as we conceive of it, considerable unrest had been created during the intervening years by novel methods of prophetic interpretation, especially with reference to the blessed hope of the Lord's return for His saints. Many were engaging in doubtful disputations to no personal profit, and in a general way the disturbance seemed to affect detrimentally the life and testimony of the household of faith in some important areas.

The need for a clearing of the atmosphere was so keenly felt that all the honored brethren whose messages are contained in this volume were willing to leave their appointed places of ministry in order to meet at Calvary Baptist Church, New York City, the week of November 6-13, for fellowship in, and conference and testimony about, the Word of God in relation to the future.

The Lord very graciously made Himself known among us. We were a band of people whose hearts had been touched by Him. No one expected or received any remuneration. To be with other brethren in the Lord's presence was reward enough. Strong men accustomed to bearing the burdens and heat of the day had tears in their eyes when parting time came. It was good and pleasant to dwell together in oneness of mind and heart, and the anointing of the Spirit rested on the exposition of the Word like the dew of Hermon on the fields of God.

The Congress was blest by the chairmanship of Dr. V. Raymond Edman, president of Wheaton College; the generous hospitality of Dr. John S. Wimbish, the Rev. Richard Hamilton, and the staff, officers, and congregation of Calvary Baptist Church; the general directive genius of Dr. A. B. Machlin; and the financial backing of the American Association of Jewish Evangelism, without which this tremendous undertaking could not have been accomplished.

The proceedings of the Congress, expressing the innermost faith of those who took part in it, are now placed in your hands in the form of this book. You will find no shibboleths in it, but a wonderful unity on essentials, characterized by a complete freedom of expression.

It is the hope of the editors that this volume will find a place in your heart and home; and may the truth of God here contained illumine the path of your Christian pilgrimage until the dawning of the perfect day.

Maranatha!

WILLIAM CULBERTSON
HERMAN B. CENTZ

Chicago, Illinois

CONTENTS

Foreword 5

1. Understanding the Times................................... 9
   William Culbertson

2. Premillennialism as a Philosophy of History................... 20
   Alva J. McClain

3. The Various Times of Divine Revelation...................... 26
   John G. Mitchell

4. The Various Methods of Divine Revelation.................. 33
   John G. Mitchell

5. The Crown Rights of the Crucified............................. 44
   William Culbertson

6. The Conflict of the Ages... 53
   Wilbur M. Smith

7. Christ Incarnate in Conflict with Satan........................ 73
   Wilbur M. Smith

8. The Lord's Return in Patristic Literature..................... 84
   William F. Kerr

9. Tribulation for the Church — But Not the Tribulation.. 98
   William F. Kerr

10. The Prophets Speak to the Twentieth Century...........107
    Richard A. Elvee

11. The Times of the Gentiles....................................116
    John F. Walvoord

12. Will the Church Go Through the Tribulation?...........125
    John F. Walvoord

13. The Mystery of Godliness.....................................135
    Roy L. Laurin

14. Current Trends in Eschatological Beliefs....................142
    Herman A. Hoyt

Contents

15. The Blessed Hope and Holiness of Life......................152
    Claude A. Ries

16. Eschatology According to Christ.............................159
    S. Maxwell Coder

17. The Marriage Supper of the Lamb.............................171
    Robert T. Ketcham

18. Shadows of Armageddon......................................180
    W. R. Wallace

19. Ecumenicity, the True and the False........................190
    Harry J. Hager

20. The Pretribulation Rapture and the Commentators...........198
    Alva J. McClain

21. The Parables of the Kingdom...............................208
    John F. Walvoord

22. The Threefold Ministry of Christ—Prophet, Priest, King..219
    Peter Hoogendam

23. The Testimony of Jesus in the Book of Revelation......228
    Peter Hoogendam

24. Israel and the End of History.............................236
    Roy L. Laurin

25. The Doctrine of the Lord's Return in the Scriptures.......242
    William F. Kerr

26. Arnold Toynbee and the Jews..............................251
    Frank E. Gaebelein

27. The Spirituality of the Millennial Kingdom...............264
    Alva J. McClain

28. As It Was In the Days of Noah............................271
    M. R. DeHaan

29. The Trump of God...279
    Herman A. Hoyt

1

UNDERSTANDING THE TIMES

by WILLIAM CULBERTSON, D.D.

I invite you to open your Bibles to the twelfth chapter of I Chronicles. There has been assigned to me the responsibility and the privilege of speaking on the Congress theme, *Understanding the Times,* taken from verse 32: "And of the children of Issachar, which were men that had understanding of the times, to know what Israel ought to do; the heads of them were two hundred; and all their brethren were at their commandment."

The Lord Jesus Christ, when He was on earth, made it plain that He was to be found in every part of the Old Testament. Of the sacred writings He said, "Ye search the Scriptures . . . and these are they which bear witness of me" (John 5:39, ASV). To a group of incredulous disciples, He said, ". . . all things must be fulfilled, which were written in the law of Moses, and in the prophets, and in the psalms, concerning me" (Luke 24:44). So the child of God is justified in looking for the Lord Jesus in all portions of the Old Testament.

Now one of the ways that we see Him on the pages of the Old Testament is in the lives of God's men whose experiences anticipated His. Often these characters and incidents become types of Him: They present a "divinely purposed illustration of some truth."

For example, we understand that Adam is typical of our Lord and Saviour Jesus Christ. Two quotations from the New Testament prove the fact. In I Corinthians 15:45, "The first man Adam was made a living soul; the last Adam a quickening spirit." And in Romans 5:17, ASV, ". . . if, by the trespass of the one

9

[Adam], death reigned through the one; much more shall they
that receive the abundance of grace and of the gift of righteousness reign in life through the one, even Jesus Christ." In these
comparisons and contrasts Adam prefigures our Lord.

We cannot read far in the Old Testament until we come
upon another person prophetic of our Lord—Isaac. You remember the twenty-second chapter of Genesis, to select just one
episode which reminds us of the Lord. Isaac's father took him
to Mt. Moriah, and there Abraham's only son willingly allowed
his father to bind him upon an altar and prepare to slay him.
And as the knife in Abraham's hand flashed in the Palestinian
sun, there was a voice that stayed his hand and directed Abraham to a ram caught in a nearby thicket. Strangely prophetic,
for many hundreds of years later God's only Son died on
Mt. Calvary for sinful men. Then there was no voice from
heaven to stay the sacrifice. He, the spotless Lamb of God,
died, "the righteous for the unrighteous, that he might bring
us to God" (I Pet. 3:18, ASV).

And then there is Joseph—hated of his brethren, sold for
twenty pieces of silver, and ultimately acknowledged as their
lord. And who among us does not know the New Testament
story of our blessed Lord who "came unto his own, and his
own received him not" (John 1:11), sold for thirty pieces of
silver, ultimately to be acknowledged as their Lord when they
see Him as the One whom they have pierced (Zech. 12:10).
And Jerusalem shall then echo with the mourning of a peni-
tent people.

There is also David, who in the time of his great sorrow
was betrayed by his own familiar friend. Our Lord applied to
Himself Psalm 41:9 when He said, "I speak not of you all . . .
but that the scripture may be fulfilled, He that eateth bread
with me hath lifted up his heel against me" (John 13:18).
David, when he wrote those words, undoubtedly was thinking
of the defection of Ahithophel; but our Lord said the incident
pointed to His betrayal by Judas Iscariot.

There are many personalities and incidents in the Old Testament which prefigure the Lord Jesus Christ, and those con-

tained in I Chronicles 12 are no exception. Pause with me, then, while I try to tell something of the story.

The chapter from which the theme of this Congress is taken contains in part the record of a period the days of which were filled with perplexity for David. He was the man God had anointed to reign over His people, Israel; but David was now a fugitive. Saul, although rejected by God, was still serving out his time as king, and David, hunted and hounded from pillar to post, had to flee from his presence. The last meeting of the two was when David, not for the first time, had Saul in his power. In pursuit of David, Saul and Abner had come down into the southern part of Palestine. Wearied by the hunt, Saul went to sleep in a trench, unaware that the object of his quest was near at hand. Abner and his company also went to sleep, and the king was left unprotected. Stealthily, David and Abishai made their way down into Saul's camp, even to the very trench where the king was sleeping. Abishai, one of those bloody sons of Zeruiah, said to David, ". . . let me smite him, I pray thee, with the spear to the earth at one stroke, and I will not smite him the second time," but David stayed his hand, saying in substance: Abishai, we can't with impunity lift our hands against God's anointed (I Sam. 26:1-9). So, taking Saul's spear and cruse of water, David departed. When Saul realized what had taken place, he sought a reconciliation, but David did not trust him. Instead David went down to Philistia, where his friend Achish gave him Ziklag, a city in the country, for his dwelling and center.

Seeking to find favor with Achish, David went out on several expeditions. He went out against the Amalekites actually, but when he made the report, he made it sound as though he had gone out against Israel. Achish believed David, and he was sure that David had made himself obnoxious in the sight of King Saul and in the sight of his brethren. So, for over a year and four months, according to the scriptural record (I Sam. 27:7), David dwelt among the Philistines. And then came the critical moment when the war between the Philistines and the Israelites was to be joined once again. While Achish was away at war, the Amalekites attacked Ziklag and David pursued them

and came back victorious. Meanwhile the Philistines fought at
Gilboa, up in the north, and Israel was defeated. Saul, having
tried at last to find out what God might say, and finding the
heavens above him as brass, had gone to the Witch of Endor,
but there was no help for him. He perished, and three of his
sons, Jonathan among them, perished with him on the ill-fated
slopes of Mt. Gilboa (I Chron. 10). Word about the tragedy,
came to David at Ziklag and one of the most tender laments
in all Scripture—a threnody that beggars description—is unfolded in the first chapter of II Samuel. David wept his heart
out for Saul and for Jonathan. He then asked God where he
should go. God said, "Unto Hebron."

This twelfth chapter of I Chronicles tells us of various men
who joined David, first at Ziklag and then at Hebron. It is an
imposing list. Men from Benjamin, from Saul's own tribe,
thoroughly disgusted by Saul while he was still king, joined
David in Ziklag. They were men who used slings, and were
able also to use bows and arrows. You read about them in the
early verses of I Chronicles 12. Another tribe was represented,
the tribe of Gad. They used the shield and spear, and the
Word of God says they had faces like lions and were swift as
roes upon the mountains. Ah, what men! Men who would en-
danger their lives for the cause of God's anointed! Then came
men from Benjamin and Judah. And there is an interesting word
about them in the earlier verses of I Chronicles 12, for when
these men came, David was not certain of them, and he asked
of them their intent and purpose. Amasai acted as their spokes-
man, and celebrated words are his (v. 18): "Thine are we,
David, and on thy side, thou son of Jesse: peace, peace be unto
thee, and peace be to thy helpers; for thy God helpeth thee."
That was true loyalty! According to the record one other tribe
was represented: Manasseh. These men had gone to David
while he was in exile. They had acknowledged their fealty to
him while he was a fugitive. Noble men they were!

Then David went to Hebron and these men went with him.
And during the seven and one-half years that he was there
others came, first from one tribe, then from another. All
thirteen tribes are represented here (yes, I mean thirteen—

Levi is included), and the number of them is given. Men armed for war, mighty men of valor, men not of a double heart— altogether over 340,000 in number came to Hebron to make David king.

But of this great number, two hundred men representing the thousands of Issachar are especially singled out. Look at it again (v. 32): "And of the children of Issachar, which were men that had understanding of the times, to know what Israel ought to do; the heads of them were two hundred; and all their brethren were at their commandment."

In this connection, I became interested in another passage where I came across 200 other men. This is a chapter from David's later life. Here it is, in II Samuel 15:12, ASV—"And Absalom sent for Ahithophel the Gilonite, David's counsellor . . . while he was offering the sacrifices. And the conspiracy was strong; for the people increased continually with Absalom." That day it seemed as though Absalom's revolt against his father David was just about to succeed. Now look at verse 11, ASV: "And with Absalom went two hundred men out of Jerusalem, that were invited, and went in their simplicity; and they knew not anything." They just went along! Someone said, "Let's go," and they said, "We're coming." No thought of seeking the mind of God; just going along.

I wonder, would it be too harsh to suggest that there were some who came to Hebron in a spirit like that? They just went along. You know how it is. When a movement gets started, there is a mob psychology that sweeps men along. But if you had taken each individual off to a corner and said to them, "Do you really believe that David is going to be king? Are you absolutely sure? So sure of it that you'd be willing to stake your life on the outcome of his cause?" Do you think that, so confronted, some of them might have started to waver a little bit? Or that perhaps there were others who were quite sure that David was going to be king, but were not at all sure that his strategy was right? But these men of Issachar were different. They had an understanding of the times and they knew what Israel ought to do.

Well, what ought Israel to do? In the first place, they knew they were not to make Ishbosheth, Saul's son, king in the room of his father. They were sure of that. You see, for a while there were those in Israel who thought that was the direction in which to move. Among them was Abner, the son of Ner, Saul's general. He was sure of it. But even Abner had to come to the conclusion that he had been wrong; so it is recorded in II Samuel 3:17, 18, ASV, that Abner said to those who followed him, "In times past ye sought for David to be king over you: now then do it; for Jehovah hath spoken of David, saying: By the hand of David I will save my people Israel out of the hand of the Philistines, and out of the hand of all their enemies." But you see, the sons of Issachar knew that from the beginning. They were not misled. They believed God and knew what His plan was.

I am sure there were those in Israel who said, "Why, that's all wrong. That's not the thing to do, and that is not the way to do it." But these children of Issachar stuck to their decision and history has proved them to be right. Now pardon me if I labor the point — some of you probably have it already. *It always pays to believe God.* I'd rather be on God's side and thought of by men as a fool, then to be lauded as the wisest man on earth and be accounted as a fool in God's sight. The sons of Issachar were that way. They had an understanding of the times and knew what Israel ought to do.

Now all this is an analogy. There is a parallel here, and it is this parallel which, under God, I'd like to stress in the rest of the message:

We are living in a day when men are not sure. Men have their notions and preferences, but all are agreed that these are difficult days. Therefore, say some, "The thing we need is a democracy where everyone has equal rights." Others say, "A benevolent dictator, that's what we need. Someone to make all the decisions for us." Well, others have tried that, and to their sorrow. Now, thank God for a democracy. I thank God for all the blessings that are mine as a citizen of the United States of America. But you and I know full well that neither democracy nor dictatorship is God's final answer for the times in which we are living, when there is war, crime, worldliness, materialism, godlessness, such as the world has never known before.

After all this, you are probably thinking, "What, then, is the answer? What is God aiming at? What is the ultimate in His program for man?" Well, let me say that there are people living in these days when God's King is rejected and is, to use a figure of speech, tarrying at Hebron, who like the sons of Issachar have an understanding of the times and know what God's people ought to do. This knowledge is theirs by the Word of God. For God has a program, and I think this program can be outlined in a few very meaningful Scripture texts.

But before we consider the several parts of this program, let us first put at the head of it God's over-all purpose as declared in predictive terms by Ezekiel 21:26, 27, ASV: "Thus saith the Lord Jehovah: Remove the mitre, and take off the crown: this shall be no more the same: exalt that which is low, and abase that which is high. I will overturn, overturn, overturn it . . . until he come whose right it is; and I will give it him"; or as restated in I Corinthians 15:25 as part of the New Testament revelation: "For he must reign, till he hath put all enemies under his feet." However long a period may intervene before these declarations of Holy Writ are fulfilled; and whatever may enter into the fabric of history, whether it be evil (Cf. II Tim. 3:13), or apostasy (Cf. II Thess. 2:3), or wars (Cf. Matt. 24:6); of this one thing we may be altogether confident: Even though for the time being it seems that right is on the scaffold and wrong on the throne, this state of affairs will not prevail forever. God is untiringly working toward the accomplishment of His ultimate purpose: "That in the dispensation of the fulness of times he might gather together (sum up) all things in Christ" (Eph. 1:10). "And he (the Lord Jesus Christ) shall be a priest upon his throne" (Zech. 6:13b), "and shall execute judgment and justice in the earth. . . . And this is his name whereby he shall be called, THE LORD OUR RIGHTEOUSNESS" (Jer. 23:5, 6).

And now that we have noted God's long range purpose, let us get back to His program for the present hour. I shall try to confine myself to four points:

First, according to Acts 15:14, ASV, it is a part of God's program "to take out from among them (the Gentiles) a people for his name." He has been doing that since the Day of Pentecost, saving men and women from among all nations and tongues who believe and trust His Son.

Second, according to Romans 11:5, God is also saving Jews. This is a wonderful word about Israel, that just as there were seven thousand of them in Elijah's day who had not bowed the knee to Baal, so there are today those who believe God's testimony concerning His Son and own Him as their Saviour: "the remnant according to the election of grace."

Third, believing Gentiles and believing Jews are being brought together and made one in Christ Jesus (Eph. 2:13-18), the middle wall of partition having been broken down and the Lord Jesus Himself becoming our peace. This, in the truest sense, is the Church. And the Word of God assures us that the day will come when even the "hardening in part (which) hath befallen Israel, until the fulness of the Gentiles be come in" will be taken away, and "all Israel shall be saved" (Rom. 11:25, 26, ASV). Meanwhile the Church waits for its completion, and there is the prospect that some Christian will one day have the privilege of bringing to Christ the last person to be added by the Spirit to the Body of Christ. What a privilege that will be! The completion of the Church will be signalized by the return of our Lord from heaven "with a shout, with the voice of the archangel, and with the trump of God." Then all of His redeemed, resurrected and living, shall be caught up together to meet the Lord in the air, to be forever with Him.

Long ago, in the days of Zerubbabel, a temple was built. When the builders were fitting the headstone into its place, the people shouted, "Grace, grace unto it" (Zech. 4:7, ASV). Somehow I cannot help believing that on that day when the temple not made with hands, the Church of the living God, in which the Holy Spirit is now resident, will be completed, the angelic hosts of heaven will raise the shout "Grace, grace unto it," for the glorious Son of God, the Stone which the builders rejected, will crown the whole structure as the apex stone — the head of the corner.

Fourth, God's program is manifold. It includes the winning of Jews to Christ, the calling out of a people for His name from among the Gentiles, and the completion of the Church. But He also has a purpose to accomplish in the political activities of the governments of men. For be men ever so unruly, God is still on His throne. And it is for precisely this reason, because "the heathen rage, the people imagine a vain thing, the kings of the earth set themselves, and the rulers take counsel together against the Lord and against his anointed" (Ps. 2:1,2), that this age will be climaxed by a gigantic conflict between the kingdoms of this world in the passing and the coming Kingdom of our God and of His Christ, in which Jerusalem and the people of Israel will be the principal battleground. Zechariah speaks of all nations being gathered against Jerusalem to battle (14:2), and in the Olivet Discourse our Lord gives us in His own words a vivid description of the crucial part of the conflict: "And they (the people of Israel) shall fall by the edge of the sword, and shall be led away captive into all nations: and Jerusalem shall be trodden down of the Gentiles, until the times of the Gentiles be fulfilled" (Luke 21:24).

Now the times of the Gentiles were initiated when God gave the people of Israel into the hands of Nebuchadnezzar, head of the mighty kingdom of Babylon, and the world empires figuring in prophecy have to run their course. But our Lord told us in the clearest of terms that the times of the Gentiles will be at an end when Jerusalem is no longer trodden down of the Gentiles. In other words, the day is coming when the Lord shall say, "It is enough." Then the Son of David — the Lord who is now at the Father's right hand, will have His enemies made the footstool of His feet. God's program, in its ultimate reaches, provides that the Stone cut out of the mountain without hands, falling upon the feet of the image of human government, shall become a mountain in the earth (Dan. 2:34). Then "the earth shall be filled with the knowledge of the glory of the Lord, as the waters cover the sea" (Hab. 2:14).

Think of it! God wants us to be the spiritual descendants of those two hundred children of Issachar. He wants us to under-

stand the times, to know the significance of world currents
swirling all around us, so that we shall never be subject to
them, never be found in consternation or fear, but always understand what the will of the Lord is. The children of Issachar
had an understanding of the times, and they knew what Israel
ought to do. You and I also have our work cut out for us. If
I were to sum up our responsibility as Christians in the present
hour, it would be in these words: *Believe — Stand — Live — Pray
— Work — Win.*

The first word, then, that I want to underscore is *Believe.*
It is this word that so truly characterized the early disciples, for
they, first of all and above all, were *believers.* As His children we
must believe God. Whatever men may say, however they may
scoff and ridicule, with this one thing we stand or fall: The
Bible is the inerrant and infallible Word of God. God has
spoken. *Believe!*

The second word is *Stand.* Beloved, these are days in which
men are not standing, but are being swept along with the
crowd, like the two hundred that followed Absalom. But the
Lord expects us to stand our ground! This effeminate kind of
Christianity which goes along with anything is not for us.
Do not be ashamed to stand for the Word of God. It will
seem infinitely worth while at the judgment seat of Christ.
Therefore, *Stand!*

The third word is *Live.* I have no use for the kind of
Christianity that is all theoretical. Unless you get down to
practical living, where being a Christian makes a decided difference, you haven't the right brand. These are days when we
must live for God, and that means purity of heart, sincerity
of soul, courage of spirit, and a heart concern for the souls of
others. It means out-and-out living for God. And in these days
when the lines between worldliness and Christianity are being
obliterated more and more, it is going to cost something. God
calls us to be separated unto Him. He calls us saints! Don't
go along with the world because others do. *Live* for God.

The fourth word is *Pray.* Oh, the need and power of prayer!
John Bunyan used Paul's phrase, "Praying with all prayer and

supplication in the Spirit." What do we know about that these days? *Pray!*

The fifth word is *Work*. Yes, the night is coming. Thank God, the day is coming too. But what about today's opportunities for God? I'm sure that if there are tears to be shed at the judgment seat of Christ, some of us are going to weep out our hearts because of the opportunities we have allowed to slip away while we were looking for something bigger. Five minutes in the presence of Christ will make us wish we had spent more time in prayer, witnessing, and learning to help others down here. But then it will be too late. *Work!*

The final word is *Win*. Oh, win souls for Christ! The children of Issachar understood the times. It did not matter what others said; it did not matter what others did. They had one purpose, and that was that their will and God's should coincide. They wanted what He wanted! And that was to make David king. Although David was an outcast, a fugitive, and his name a byword, they stood by David! I am asking you to stand for David's Greater Son. Stand with Him at "Hebron." Because just as David reigned from Jerusalem, so one day will David's Greater Son — the Lord Jesus Christ. And the law will go forth from Jerusalem, and the glory of God will encompass the world. Then will be realized the answer to our prayers: "Thy kingdom come. Thy will be done, in earth, as it is in heaven."

2

PREMILLENNIALISM AS A PHILOSOPHY OF HISTORY

By Alva J. McClain, D.D., LL.D.

Christianity is not a philosophy. But Christianity *has* a philosophy — the best and the brightest of all philosophies. In fact, it will be the *final* philosophy, not only because it is founded upon divine revelation, but also because it does justice to all points of view which have any value. Most philosophies are extremely narrow, often based upon only one aspect of reality. From the "very rich" variety of the world, the philosopher may select one segment of reality which seems most impressive to him, and then proceed to explain the universe in terms of that one thing, which then becomes the "type-phenomenon" of his system. Thus one man may be impressed by the fact of *mind*, and he becomes an idealist. Another is intrigued by the wonders of *matter*, and he becomes a materialist. But in Christian philosophy both mind *and* matter are recognized as worthwhile realities, each being given its proper place and function in the Kingdom of God.

Thus a good philosophy should have at least three marks: First, it should be able to give due recognition to every aspect of reality, excluding none. Second, it should fit into a rational scheme of thought; that is, it should make sense. Third, it should have beneficial practical effects here and now. I am not a pragmatist, but the pragmatists have a point. Their great mistake was to exalt this point into a theory of truth. Things are not true because they work; they work because they are true.

Now the Bible divides all human existence into two stages

or kinds: With respect to their *nature*, the one is called "natural"; the other "spiritual" (I Cor. 15:46). As to their *derivation*, the first is called "earthy"; the second "heavenly" (v. 48). As to their *duration*, the first is called "temporal"; the second "eternal" (II Cor. 4:18). As to their *time relationship*, the one is described as "the life that now is"; and the other as "that which is to come" (I Tim. 4:8).

Toward this present life on earth there have been two extreme attitudes: Some have wrongly regarded this life as the only existence worthwhile, scoffing at the idea of anything higher and beyond. Thus according to the consistent Marxians there is no substance to the promise of "Pie in the sky, by and by." Others, also wrongly, have scorned the present life as of small or no value, even arguing that salvation consists in getting loose from it altogether. On this philosophic road, at various stages, were the Hindu religionists, the monastics of the middle ages, even Plato, and a few theologians who should have known better. Now the Bible, with its unerring philosophic balance, recognizes certain values in both the present life and that life which is to come. Life on the present earthly stage is, of course, not the best; but it is "good" (Gen. 1:31). The Bible writers are never hard put, as was Plato, to explain how the eternal world of spirit ever became entangled in the stuff of physical existence.

Now it should be obvious, of course, that history can deal only with the present life, that which is temporal. History can have nothing to do with the world to come, which is eternal. Likewise, any genuine philosophy of history must be subject to the same limitations. Such a philosophy, if it lays claim to any truth, must give some rational account of the life which now is.

Let us inquire now briefly into the answers on this point which appear in certain types of theology. Classical *Postmillennialism* had plenty of defects, but it did make a serious attempt to deal with human history. The same thing was true of the *Liberalism* of the last generation. Both had a goal in human history, more or less clearly defined. God was making progress, they said; slowly at times, but surely. *Science* also, although

not too sure about God, had its own philosophy of progress toward a goal. This optimistic theory of human progress had
much its own way for the half-century ending in World War
I of 1914. After that the foundations were badly shaken;
prop after prop went down, until today the whole theory is
under attack from every side. Devout Postmillennialism has
virtually disappeared. Liberalism is hard put to defend itself
against new enemies. Some of the greatest names in science
are feeling a pessimistic "guilt" which is almost pathological.

In the midst of this debacle a new and powerful school of
theology has arisen, laying claim to some of the most brilliant
minds of our generation. This is the "Theology of Crisis" of
Barth and Brunner; also closely related is the so-called Christian
Realism of such men as John C. Bennett and Reinhold Niebuhr,
whose ideas have been developed largely under the influence
of Kierkegaard. To the great consternation of Liberalism, these
men and their followers are taking refuge in pessimism so far
as human history is concerned. According to their expressed
views, the Kingdom of God has little, if any, relation to the
present world and human history. The Kingdom to them, is
wholly "eschatological." But by this term the theologians of
"crisis" do not mean what is meant ordinarily. In the Bible
eschatological events are found at the end of but *within* human
history. But the "eschatology" of Barth is both above and beyond
history, having little or no vital relation to history. Dr. Berkhof
has written a valuable summary and critical evaluation of this
new school of "eschatology" (*The Kingdom of God,* pp. 114-131).

But what Berkhof fails to see, it seems to me, is that his
own Amillennial school of thought is in some measure "tarred
with the same brush," at least in its doctrine of the established
Kingdom of God. According to this view, both good and evil
continue in their development side by side through human
history. Then will come catastrophe and the crisis of divine
judgment, not for the purpose of setting up a divine kingdom
in history, but *after* the close of history. Hope lies only in a
new world which is *beyond* history. Thus history becomes merely
the preparatory "vestibule" of eternity; and not a very rational
vestibule at that. It is a narrow corridor, cramped and dark, a

kind of "waiting room," leading nowhere *within* the historical process, but only fit to be abandoned at last for an ideal existence on another plane. Such a view of history seems unduly pessimistic in the light of Biblical revelation. While we who are Premillennial in theology cannot, of course, accept the Liberal illusion of human progress; we must nevertheless reject likewise the "historical" despair of the theology of crisis.

What then can we learn from history *past* in order that we may be able to infer something reliable about what to expect in the *future?* Well, if there is anything crystal-clear in Biblical history, it is that the existence of our sinful race falls into periods of time (call them eras, ages, dispensations, or whatever you will), and that each age represents an advance over the preceding age, when looked at from the standpoint of what God is giving and doing for man. It is true that sinful man is always failing; but where sin abounded, always grace did much more abound. Thus to the old question, "Is the world getting better or worse?," from one standpoint we might answer, "The *age* is getting worse, but the *course of history*, by the grace of God, is moving forward."

On the basis of this law of divine progress in ages past, therefore, we may legitimately argue that "the life which now is" should have some proper goal. *It ought to go someplace.* And it should not be finally adjudicated and brought to an end until all its known possibilities have been fulfilled within the admitted limits imposed by that which is finite and sinful. Let me try to clarify this point further. Forgetting for the moment what has been accomplished in the natural world by those great intrusions of supernatural power in the course of history, and confining our attention wholly to what man has done, we know that *some* physical diseases have been conquered, *some* wars have been prevented, *some* hazards to life and safety have been eliminated, *some* years have been added to the brief span of human life, *some* social and political evils have been corrected. If this be so, why then should there not be an age when *all* wars will be stopped, *all* diseases cured, *all* the injustices of government rooted out, and *many* more years added to human life? Why should there not be an age in which all such un-

realized and worthwhile dreams of humanity will at last come
true on earth? If there be a God in heaven, if the life which
He created on earth is worthwhile, and not something evil per
se, then there ought to be in history some worthy consummation
of its long and arduous course.

It is just there that we must part company with any theological school which dogmatically asserts that there never will be
such a "Golden Age" upon earth in history; which argues that
for the present we must be satisfied with a mere pittance of
progress in such matters; that the world which now is must
continue with its terrible needs, its tragic handicaps, struggles
and problems, to the very end. And then God will suddenly
write a catastrophic *finis* to the whole of it, abolish human
existence on its first and natural plane, and thrust us all, both
saved and unsaved, out into the eternal state.

I am quite well aware of the peril of basing eschatology on
philosophic considerations. The Word of God alone must be
our base of authority. But where Biblical interpretation may be
in question, surely the right view should display clearer marks
of rationality than the wrong one, and such a philosophy of
history as I have been describing seems to me to be utterly
irrational. For, remembering that history has to do *only* with
the life that now is, such a philosophy of history has no proper
goal. To borrow a figure once used by the late President Mullins
in another connection, it is like a man building a great stair-
case. Step by step he sets it up, laboring wearily, often suffering painful reverses because of tragic hazards and poor ma-
terials. And now at last it is finished. But lo, it is a stairway
that goes no place! Such a philosophy of history not only flies
in the face of the clear statements of Scripture, but also runs
contrary to the reason of man in his finest moments and aspirations.

The Premillennial philosophy of history makes sense. It lays
a Biblical and rational basis for a truly optimistic view of human history. Furthermore, rightly apprehended, it has practical
effects. It says that life here and now, in spite of the tragedy
of sin, is nevertheless something worthwhile, and therefore all
efforts to make it better are also worthwhile. For all the true

values of human life here and now will be preserved and carried over into the coming Millennial Kingdom; nothing worthwhile will be lost. Furthermore, we are encouraged in the midst of devilish opposition and appalling reverses by the assurance that *help is on the way.* Supernatural help—Jesus is coming! "Give the King thy judgments, O God. . . . In his *days* shall the righteous flourish. . . . All nations shall call him blessed" (Ps. 72:1, 7, 17).

3

THE VARIOUS TIMES OF DIVINE REVELATION

by John G. Mitchell, D.D.

The two topics assigned to me are, "The Various Times of Divine Revelation" and "The Various Methods of Divine Revelation." While other men on the program give you the detailed picture of the various phases of prophecy, it is my purpose to give more of a telescopic view of the subject. There are certain well-defined pathways in the Word of God to guide us in the study and understanding of prophecy.

God has a purpose in history, and a purpose for man on earth. Being righteous, He must of necessity see to it that His purposes are fulfilled. "Remember the former things of old; for I am God, and there is none else; I am God and there is none like me. Declaring the end from the beginning, and from ancient times the things that are not yet done, saying, My counsel shall stand and I will do all my pleasure . . . Yea, I have spoken it, I will also bring it to pass; I have purposed it, I will also do it" (Isa. 46:9-11).

"The Lord of Hosts hath sworn, saying, Surely as I have thought, so shall it come to pass; and as I have purposed, so shall it stand. . . . This is the purpose that is purposed upon the whole earth: and this is the hand that is stretched out upon all the nations. For the Lord of Hosts hath purposed, and who shall disannul it? And his hand is stretched out, and who shall turn it back?" (Isa. 14:24, 26, 27). "Known unto God are all his works from the beginning of the world" (Acts 15:18). "The counsel of God standeth for ever" (Ps. 33:11).

What is God's purpose for man? God made him to be a

worshiper and a worker, and to have dominion over the works of His hands (Genesis, chapters 1-3, and Psalm 8:4-6). Man sinned and his fellowship with God was broken. He failed in the Grace of God, the Word of God, and the Person of God (Gen. 3). Judged by God and cast out of the Garden of Eden, man, though restored to fellowship with God, was not restored to his place of dominion. In Hebrews 2:5-9 we find that God is going to restore man to his place of dominion, and that He guarantees it in His Son, Jesus Christ. "But now we see not yet all things put under him. But we see Jesus, who was made a little lower than the angels for the suffering of death, crowned with glory and honour" (vv. 8, 9a). The representative Man, Christ Jesus, crowned, is the guarantee that man again shall have dominion over the works of His hands.

THE PRIMITIVE REVELATION

As we read the Word of God, we see that man was put under certain responsibilities at different times in his history, and in each case man proved an utter failure and unfit to have dominion. What then will God do with respect to His purpose for man? In the Scriptures He has revealed how and when He will fulfill that purpose which is centered in His Son, Jesus Christ.

God first revealed to Adam that He would send a redeemer. In Genesis 3:15 we read, "The seed of the woman shall bruise the serpent's head." This redeemer would deliver man from sin, death, and the devil, and the basic fulfillment of this is seen in John 3:16.

WHEN MANKIND WAS UNITED

Between Adam and the flood, we have one race of people, and in that period a further revelation concerning the promised Redeemer. Enoch, the seventh from Adam, prophesied to his generation before the flood of the coming of the Lord to judge them in righteousness; however, the Spirit of God carries it over to the last days, for we read in Jude 14, "The Lord cometh with ten thousands of his saints to execute judgment upon all." Conditions which existed in Enoch's day parallel those of the present generation. They were indifferent to the person of

God, ignorant of the program of God, and careless in their morals. This same message was delivered by Noah to his generation (see II Pet. 2:5). God in every time of declension reveals His purpose and program, and raises up witnesses to declare them.

It is to be noted that from the creation of man until the scattering of the people at Babel (Genesis 11), the human race was one, having one language. The division between Jew and Gentile did not come until after the calling out of Abraham. In the period between the flood and Babel, no testimony for God was given, except possibly the prophecy of Noah concerning his three sons.

GOD MAKES A NEW BEGINNING

With the call of Abraham (Genesis 12), and running through the Gospels, God deals with two groups: Jews and Gentiles — Israel and the nations of the earth. Although there are many precious truths for us today in the portion of the Scriptures covering this long period, nevertheless, God's dealings are primarily with Israel and the nations.

The call of Abraham ushers in a new era in divine Revelation. God called Abraham when he was but one. "Look unto Abraham, your father, for I called him alone" (Isa. 51:1, 2). To this man God gave the promise of both a heavenly and an earthly seed (Genesis 12-17), and began to reveal His divine purpose in a special way. As we see in Romans 1:24-32 and Acts 17:30, the human race was given up to uncleanness because they changed the glory of the incorruptible God into an image; they were given up to vile affections because they changed the truth of God into a lie; and they were given up to a reprobate mind because they refused to retain God in their knowledge. From this time and on the purpose of God in the earth is linked with the descendants of Abraham, even the people of Israel.

To Abraham was given also the promise of a land, and it is noteworthy that all through the Scriptures the people Israel and the Promised Land are inseparably bound together. The prophets speak continually of the people and the land. The people are blessed in the land, and the opposite is true when they are out of their land. You cannot divorce the people from the land, no matter how much you try to spiritualize it. It is God's land, and His program for the earth is that Israel shall be in her land. It was given as an everlasting possession, just as eternal as the heavens (read Amos 9:11-15; Isa. 66:22-24).

The Lord revealed to Abraham that his seed (earthly) would be strangers in a land that was not theirs, would serve in bondage for 400 years, and afterward they would come out with great substance (see Gen. 15:13, 14). To recapitulate, God revealed to Abraham that he would have a heavenly seed (Gen. 15:5, 6, fulfilled in Christ, Gal. 3:16); an earthly seed like the sand by the seashore for multitude (Gen. 13:16); and a land for an everlasting possession.

A THREEFOLD REVELATION

The next revelation of God's purpose in history was given to Moses, the servant of God and the great lawgiver. It was a threefold revelation. First, the coming of the Son of God as a prophet. "The Lord thy God will raise up unto thee a Prophet from the midst of thee, of thy brethren, like unto me; unto him ye shall hearken" (Deut. 18:15, 18). The hope of the coming of this prophet became deeply rooted in the faith of Israel, so that when John the Baptist came preaching the kingdom of heaven, the people asked him, "Art thou that prophet?" (John 1:21). We find this faith alive in Philip (John 1:45); in Peter (Acts 3:22); and in Stephen (Acts 7:37).

Secondly, Moses predicted the history of Israel, both the blessings and the curses which God would cause to fall upon His people. Deuteronomy, chapters 28 to 30, is a remarkably detailed preview of things which have for the most part been fulfilled. No one can read these passages of Scripture without realizing that they are the direct result of revelation. That which was spoken 1500 years before Christ is for the most part history today.

In the next place, Moses also prophesied the return of the Lord for and to His people Israel, and their restoration to the promised land with His abundant blessing (Deut. 30:1-10; note especially the word "return" in verse 3). This regathering of Israel to their land is dependent upon their confession, repentance and obedience. Moses declared that if they would not hearken and do God's commandments, they would come under His judgment, even until the land would enjoy her sabbaths (Lev. 26:40-45). We see here the truth that whether in the case of a nation or an individual, confession comes before restoration (see Daniel 9, Zechariah 12 and 13, Ezekiel 20).

CHRIST AND ISRAEL

Down through the centuries the prophetic utterances concerning the nation Israel and their land were always interwoven with the sufferings of Christ and the glory that should follow (I Pet. 1:11). Indeed, God's purpose in history, whether revealed to Adam, Enoch, Abraham, Moses, or the other prophets, is always predicated upon the redemptive work of our Lord and Saviour Jesus Christ. Hosea is very bold in that he reveals the time of our Lord's return and of the regathering of Israel. God speaks: "I will go and return to my place *till* they acknowledge their offence, and seek my face: in their affliction they will seek me early. Come, and let us return unto the Lord: for he hath torn, and he will heal us; he hath smitten and he will bind us up. After two days will he revive us: in the third day he will raise us up, and we shall live in his sight" (Hos. 5: 15; 6:1,2). And so also said our Lord, "Behold your house is left unto you desolate. For I say unto you, Ye shall not see me henceforth, *till* ye shall say, Blessed is he that cometh in the name of the Lord" (Matt. 23:37-39).

Daniel prophesies the history of Gentile world powers in chapter 2, and the character of the Gentile powers in chapters 7 and 8. When these have run their course, there will be set up the everlasting kingdom of our God, a kingdom that will never fade away, where the Lord will reign in righteousness, and where peace shall be man's universal experience. "And the work of righteousness shall be peace; and the effect of righteousness quietness and assurance for ever. And my people shall dwell in a peaceable habitation, and in sure dwellings, and in quiet resting places" (Isa. 32:17,18). There never can be any

real, satisfying peace until the Righteous One comes to reign
on the earth. He will reign not only in righteousness, but also
in love. Power without love leads to destruction, sorrow, suffering. We have seen this evidenced so much among the nations
even in our day. Thank the Lord, when He comes, He will
wield power by love and reign in righteousness.

BEHOLD THE KING

Now we come to the revelation of His purpose in the New
Testament. Here the Scriptures speak of three classes of people
in the earth, "the Jew, the Gentile and the church of God"
(I Cor. 10:32). God is speaking now not through the prophets,
but in His Son (Heb. 1:1,2; John 1:18). It would be impossible to give in brief the truth set forth by our Lord during
His ministry on earth. It is sufficient for me to say that in
Matthew, the Book of the King, our Lord begins to instruct
His disciples concerning His purpose and program. He proves
His legal right to the throne in chapter 1; His moral right to
the throne in chapter 4; His judicial right to the throne in
chapters 5-7; His prophetical right to the throne in chapters
8-10; and He is then opposed and rejected by Israel in chapters 11, 12. After His rejection by the nation, He begins to
reveal to His disciples in chapters 16, 17 His purposes for His
own. In this passage there is given to us the revelation of His
Person ("Thou art the Christ, the Son of the living God"); the
revelation of His *Purpose* ("Upon this rock I will build my
church"); the revelation of His *Program* ("He must go to
Jerusalem, and suffer many things of the elders and chief priests
and scribes, and be killed, and be raised again the third day").
We have here also the *Opposition* to His program and its
source ("This be far from thee, Lord . . . Get thee behind me,
Satan"); the revelation of His *Followers* (the definition of dis-
cipleship, 16:24,25); the revelation of His *Return to the Earth*
("The Son of man shall come in the glory of his Father with
his angels. . . . There be some standing here, which shall not
taste of death, *till* they see the Son of man coming in his kingdom"). This is followed by the transfiguration of our Lord,
which is a miniature of His return in glory. John speaks of

this in John 1:14, "And we beheld his glory." Peter also speaks confidently of this event, "For we have not followed cunningly devised fables, when we made known unto you the power and coming of our Lord Jesus Christ, but were eye-witnesses of His majesty . . . when we were with him in the holy mount" (II Pet. 1:16-18). Peter, James and John, all three, saw the Lord in His majesty on the mount of transfiguration.

In Matthew 24 and 25 we have the predictions of the King. Here are given the signs of His coming to the earth, and a description of the condition of the world at the end of the age. Compare also Luke 21.

THE CHURCH — HIS BODY

Finally, He reveals His purpose through His apostles. Our Lord told His disciples that the Holy Spirit, the Spirit of truth, would bring all things to their remembrance; would show them things to come; would take the things of the Lord and declare them unto them (John 14:26; 16:13-15).

The revelation of the Church, the Body of Christ, was given to the Apostle Paul, especially in his Epistle to the Ephesians. The Church, a mystery hidden in God in past ages, is now revealed as a new race of people, born of God, partakers of the divine nature, members of the body of Christ. To build this Church, God is now gathering out from among all nations a people for His name (Acts 15:14), after which He will return and gather Israel back to Himself. Through this new company, the Church, He is going to reveal His wonderful grace in the ages to come, and display His marvelous wisdom to all created intelligences (Eph. 2:7; 3:10,11). Having completed His body, the Church, He will take it up to glory, to be forever with Him. Then each believer will be conformed to the image of Jesus Christ (Rom. 8:29; I Thess. 4:13-17; I Cor. 15:51,52).

To the Apostle John was given the revelation of Jesus Christ as the Judge. In the Book of Revelation we see our Lord as the Judge in the midst of the churches, Israel, and the nations. The final two chapters speak of the new heavens and the new earth, where God is in the midst of His people. When we see God's program thus set forth from Genesis to Revelation, our hearts respond eagerly with John, "Even so, come, Lord Jesus."

4

THE VARIOUS METHODS OF DIVINE REVELATION

by JOHN G. MITCHELL, D.D.

Our subject is the Methods of Divine Revelation, and I would like to read again the three verses of Hebrews 1:1-3— "God, who at sundry times and in divers manners spake in time past unto the fathers by the prophets, hath in these last days spoken unto us by his Son, whom he hath appointed heir of all things, by whom also he made the worlds; Who being the brightness of his glory, and the express image of his person, and upholding all things by the word of his power, when he had by himself purged our sins, sat down on the right hand of the Majesty on high." I am much tempted to spend this hour on these verses, thinking of the sevenfold glory of the person of our Saviour. However, we will just make these verses our starting point as we think together of the various manners of the revelation of God in the Scripture, especially with reference to prophetic truth.

GOD KNOWN THROUGH CREATION

God was first of all revealed through creation. You remember the 19th Psalm, "The heavens declare the glory of God; and the firmament sheweth his handywork. Day unto day uttereth speech, and night unto night sheweth knowledge. There is no speech nor language, where their voice [the voice of creation] is not heard."

We have the same thing in Romans 1:20, "For the invisible things of him from the creation of the world are clearly seen, being understood by the things that are made, even his

eternal power and Godhead; so that they are without excuse."
Also in Acts 14:15-17 and 17:20-29 the same truth is expressed.

HE SPAKE THROUGH PROPHETS

As I read the Scriptures, I find that God was pleased to raise
up men who became His channels of expression. That is what
the prophets were, God's channels of expression. You and I
can talk all we want to about the indwelling Spirit of God, but
does the Spirit of God use us as His channels of expression
to our generation? God through the centuries has chosen men
and made them the vehicles of His divine purpose. For example,
a prophet is one who represents God to the people, and a priest
is one who represents the people to God. A prophet is God's
messenger; his message is from God. All of the prophets were
distinguished by the privilege of prefacing their utterances with
"Thus saith the Lord." They were His mouthpieces. The
Word of God burned in them. You remember Jeremiah, chapter 20, where the prophet says, in substance, "Lord, I shall
speak no more for you. Every time I speak they abuse me; they
call me a traitor; I shall speak no more in your name." But
Jeremiah tells us that the Word of God burned in His bones
and he could not but speak out. He was one man who knew
the heart of God. When you read the prophet Jeremiah, you
almost feel like he did when he said, "Oh that my eyes were a
fount of tears, that I might weep day and night for the slain
of the daughter of my people." That's the kind of men God
used as prophets. As I Peter 1:11 declares, they spake of "the
sufferings of Christ and the glory that should follow." How
did they speak? By the Spirit of Christ that was in them.

ONE TAKEN OUT OF IT — ONE DELIVERED THROUGH IT

In the period of time between Adam and Abraham two men
stand out before us whom God used to give forth some measure
of the truth concerning His purpose in the earth. These two
were Enoch and Noah. Both were men who walked with God.
Did you ever stop to meditate upon the difference between
these two men? The history of Enoch is very brief. Genesis,
chapter 5, "And Enoch walked with God after he begat Methu-

selah . . . and he was not; for God took him." Hebrews 11:5, 6,
". . . Enoch was translated that he should not see death . . . for
before his translation he had this testimony, that he pleased
God. But without faith it is impossible to please him." Jude 14,
15, "And Enoch also, the seventh from Adam, prophesied saying,
Behold, the Lord cometh with ten thousands of his saints, to
execute judgment." How did Enoch know these things? What
did he prophesy? The coming of the Lord in judgment at the
flood? Certainly, but the Spirit of God also prophesied through
him concerning the conditions today. Jude is one of the books
of the last days. For example, Jude 11 gives us the character of
the leaders of the last days. How did Enoch know? Because
Enoch walked with God. Enoch was not given faith to make
this a better world. Enoch was given faith to walk with God.
The important thing about Enoch is not that he was translated,
but that he walked with God. I am of the persuasion that
Enoch experienced God's initial purpose for man. It was not
God's purpose that man should die, but that man should live
in fellowship with Him. Enoch was close to God, and he so
walked with God, that he realized and experienced the purpose
of God for man. "He walked with God and was not." The
world said, "He disappeared." God said, "He walked with Me,
and I took him home." He didn't see death because he saw
God.

The second man is Noah, and he, too, walked with God.
Why didn't God take him home? Because He had a different
purpose for him. Noah was God's witness to that generation
about the coming judgment. He did not build the ark to save
the world; he built the ark to save his house in case the world
wouldn't believe. Noah was more intensely occupied with the
coming flood than he was with the life around him. It is
about time, my Christian friends, that we learned that lesson.
You and I ought to be more occupied with the coming of our
Saviour than with the life around us. The faith he has given
to you is not intended to transform this world. God Himself has
to do that. So He has given you faith to walk with Him and
live in the glorious anticipation of His Son's coming. Enoch
was delivered before the flood; Noah was kept through it. And,

when I come to the New Testament, I find the exact counterpart to these strongly typical events. But make a mental note of this; we shall return to it presently.

Between Adam and Abraham there was one race of people. Two men walked with God — two men of faith. In Hebrews 11, we read of other men and women of faith. We see in Abel the sacrifice of faith; in Enoch the walk of faith; in Noah the work of faith; in Abraham the obedience of faith; in Sarah the sufficiency and the anticipation of faith. But through the whole period Enoch and Noah stand out, these two men who walked with God. Both were vehicles through whom God expressed Himself. One was caught up to heaven in fellowship, the other was left on earth to witness.

BETWEEN THE FLOOD AND MOSES

One man stands out before us in the period between the flood and Moses. This man is Abraham, the friend of God. Abraham was given the remarkable promises of a heavenly seed, an earthly seed, and of a land which was to become his eternal possession. Abraham also prophesied, but in a limited way. His prophecy was mainly about his descendants, that they would be strangers in a land for four hundred years, would be afflicted, and in the end would come out with great substance. I am sure you remember the content of Genesis 15. There we see the *reward* of Abraham's faith, namely, a heavenly seed and a land forever, both integral parts of God's eternal purpose. But there was another man who was raised in the same family. His name was Lot. Why didn't God reveal Himself to Lot? Lot was a righteous man. You would not believe that if it was not written in the Epistle to Peter. But God could not bring judgment upon the city of Sodom until Lot, the righteous man, had been taken out. And he *was* taken out. In Genesis 18 we see the energy of faith in Abraham's intercession for Sodom and Gomorrah. In the 19th chapter God remembers Abraham and delivers righteous Lot. The judgments of this world, of which we have been hearing these days, can never fall upon the world so long as God's righteous people are still here.

BETWEEN MOSES AND CHRIST

But now let us come back to the period from Moses to Christ. We were speaking of Moses yesterday in connection with the times of divine revelation, and you will remember that amazing passage in Numbers 12:6-8, where God deals with Aaron, Miriam, and Moses. Listen again to these words, "Hear now my words. If there be a prophet among you, I the Lord, will make myself known unto him in a vision, and will speak unto him in a dream. My servant Moses is not so, who is faithful in all mine house. With him will I speak mouth to mouth, even apparently, and not in dark speeches; and the similitude of the Lord shall he behold: wherefore then were ye not afraid to speak against my servant Moses?" To others, God says, I will speak in a vision or in a dream, but to my servant Moses, who is faithful in My house, I will speak to him mouth to mouth, and the similitude of the Lord shall he behold.

In Exodus 30, 32, and 33, we read that God did speak to Moses face to face, as a man talks to his friend. And when Moses said, "Show me now thy way, that I may know thee," the Lord answered, "My presence shall go with thee." And when Moses asked, "Show me thy glory," as if he was reaching out to apprehend that for which he was apprehended, God said, in substance, "Wait a minute, Moses, you can't see me in my glory." Instead, He hid him in the cleft of the rock and allowed him to see the one who is to come afterward. Moses! The man whom God knew face to face. Who knows the purposes of God? To whom will God reveal His program? To those whom He knows face to face, of course. It does not say that *Moses* knew God face to face. No. It may be a fine point, but Moses was the man whom *God* knew face to face.

Allow me, my Christian friends, to drop a few words into your hearts, just for yourselves, along this line. In John 14:21, 23, Jesus said, "He that hath my commandments, and keepeth them [he was not talking about the law of Moses], he it is that loveth me . . . and my Father will love him, and we will come unto him, and make our abode with him." "We will reveal ourselves to him." In verse 21, obedience brings revelation;

in verse 23, obedience brings intimacy of fellowship. My friend, examine your life. If you are empty, shallow, know nothing of His purpose and counsel; remember that obedience brings the intimacy of His fellowship. Of Moses God said, "With him will I speak mouth to mouth" (Num. 12:8).

To Moses was given the marvelous revelation of the coming of the Lord as the Prophet. And by the way, I believe that Moses knew something also about the death and resurrection of Christ. Otherwise how could he discuss that matter with our Lord on the Mount of Transfiguration? Some people think that God was a little bit unfair with Moses when on Mount Pisgah, in sight of the Promised Land, He said to him, "Thou shall not go over thither." But the truth is that God had something much better for Moses than going into the land with a stiff-necked people. On the Mount of Transfiguration Moses had a preview of the Lord in His glory, and when he finally enters the land he once saw afar off, he will be among the *entourage* of the King of Glory. Familiar sights will meet Moses' eyes, because "the Lord will create upon every dwelling place of Mount Zion . . . a cloud and smoke by day, and the shining of a flaming fire by night" (Isa. 4:5). Meanwhile the Lord will have spared His loved servant all the gory history of the people and land that have known little else than desolation. It is remarkable that from Moses and right down through all the prophets, God took these amazing men like Isaiah, Jeremiah, Ezekiel, and laid bare before them the marvels of the person and purpose of God in His Son.

So, between Adam and Abraham we have Enoch and Noah. One was taken out; the other left to witness. Between Abraham and Moses we have the deliverance of Lot, the righteous man, from judgment through the intercession of Abraham. Hence it is not at all strange when we find the same truth emphasized between Moses and the coming of Jesus Christ our Lord. In the middle of this period we again find two characters who serve as instruments and exemplars of God's method and purpose in history. There is *Elijah*, the man who stood for God even though he thought himself to be alone. There were seven thousand who had not bowed the knee to Baal, but these were known only to God.

I can imagine that dear man. After his great victory over the prophets of Baal on Carmel, discouragement set in, the smouldering embers of it fed by the threats of that wicked queen Jezebel. Constantly sounding in his ears must have been the woman's words, "Wait until I get my hands on that Elijah." It was then that he ran for his life. But this is not the end of the story. God fed and rested His weary servant, He sent him back to finish his job, then He took him home to glory in a whirlwind. Elijah did not see death. He also experienced something of the purpose of God for man.

Then there is *Elisha,* a different character altogether, who performed more miracles than Elijah. Why did not God take Elisha home? Because it was Elisha's appointed mission to stay on earth and witness to his decadent generation. These experiences of God's men of old point us in no uncertain way to truth now revealed in our New Testament.

BETWEEN THE TWO ADVENTS — HIS SON

Our brief study in the history of revelation has, I believe, demonstrated in every detail Hebrews 1:1, 2, the passage we took as our foundation text. Ours is the God who speaks. In the past He had spoken through the prophets, using time in its various divisions as His laboratory, and men in the variety of their experiences as the objects of His demonstration. To take one example, in a period of human perverseness and wickedness, by taking one man — Enoch — to heaven without dying, God demonstrated what one day He is going to do with all of His redeemed heritage in the earth. God's method in revelation has been eschatological throughout. He has been guiding everything to a predetermined *end.*

Now, and ever since history arrived at that junction of the ages which in Scripture is called the fullness of time (Gal. 4:4), God is speaking to us in His Son. In Him we see all of the personality of God (Col. 2:9; John 14:9), and by Him we see God's eternal purpose being worked out in history (Phil. 2:9-11; Eph. 1:10).

When we come to the New Testament revelation, we find it following a pattern with which we have become so well acquainted: These are the "last days," and God is now speaking *in* His Son, but the message still comes to us, as the Greek text has it, *polumeros kai polutropos,* in or about various periods of time, and in a variety of ways.

In the Gospels, the first grand division of the New Testament, we have the fourfold presentation of the incarnate Son of God, the Messiah of prediction who is now the Jesus of history. "The Word became flesh and dwelt among us" (John 1:14). This is a message no longer subjective, but personified, revealing in a human form the thought and character and purpose of the invisible God. "No man hath seen God at any time; the only begotten Son, which is in the bosom of the Father, he hath declared him" (John 1:18). So real was this revelation to the early Christians, that John could write, "That . . . which we have looked upon, and our hands have handled, of the Word of life . . . declare we unto you" (I John 1:1-3).

God has fulfilled His promises spoken through the prophets and the expected One became a neighbor among men. But let us not forget that the Gospels end in a cross. God revealed Himself in Jesus Christ, but when we looked at Him, "his visage was so marred more than any man, and his form more than the sons of men" (Isa. 52:14). Without the cross there would be no New Testament. You see, He came not only to fulfill a promise, but to accomplish a purpose. "Wherefore when he cometh into the world, he saith, Sacrifice and offering thou wouldest not, but a body hast thou prepared me. . . . Then said I, Lo, I come (in the volume of the book it is written of me), to do thy will, O God" (Heb. 10:5-7). Here is the link between the Gospels and the Old Testament; between the Jesus of history and the Christ of the ages. The Old Testament said, "He is coming"; the Gospels shout, "He has come"; and all Scripture asserts, "He is coming again."

This leads me to suggest that, in addition to the generally accepted depictions of Christ in the four Gospels as King, Servant, Man, and God, our Lord is also presented there as the sacrifice once for all offered: In Matthew He is the Trespass

Offering; in Mark, the Sin Offering; in Luke, the Peace Offering; in John, the Burnt Offering; and in all four Gospels He is the Meal Offering. "Behold the Lamb of God, which taketh away the sin of the world" (John 1:29).

Coming to the Epistles, we realize that it would be quite impossible to deal with the truth contained in them in the limited scope of this address. However, to preserve the unity of God's total revelation, of which the Epistles are an integral part, certain things concerning them should be pointed out.

The Epistles partake of the nature of the Church for whom and about whom they were written. The Church is "the mystery . . . which in other ages was not made known unto the sons of men . . . [but] is now revealed unto his holy apostles and prophets by the Spirit." Try to apply the teaching of the Epistles to any other body or kind of people and it becomes wholly unintelligible. The Church is not Israel. It is not the subject of Old Testament prediction, and by no stretching of Biblical terms can one be taken for the other. The Bible draws a very clear line of demarcation between the nation Israel, which, with its land, is eternal in the purpose of God, and the Church, the body of Christ. I think that most differences of opinion on matters of prophecy are concentrated here. Many of our problems would be settled, even the dispute about the Tribulation (I believe in the pretribulation translation of the Church), if we could agree on the right answers to the questions: What is the Church? and, Is the nation Israel going to possess her land, never to be removed from it?

The Church is a new race of people. God does not take Adam's race and patch it up. He brings in something entirely new: A new creation with a new nature; a new life with new aspirations; a new hope with a new destiny. Indeed, we do not even belong down here. When you build your doctrine for the Church, remember that the purpose of God for the Church is found in the Epistles of Paul from Romans to Thessalonians, although I believe that the whole Bible is *for me*.

The well-established methods of God in redemption persevere in the Epistles. Remission of sins is still by sacrificial shedding of blood, as in Abel's time, except that for us God has provided

His Lamb, foreordained before the foundation of the world (I Pet. 1:18-20). Salvation is still by grace, through faith, as in Abraham's case. Fellowship is still walking in step with God, as in Enoch's experience. Rapture is still God's favorite way of taking His children home, for Elijah, and, please God it may be soon, for us. All the Epistles, from Romans to Jude, testify to this.

And now, as we come to the close of this address, we want to call attention to an act of great kindness on the part of our God, all of whose acts are the expressions of His nature, by which He has shown His unfailing love and tender solicitude for Israel, the people of His two covenants (Rom. 9:4), even though the New Covenant still waits for acceptance by the party of the second part (Hos. 5:15).

You are probably aware that, although God is now gathering out from the nations, Jews and Gentiles, a people for His name, He has nevertheless caused His thoughts concerning Israel to be recorded in Romans 9-11, and, briefly, here are the facts:

1. Israel is blinded, but only partially (Rom. 11:25), and temporarily (Matt. 23:39). When Christ returns to earth, the blindness will be removed.

2. Israel is seeking that which the "remnant according to the election of grace" have found, but without success (Rom. 11:5). They must be enlightened, because, for individuals, faith *now* removes the blindness (Rom. 10:12-15).

3. God loves Israel (Rom. 11:28), and one day, according to a standing and irrevocable covenant (Rom. 11:29), He will save the whole nation (Rom. 11:26, 27).

4. How He is going to do it has already been demonstrated in the experience of Saul of Tarsus on the Road to Damascus (I Cor. 15:8). He saved *one* ahead of time, so we may know that He is going to save *all* in due time. Upon this day much of prophecy converges. Read Zechariah 12:10; Acts 9:1-20; 15:13-18).

At this point the hope of Israel becomes contingent upon the hope of the Church (I Thess. 4:16-18), for the Christ who comes into the air to rapture the Church, returns to earth to rescue beleaguered Israel (Zech. 14:1-9).

"Oh, Lord Jesus, how long, how long ere we shout the glad song? Christ returneth." Listen, my friends. Noah lived, believed, looked forward to the fulfilling of the word which he preached. His heart was more occupied with the message of God, even though it was a message of judgment, than with the life around him. God grant that you and I shall be living so in the expectation of the coming of our Saviour, that the life around us will not affect the desire of our hearts, nor tarnish the love of His appearing. And again I say with John, "Amen. Even so, come, Lord Jesus."

THE CROWN RIGHTS OF THE CRUCIFIED

by WILLIAM CULBERTSON, D.D.

At the Cross of Calvary our blessed Lord purchased for Himself His crown rights — the rights to a redeemed people, a redeemed creation, and an unquestioned sovereignty.

This third right, the right of our Lord Jesus Christ to be the unquestioned sovereign Ruler of the universe rests upon three considerations. First of all, He has a right to rule because He is God. Second, He has a right to rule because He is the Son of David. And third, He has a right to rule because He is the crucified Lord of heaven.

In the Word of God these three themes are played over and over again until, mingling and swelling, they break at last into a heavenly chorus in which all unite to crown Him Lord of all (Rev. 19:16, ASV): "And he hath on his garment and on his thigh a name written, KING OF KINGS, AND LORD OF LORDS."

FIRST, let us look at some scriptures which deal with our blessed Lord's right to rule *because He is God*. Reading from the American Standard Version, published in 1901, I turn to the second Psalm, the psalm that tells us of the opposition of men, but which tells also of the certainty of God's ultimate triumph.

You know the scene. Nations are raging, peoples are meditating, kings of the earth have set themselves, rulers are taking counsel together against Jehovah, and against His Anointed. And all their schemes, all their imaginations are directed to one end: "Let us break their bonds asunder, and cast away their cords from us." God dethroned, the Anointed of the Lord taken from His place of sovereignty — that is their purpose.

But what does *God* say? Look at verse 6: "Yet I have set my king upon my holy hill of Zion." Whatever men say, however unruly the nations are, however hateful and antagonistic they may be, God says, "I have set my king." In the purposes of God it is as though He had already reigned in the Millennium.

Now listen to the Lord Jesus as He speaks in verse 7, ASV: "I will tell of the decree." You see, there is a decree involved here, and God the Father has made it. The Lord Jesus says: "I will tell of the decree: Jehovah said unto me, Thou art my Son; this day have I begotten thee. Ask of me, and I will give thee the nations for thine inheritance, and the uttermost parts of the earth for thy possession. (Remember, it is God the Son who is speaking, and He is telling us what God the Father said to Him.) Thou shalt break them with a rod of iron; thou shalt dash them in pieces like a potter's vessel."

Why? Because He is God's Son. Inherent in His royalty, inherent in His dignity, is the right to rule. God has given Him that right, and there is no question about it. It is signed, and sealed, and finished.

And this passage does not stand alone. In Psalm 45:6, ASV—and what a powerfully moving verse this is!—we read: "Thy throne, O God, is for ever and ever: a scepter of equity is the scepter of thy kingdom. Thou hast loved righteousness, and hatest wickedness: Therefore God, thy God, hath anointed thee with the oil of gladness above thy fellows."

"Thy throne . . . is for ever." Whose throne? God's throne. "Thy throne, O God, is for ever." But let me ask you, which Person of the holy and blessed Trinity is addressed in this verse? We are not left to our own ingenuity. This is not something for which we have to make up our own answer.

Turn to the first chapter of Hebrews, where is contrasted the regal, high exalted sovereignty of the Lord Jesus with the position of the angels. The writer of the epistle to the Hebrews, led of the Holy Ghost, went back to that forty-fifth Psalm and quoted the very same verse I have read. Look at it—Hebrews 1:8, "But of the Son he saith"—there it is—". . . of the Son he saith, Thy throne, O God, is for ever and ever."

Those of you who do not believe that the Bible says the Lord Jesus is God, what are you going to do with that verse? "Of the Son he saith, Thy throne, O God, is for ever and ever." And why is it forever? Because He is God, the everlasting Son of the Father.

Let us look again in the Old Testament in Micah 5:2, ASV, "But thou, Bethlehem Ephrathah, which art little to be among the thousands of Judah, out of thee shall one come forth unto me that is to be ruler of Israel; whose goings forth are from of old, from everlasting."

Who is this? Who alone has eternity in being, who alone is from everlasting? The One who was born as a Babe in Bethlehem, He is the One. He is to be ruler over His people Israel, and His goings forth have been from all eternity.

Look at one other Old Testament passage, Psalm 110, which is frequently quoted on the pages of the New Testament: "Jehovah saith unto my Lord, Sit thou at my right hand, until I make thine enemies thy footstool" (v. 1). It was this passage that our Lord Jesus used to bring consternation to the representatives of the Pharisees who came with their captious questions.

I have often thought about that day of questioning in holy week, how when it was all over — or at least when the representatives of the Herodians and Sadducees and Pharisees thought it was all over — suddenly the Lord Jesus said to the Pharisees, "I have a question that I want to ask you. The Messiah, whose son is he?"

Can you not see them breathing a sigh of relief and saying one to another, "I thought he was going to ask us something we could not answer. Any school boy knows that the Messiah is the son of David." I can see them turning to go away, when the Lord Jesus says, "Wait a minute. I have another question for you. If the Messiah is the son of David, how then does David in the Spirit call him Lord, saying, 'Jehovah said unto my Adonai, Sit thou on my right hand'? How did he do that?"

They had no answer to that question, neither did they dare from that day on to ask Him any more questions (Matt. 22: 41-46). But you know the answer to that question, don't you?

It was because Messiah is the Son of God as well as the Son of David.

Psalm 110 is a tremendous psalm. Look at those words again. "Jehovah saith unto my Lord, Sit thou at my right hand, until I make thine enemies thy footstool."

Now, just as we found in Psalm 2, so here, the psalmist reports: "Jehovah will send forth the rod of thy strength out of Zion." Jehovah is going to send the Lord Jesus. And He, Jehovah, said unto Thee, Adonai, "Rule thou in the midst of thine enemies."

Now look at verse 5. The psalmist is speaking, and describing the Lord Jesus in His relationship to the Father. The psalmist is looking at God the Father and saying, "The Lord at thy right hand . . . [And who is the Lord at the right hand of the Father? The Lord Jesus.] The Lord at thy right hand will strike through kings in the day of his wrath."

Now verses 6 and 7: "He will judge among the nations, He will fill the places with dead bodies; He will strike through the head in many countries. He will drink of the brook in the way: Therefore will he lift up the head." These verses all speak of Adonai, the Lord Jesus, God.

And so our Lord has a right to rule because He is God.

SECOND, He has the right to rule *because He is the Son of David*. Turn to II Samuel 7, ASV, where the Davidic covenant is enunciated, and look at three verses, beginning with verse 12.

God is speaking to David: "When thy days are fulfilled, and thou shalt sleep with thy fathers, I will set up thy seed after thee, that shall proceed out of thy bowels, and I will establish his kingdom. He shall build a house for my name, and I will establish the throne of his kingdom for ever."

Plainly, there is someone of the seed of David who is to be an everlasting monarch, one who is to have a throne and a kingdom that will last forever. That is God's covenant with David. Now look at verse 16, ASV: "And thy house and thy kingdom shall be made sure for ever before thee: thy throne shall be established for ever."

Now, the only part that David could possibly have in that covenant would be that he have a son, and this was already accomplished. God was saying, in effect: "Somewhere in your posterity, David [He did not say where], there is going to be a King, and that King, by right of His relationship to Me, as being involved in this Davidic covenant, will sit on a throne that will last forever."

This same covenant is reiterated in Psalm 89, ASV. As I read this psalm in preparation for this message, my soul was stirred. Let me read just four verses, 34 through 37: "My covenant will I not break, nor alter the thing that is gone out of my lips. Once have I sworn by my holiness: I will not lie to David: His seed shall endure for ever. And his throne as the sun before me. It shall be established for ever as the moon, and as the faithful witness in the sky. Selah."

God promised to David a kingdom in perpetuity, a throne, and *David's seed is to sit on that throne.*

Now as we turn to the New Testament, and the Gospel story comes before us, what do we read? In the Gospel according to Luke, the first chapter, we read that Gabriel, the angel of God, was sent to visit the virgin Mary. And among other things he said to her in verse 32 of Luke 1, ASV: "He shall be great, and shall be called the Son of the Most High: and the Lord shall give unto him the throne of his father David; And he shall reign over the house of Jacob for ever; and of his kingdom there shall be no end."

There is the New Testament "Amen!" There is Gabriel's word to Mary concerning the One of whom God was speaking back in the Old Testament days, when He told David that of his seed would One arise to sit upon the throne of His kingdom, and that He would rule forever. The Lord Jesus Christ is that One. I say to you, He has a right to sovereignty because of the inviolable, immutable covenant which God made with David.

Now our Lord's right to rule as the Son of David is also clearly established in the genealogical tables of Matthew 1 and Luke 3.

You know, of course, that Matthew's genealogy begins with Abraham. And when you get down to verse 6 you come to David and the kings. Here they are, beginning with Solomon in verse 7, ASV: then Rehoboam, Abijah, Asa, Jehoshaphat, Joram . . . and so all the way down to the Lord Jesus.

What I'd like to emphasize, without going into it too deeply, is that here is recorded one dynasty, one family, until He should come whose right it would be to sit on the throne of David forever, and His line of succession must be unbroken.

It is amazing how many family trees are broken somewhere along the line. Either there is no son born to carry on the family name, or he is born and dies before he has posterity. So easily is the line broken — by disease, war, failure to marry, inability to have children. But generation after generation, generation after generation, here is the line! And so the Lord Jesus is born. I suggest to you, here is an indication of the providential rule of Almighty God, seeing to it that the Seed of David would be born.

But you know and I know that according to this first chapter of Matthew there is a man in the genealogy who beclouds all of it. This man is Jechoniah, or Coniah, whom Jeremiah talks about when he says (Jer. 22:30), "Write this man childless . . . for no more shall a man of his seed prosper, sitting upon the throne of David." That is enough for me to know that Matthew's genealogy is the genealogy of Joseph and not of Mary.

So I turn to the genealogy recorded in Luke 3. Oh, there is so much in this Book, so wonderful it is! If you look at Luke 3:31 you will see recorded there the descent of our Lord through Mary, traced through Nathan, another son of David — notice, not through Solomon, but through Nathan.

So our Lord has the right to rule as the son of David so far as *legal* genealogy is concerned, since Joseph was his foster father. And He has the right also so far as *direct* lineage is concerned, because that line goes back to David through Mary.

My friends, that covenant of God with David is, I repeat, inviolate, for God cannot lie. And some day the law will go forth from Jerusalem, and our blessed Lord will rule from the river to the ends of the earth. That is His right; He is the son of David.

THIRD, He has the right to rule *because He is the crucified One*. What happened at Calvary? I do not know whether John

12 strikes fire in your soul, but I never read it without a hallelujah in my heart and a desire to take the crown and put
it on the brow of my blessed Lord!

Listen. The Lord Jesus is standing just hours away from
Calvary, standing in the place where He Himself said, "This
is your hour, and the hour of darkness." All the avalanche of
hell is about to fall in upon Him. And He has the audacity,
the temerity to stand up and say — look at it — John 12:31: "Now
is the judgment of this world."

Why, why — you are wrong! This is *your* judgment! Do you
not understand? There is Pontius Pilate, the Pharisees, the high
priest, the Roman soldiers, the Roman authorities. *They* are
judging *You!*

Oh, no, says the Lord Jesus, "Now is the judgment of this
world."

Listen to me, my friends. By the Cross of Christ the world
is judged. And every last mortal in this world stands or falls
with regard to his attitude toward that Cross. The Lord Jesus
said: "Now is the judgment of this world: now shall the prince
of this world be cast out."

What? At the Cross the prince of this world cast out? Yes!
Yes! For do you not see, do you not understand? Hell and
heaven were locked in mortal combat on Golgotha's hill, and
there our blessed Lord cast out the prince of this world!

I am glad that as a preacher of the Gospel I have this kind
of Gospel to preach. Listen, there is no soul so depraved, there
is no sinner so low but my Lord can take him up and clean
him up and make him a citizen of heaven. Glory to God, I
have seen Him do it.

Then that passage in Colossians 2, ASV — oh, what a tremendous word that is! I'll read only verse 15: "Having despoiled the
principalities and the powers, he made a show of them openly,
triumphing over them in it." That is the triumph of Calvary!

On two occasions I have stood by the arch of Titus in Rome.
There I have closed my eyes and tried to envision those Roman
armies. I see them marching with heads high — Titus, the
Roman general, at the forefront, and the cringing captives being

dragged along behind. And behind are the spoils — the candle-stick, and the table, and the gold from Jerusalem.

That was celebrating a triumph over them, making a "show of them openly." That is what Christ did to evil principalities and powers at Calvary. Christ has the right to rule, for He has overcome.

Read Revelation 5:5-13. Will you notice there that the Lord's right to dominion is based upon the fact that He is a Lamb slain from the foundation of the world? It is on the basis of Calvary that He assumes the sovereignty.

See it in Isaiah 53:10-12. Why is it that He has a right to divide the spoil with the strong? Because He poured out His soul unto death, that is why!

Or look at it in that tremendously moving passage of Philippians 2:8-11, ASV: "And being found in fashion as a man, he humbled himself, becoming obedient even unto death, yea, the death of the cross." And for what end? "God highly exalted him, and gave unto him the name which is above every name; that in the name of Jesus every knee should bow . . . and that every tongue should confess that Jesus Christ is Lord." His right to rule is based upon His death on Calvary.

WHEN our Lord enters into His sovereignty, when He takes to Himself His great power and rules and reigns — oh, what a day that will be! Today I would direct your eyes to the form of Him who is altogether lovely, the chiefest among ten thousand, the One who is "over all, God blessed for ever."

Behold the sweetness of His countenance, the penetrating glance of His eyes; see the grace of His lips, how majestic His appearance! He is glorious in His apparel; He walks with the carriage of a king; hosts prostrate themselves before Him and cry, "Holy, holy holy, Lord God of Sabaoth!" Ransomed sinners bow before Him and sob out their gratitude for His mercy and His compassion. Strong men claim Him as their strength. Helpless women look to Him as their stay and support. Little children love Him. Demons see Him, confess Him as the Son of God, and flee. Armies flee from His presence.

Oh, behold Him! Some day, some blessed day, He whose right it is to rule because He is God, because He is the son of

David, because He died for sinners on Calvary—some blessed day His glory shall cover the heavens, and the earth shall be full of His praise. Men will have to shield their eyes from the brightness of His glory. And when He stands to measure the earth, the everlasting hills shall bow before Him.

> Lo, He comes, with clouds descending,
>   Once for favored sinners slain;
> Thousand, thousand saints attending,
>   Swell the triumph of His train;
> Hallelujah! Hallelujah!
>   God appears on earth to reign!
>
> Yea, Amen! Let all adore Thee,
>   High on Thine eternal throne:
> Saviour, take the power and glory;
>   Claim the kingdom for Thine own.
> O come quickly, O come quickly,
>   Hallelujah! Come, Lord, come!

Just this word and I am done. There is little use talking about His coronation then, if we have not crowned Him now. His crown rights, based on the eternal verities of God, are unassailable, and they demand our full allegiance.

Is He *your* Lord? Is He your *Lord?* He has a right to be. For He is God, He is the son of David, He is the Saviour of our souls. Amen.

6

THE CONFLICT OF THE AGES

by WILBUR M. SMITH, D.D.

The first prophetic utterance in the Scriptures is found in Genesis 3:15, a divine announcement of one major aspect of the entire redemptive program of God. It is an announcement of the unceasing, age-long, bitterly-waged conflict between Satan, all the hosts under his dominion, and the Son of God, with all who are on the side of God in His redemptive purposes, who have been, and will be, redeemed by His only begotten Son. It is an announcement of conflict, suffering and final victory for the Seed of the woman. While it has been frequently acknowledged, from the time of the Church Fathers to the present, that here is one of the greatest prophetic utterances to be found in all the Scriptures, the acorn out of which the tree of God's prophetic program grows, the pronouncement itself has rarely been given extended consideration. In fact, I know of no such examination of the far-reaching implications of the verse as will be attempted in this series of studies.

The Roman Catholic Church, in this, as in many other areas of Biblical study, has far surpassed Protestant scholars in the thoroughness with which it has examined this verse, especially in recent years. I know this has been done in an attempt to bolster in every conceivable way the doctrine of the assumption of the Virgin Mary; but whatever the reason, the studies are admirably exhaustive, even if somewhat slanted in their conclusions. For example, Father Dominic J. Unger of the Franciscan Institute has recently published a magnificent discussion of this one verse extending to 325 pages of text, in which he quotes over two hundred different authors, from the

Church Fathers down to the present generation, who have given
extended consideration to this single sentence. This is by far
the most exhaustive treatment of this text that has appeared
in our language, and bears the title, *The First-Gospel,* which
is simply another way of writing the Latin title assigned to this
verse from earliest times, the *Protevangelium.*

THE DECLARATION OF WAR

In this initial message, I would like first to set forth the basic
truths to be elicited from this one sentence, made up almost entirely of monosyllables (apart from the word *enmity* and *woman,*
and two occurrences of the preposition *between*). In the Revised Version, the verse reads as follows: "And I will put enmity
between thee and the woman, and between thy seed and her
seed: he shall bruise thy head, and thou shalt bruise his heel."
I am assuming here, with almost all conservative Biblical writers
that while it was some serpentine form of animal that came
into the garden, it was Satan himself who spoke through this
animal; for, as the Apostle Paul said, it was "the serpent [who]
beguiled Eve in his craftiness," and in the Book of Revelation
the devil is actually called "the old serpent" (12:9; 20:2). It
would seem that in the fourteenth verse, the first part of the
pronouncement, the curse relates to the serpent as an animal
now doomed to go upon its belly and to eat dust; but that in
the verse we are about to study, the declaration bears directly
upon Satan, who himself initiated the temptation, and succeeded
in leading our first parents into a forsaking of the will of God
and a deliberate disobeying of God's law.

DECLARATION FROM THE THRONE

We are now ready to consider the basic truths of the verse
as it stands in the text. First of all, here is a word spoken by
God. In fact, is not the entire narrative, beginning with creation and extending to the expulsion from Eden, anything other
than a series of divine pronouncements? Each of the seven
days in the creation record, whatever might be their length,
is introduced by the phrase "And God said" (1:3, 6, 9, 14, 20),
while in the account of the sixth day the phrase is repeated
four times (1:24, 26, 28, 29), introducing on the last two oc-

casions a word spoken by God directly to man. In the second account of creation, dealing with God's rich provision for man's welfare, we read that God "commanded the man" regarding the tree of the knowledge of good and evil, of which he was not to eat; and, later, "Jehovah God said, It is not good that the man should be alone" (2:18). The temptation in Eden opens with a word from Satan, who questions the validity or reality of any announcement from God, a subject to which we shall return shortly. After the fall God speaks again, first interrogating the man (3:9-12), then the woman (3:13); and finally He speaks to the serpent, but in a pronouncement, not a question.

The second truth, so evident, is that these words (in vv. 14 and 15), addressed to the serpent, primarily concern the serpent and Satan. Notice the constant repetition of the second personal pronoun, "thou," "thee," and "thy." God speaks of what the serpent has done, of his doom, his consignment to crawl upon his belly and eat dust, of the serpent's seed, the serpent's head, the enmity that will now prevail between him and the woman, and between his seed and her seed. The one to whom God is here speaking has brought about the greatest disaster ever to occur on this earth — the fall of our first parents. In this act man deliberately chooses to disobey God, to believe Satan, and to do Satan's bidding. All the goodness, holiness, righteousness and justice of God manifested toward our first parents were not sufficient to keep them from yielding to this initial temptation. It must have been presented with great attractiveness and power. By this act sin now enters into the world, and death by sin, as the Apostle Paul reminds us (Rom. 5:12). Now begins the reign of those monstrous lords, King Sin and King Death; and what awful havoc, sorrow, shame, cruelty, they have worked in this world; what enormous schemes have been proposed to escape them; what superstitions and false philosophies have been created in attempts to deny the consequences of this original fall of man. It is a dreadful thing to say, but it cannot be denied that here Satan won a tremendous victory: he spoiled God's creation, he alienated the affection of mankind, he brought men under his dominion,

under the spell of the fear of death, and into the galling bondage of a depraved nature.

It is important, in the light of all this, to observe carefully
the mood or tone, in which these words are expressed. God's
word to Satan, following Satan's victory, is not one of be-
wilderment: God is not desperate, He is not frenzied as a
result of the disaster which has overtaken those who were
made in His image. God knows what should be done, and
what will be done: He fully knows how this present victory
will ultimately end in defeat, and how from the human race,
defeated by sin, will proceed One who will in turn destroy
the very enemy who brought about this tragedy. Neither are
these words an offer of compromise: God is not going to share
the universe with Satan now that he has won this victory, nor
is He going to do anything that would contradict or depreciate
His holiness, His justice, or His righteousness. God will un-
ceasingly wage war on Satan, on those who belong to Satan,
and on sin in every aspect of its hideousness. There is nothing
here of self-pity, no indication of weakness on the part of God.
On the contrary, note how the announcement begins with a
confident *I will*. This is the first "I will" of God in the Scriptures. The fall of man has not rendered God partially impo-
tent. He is not alarmed at the power of Satan. He does not
need to reconsider what He might be able to do. God was
omnipotent when He brought the world into existence, and He
remains omnipotent. Satan, though powerful, is not all-powerful.
Only God is almighty! Satan does have power; he has displayed
it, and he will continue to display it. He is a supernatural
being. He has worked havoc with God's creation, but he is
still within the greater power of God and he cannot escape
God's will. I have often thought that perhaps Satan attempted
to flee the garden when his vile purposes had been accomplished. But he can no more escape from God than can a man.
Satan must say with the Psalmist, "Though I make my bed
in hell, behold, thou art there" (Ps. 139:8). God held Satan
before Him as He made this pronouncement, and in this pronouncement Satan heard his ultimate doom.

Up to this point we have been examining the background

as it were, of this declaration. Now we must look into the verse itself with great care. The fundamental truth here set forth, whatever be our interpretation of the details, is that from this time on, from the day of Satan's victory in the garden, there will be two groups, if we may so call them, in history, in absolute antagonism one toward the other: on the one hand Satan and his seed, and on the other hand the woman and her seed. It would seem — though we are not arguing the point — that this classifies all members of the human race in either one or the other of these groups. There is something universal about this statement, and there would appear to be on the surface a conflict between the supernatural and the natural: Satan is certainly a supernatural being, while the woman as such is not, whatever her seed might ultimately be in the program of God. On the basis of visible facts one would expect the conflict eventually to end in victory for the one who has just made such a great opening conquest, but the text reveals the very opposite. Through the human race will come One who will defeat with finality this supernatural enemy of God.

The one word to be emphasized here is *enmity*, which expresses the attitude of Satan and his seed toward the woman and her seed. But — and this should not be forgotten — this is to be also the unchanging attitude of the woman and her seed toward Satan and his seed. This word *enmity*, even as it appears in the English text, is from the same root as the word *enemy*; indeed, not only do the English words derive from the same root, but the Greek words for *enemy* and *enmity* also derive from the same root, *echthros*, which is used in the Greek text of Genesis 3:15 as well as in the parable of the tares and the wheat, where our Lord referred to Satan as *the* enemy (Matt. 13:28, 39).

Before going further into the meaning of the passage, we might do well to dwell for a moment on some of the definitions of these words: *enemy* and *enmity*. The *Oxford English Dictionary* gives as the first definition, "one that cherishes hatred, that wishes or seeks to do ill to another; in a weaker sense, an adversary, antagonist, opponent." Already we have discovered at least one word that is often used in reference to Satan in the New Testament — adversary. It is interesting to observe that the second definition relates directly to the devil: "the enemy: the devil . . . the enemy of mankind, of souls." Following along through the various implications of this word, we come to the last: "of, or pertaining to, a hostile army or nation." Enmity is simply "the disposition or the ill-feelings characteristic of an enemy . . . a state of mutual hostility." This alone gives us some conception of what a frightful thing enmity can be, especially when it exists between an evil supernatural power and struggling mankind. Many of the very names of Satan, particularly in their Greek forms, derive from this idea of animosity, e.g., the Greek word *diabolos,* translated *devil,* meaning "an accuser"; and *apollyon,* meaning "the destroyer" (Rev. 9:11); or the words of our Lord, "The thief cometh not but for to steal and to kill, and to destroy" (John 10:10); and Peter's phrase, "The devil as a roaring lion, walketh about seeking whom he may devour" (I Pet. 5:8).

In this conflict, both sides suffer: the seed of the woman will be bruised: Satan will bruise his heel; on the other hand, the seed of the woman will bruise Satan's head. As many have pointed out, the heel is not a vulnerable part of the body; actually one could have the heel removed without his life being imperiled. The head, however, is a vital and vulnerable part of the body, and when any extensive damage is suffered in that area, the individual is rendered helpless, incapable of functioning adequately. Christ did suffer, He did die — and those engaged in putting Him to death did so by the instigation of Satan. But He was not destroyed; rather, at the time of His crucifixion, He drew, and still draws men toward Himself. But Satan will be mortally wounded, and so conclusively defeated that there will never be any possibility of his working further damage in the new creation of God.

There is one further truth to be found in this verse, and that is, the seed of the woman will ultimately terminate in a single individual, expressed by the pronoun *his.* The verdict of death was announced by God upon those who disobeyed Him, and death was the due of the Adamic race in this disobedience, but the very fact that the woman would have a seed was an indication of the grace and mercy of God. Humanity is not immediately extinguished: the full punishment for sin is not at once meted out. Death will take Adam and Eve, but children will remain; death will take the children, but grandchildren will be born; and so down through the ages until He comes who will bruise the head of Satan, who will bring this conflict to an end, who will restore to its original purity and loveliness the creation of God and defeat forever God's great enemy.

SATAN'S TWO BASIC METHODS OF DISPLAYING THIS ANIMOSITY

I do not recall having seen any serious attempt to define the principal methods which Satan has used down through the ages to reveal his unchanging hostility to the redemptive program of God, and to those whom God intends to use to accomplish this program. These methods are primarily in the areas of destruction and deception. The titles given Satan; our Lord's characterization of Satan; the work of Satan as seen in the Gospels, in the Early Church, in the Book of Revelation; all these can be related to one or the other of the subtle but vast programs of the devil. Without enumerating all the relevant passages, we might recall but two verses in John's Gospel, in which Christ refers to Satan first as a deceiver and a liar (8:44, 45), and then as a murderer from the beginning. May I then dare to suggest that, according to the Biblical records, Satan's primary activity from the beginning of Old Testament history down to the death of our Lord upon the Cross seems to be in the area of destruction; that from the ascension of Christ down to the end of this age his main work will be that of deception; and that during the concluding years of this age, the dark and dreadful era in which Antichrist will be supreme on earth, this deception will be revealed with a terribleness beyond anything that has thus far been seen in history.

Did not the determination of Satan to destroy the godly seed, to terminate the redemptive program of God, begin with the very second generation of the human race, when Cain became a murderer — which is exactly what Satan is — and killed his own brother Abel, who had pleased God by his faith in an atoning sacrifice and by his obedience to God's command?

The first murder involves the death of a righteous man at the hands of a wicked man.

The apparent attempt to prevent the fulfillment of God's plan to establish a chosen people with the call of Abraham, and of the promises that attended this call, is not as clearly revealed as other instances we shall mention; but I do believe that a careful scrutiny of the story of Abraham's early life will nevertheless disclose a threat to the realization of God's promises to him in the invasion of one who was probably the mightiest king on earth at that time, Chedorlaomer, in confederation with a number of more or less local kings. Everyone is acquainted with the account of those early wars: the capture of Lot and his family, Abraham's pursuit of Chedorlaomer's host as far as Damascus, the rescuing of his own relatives and their return to the place from which they had been taken captive; but it has seldom been pointed out that these invading hosts seemed to have been Abraham's enemies as well as Lot's. Melchizedek in blessing Abraham said, "Blessed be God Most High who hath delivered thine enemies into thy hands" (Gen. 14:20, ASV). By this Melchizedek implies that it was only by the protecting hand of God, and an unusual power given to Abraham, that he himself escaped from the hands of these invaders. It would look as though he could have been taken captive and kept as such for the remainder of his life, had not God intervened.

The vain effort of Satan to annihilate the Israelites in Egypt is of course set forth in detail in the opening chapters of the Book of Exodus: "And Pharaoh charged all his people, saying, Every son that is born ye shall cast into the river, and every daughter ye shall save alive" (1:22, and Acts 7:19). Had it not been for divine intervention, the Hebrew race would have been ultimately extinguished in the land of the Pharaohs. At the same time there was some *deception* here by agents of Satan, in the clever imitations by which the Egyptian magicians, led by Jannes and Jambres (II Tim. 3:8), tried to deceive the royal court. As Satan sought to *destroy* the first of the godly seed, Abel, then apparently attempted to at least bring into slavery the founder of the Hebrew race, and later to annihilate Israel in a foreign land, so he also did, through various human agencies, repeatedly try to kill David. How often, for example, did this man, anointed by God to be the future king of Israel, escape from the thrown javelin of the jealous Saul, and later from the searching parties sent out by Saul to find and destroy him. It is interesting to note that whereas in the First Book of Samuel we often have the phrase, "the enemies of David" (as in 20:15), toward the end of the book these enemies are actually called "the enemies of Jehovah" (I Sam. 30:26).

Having failed to destroy the founder of the Hebrew race, the Hebrew race itself, and the founder of the royal Messianic line, Satan must of necessity bring all of his evil schemes to bear upon David's greater son, the Messiah, Jesus Christ Himself, who came to redeem men from the thralldom of the devil. One is almost amazed to discover from the gospels how many different and powerful groups of individuals sought to destroy Him.

DECEPTION, SATAN'S PRESENT METHOD

There is something very strange about Satan's determination to destroy the Lord. I John 3:8 definitely states that Christ came into the world to *destroy* the works of the devil. Now, it is interesting to note that, while there are seven different verbs in the Book of Acts used in reference to the crucifixion and death of the Lord Jesus, not once does it say that anyone *destroyed* Him: they put Him to death, they crucified Him, but they did not destroy Him. In three days He was walking in Jerusalem, in fifty days His name was preached in that same city, with the result that three thousand came out of the kingdom of darkness and received the risen Lord as their Saviour. With Christ's ascension into glory, the determination of Satan to destroy Him must be forever abandoned.

What then is there left for Satan to do now, in his unceasing effort to wreck God's program of redemption and his never-flagging animosity toward the human race? It would seem that, beginning with the ascension of our Lord, down to the end of this age, the main objective of Satan is not to make drunkards, or libertines, or thieves, or to fill our prisons: rather is it *to deceive* men and women with the intention that they may not be convicted of their sin and converted to Christ; that they will be prevented from even believing Christ to be the Saviour sent from heaven; that they shall be dissuaded from accepting the Bible as the Word of God. Indeed, the question which Satan asked of our first parents, that brought about their loss of confidence in the word of God, was "Yea, hath God said?" The same question, in various forms, he has been thrusting at men ever since Christ died and rose again. The woman herself, on the day she succumbed to this initial temptation, confessed that Satan had *beguiled* her (Gen. 3:13), a term repeated by the Apostle Paul when he refers to Eve as the woman who was *beguiled* (I Tim. 2:13).

To be *deceived* is to believe as true what is not true, to have a hope which is unjustified, or to invest one's life or means in some task or enterprise because of confidence in the word and promises of another who has not told the truth. In the deeper things of life this can mean disaster. A quack doctor can deceive a patient suffering with cancer by claiming to be able to heal him, until it is too late and the case is hopeless. When a man is deceived regarding such all-important and eternally-significant truths as the nature of God, the way of salvation, the veracity of God's divine revelation, the divine origin and deity of Jesus Christ, the need for vicarious atonement, the certainty of a life to come, his whole outlook is distorted because it is dominated by false ideas. Everything he does, his every major line of thought, his plans for the future, his general conduct, are all twisted, perverted, out of line with the truth, and he is on his way to utter disillusionment in this life, and unless saved betimes, also in the next. Indeed according to the Word of God, he is on his way to destruction.

Our Lord Himself emphasizes this deceiving work of Satan throughout His ministry. The most significant parable bearing upon this subject is that of the wheat and the tares. What are tares? They are plant growths that look like wheat, in fact, in the early stages of development only an expert could distinguish between them. They take strength from the ground, but what they ultimately produce is an absolutely worthless and even poisonous grain. Jesus says that these tares are sown

by Satan, by "the enemy," which takes us right back to the
word in our original text (Matt. 13:25, 28, 29).

Even before the coming of Christ, Satan sowed seed that
resembled some of the principles later developed in the Christian faith. Since that time also he has frequently put forth
various ideas, which seem to have a semblance of the Christian
faith. One of the better known among these is Christian Science,
whose very name, the Church of Christ Scientist, embodies two
principal New Testament words, the use of which is wholly
unjustified. Christian Science is far from the New Testament
concept of the Church. To them the Holy Spirit is the Christian Science Church. They speak of Jesus, but wholly deny
His deity, His uniqueness, His vicarious atonement, and His
bodily resurrection. According to this deception Mary Baker
Eddy was a greater prophet than Jesus, and many thousands are
so deceived that they believe it! I have even heard officers in
a Christian church, true believers, remark upon returning from
the funeral of a Christian Scientist friend, "Well, after all, there
is not much difference between our faith and theirs." This is
exactly what Satan wants men to think. There is no need to
prolong this discussion of cults and religions which, either take
their names from the Scriptures, or speak of receiving some additional light on Scriptural truth. Any suggestion that there is
some way by which man can come to God except through
Jesus Christ is Satanic deception, and the devil has been very
successful in this area!

At the end of His ministry, Christ, in His great prophetic discourse on the Mount of Olives, warned, "Take heed that no man
lead you astray" (Matt. 24:4, ASV), adding, "For many shall
come in my name, saying, I am the Christ; and shall lead many
astray." So burdened was our Lord with the necessity for ad-
monishing the Church on this point, that He returns to the
subject twice again in the same discourse: "Many false prophets
shall arise, and shall lead many astray" (v. 11, ASV). "Then if any
man shall say unto you, Lo, here is the Christ, or, Here;
believe it not. For there shall arise false Christs, and false
prophets, and shall show great signs and wonders; so as to lead
astray, if possible, even the elect. Behold, I have told you

beforehand" (vv. 23-25, ASV; see also Luke 21:8; Mark 13:
7,22).

It is, however, not only in the matter of doctrine that
Satan deceives men. The writer to the Hebrews tells us that
one of the most potent forces for deception is sin, so that
the hearts of men are "hardened by the deceitfulness of sin"
(Heb. 3:13, ASV). Paul mentions a number of ways in which
men are deceived, e.g., "the lusts of deceit" (Eph. 4:22, ASV).
through "empty words" (Eph. 5:6), the deceivable nature of
riches (I Tim. 6:10) and of unrighteousness (II Thess. 2:10).
Then there are those famous passages which apply even more
directly to our civilization today than to that which prevailed in the first century A.D., "Take heed lest there shall
be any one that maketh spoil of you through his philosophy
and vain deceit, after the tradition of men, after the rudi-
ments of the world, and not after Christ" (Col. 2:8, ASV). And
the Apostle Peter, echoing the words of our Lord in His
Olivet Discourse, warns the Church, "But there arose false
prophets also among the people, as among you also there shall
be false teachers, who shall privily bring in destructive heresies,
denying even the Master that bought them, bringing upon
themselves swift destruction. And many shall follow their
lascivious doings; by reason of whom the way of the truth
shall be evil spoken of. And in covetousness shall they with
feigned words make merchandise of you: whose sentence
now from of old lingereth not, and their destruction slumber-
eth not" (II Pet. 2:1-3, ASV).

Is it not time for the Christian Church to begin once again
to consider what Paul has to say about general world-wide
deception that is to characterize the end of this age? We
hear so much today that our hope for the future lies in a
world government, how grand it will be to have a world
church, but we are forgetting that the New Testament has
some things to say about world conditions, and says them in
searing sentences. If we believe this New Testament is the
Word of God, given by inspiration of the Holy Spirit, it is time
to examine these passages again. At the end of his life, Paul
wrote to Timothy, "But the Spirit saith expressly, that in later

times some shall fall away from the faith, giving heed to seducing spirits and doctrines of demons, through the hypocrisy of men that speak lies, branded in their own conscience as with a hot iron; forbidding to marry, and commanding to abstain from meats, which God created to be received with thanksgiving by them that believe and know the truth" (I Tim. 4:1-3, ASV).

First of all, it should be recognized that the word here translated *seducing* is from the root meaning "to deceive" and could be so translated. Demons deceive first of all in the matter of *doctrine*. Those apostatizing from the faith give heed to the "doctrines of demons." I have never seen this fascinating passage adequately unfolded, and there is no space here for a detailed study; but how easy it is to see that this particular aspect of demon activity ties in with the apostasy of the last days described in II Thessalonians 2, with the false prophets of the Olivet Discourse, with Antichrist of I John, with Satan as the great deceiver himself, and with the many aspects of deception referred to in the Apocalypse. I am more and more inclined to believe that the principal heresies of the Christian Church — denying the deity of our Lord, spurning the atonement, rejecting the resurrection, scoffing at the second advent — originate, for the most part, from these evil creatures. I would go one step further: many who from our pulpits are denouncing the cardinal doctrines of the faith, and preaching doctrines contrary to the faith, are, though they do not know it, inspired by demons. The word *doctrine* needs emphasis. The antidote for false doctrine is in II Timothy 3:16, where Paul says, "All scripture is given by inspiration of God, and is profitable for *doctrine*" (AV). The word *doctrine* is the same as that for *teaching* (ASV).

There is scarcely a more fearful passage in all the Word of God than that in Paul's Second Epistle to the Thessalonians, bearing upon universal deception: "And then shall be revealed the lawless one, whom the Lord Jesus shall slay with the breath of his mouth, and bring to nought by the manifestation of his coming; even he, whose coming is according to the working of Satan with all power and signs and lying wonders, and with all deceit of unrighteousness for them that perish; because they received not the love of the truth that they might be saved. And for this cause God sendeth them a working of error, that they should believe a lie: that they all might be judged who believed not the truth, but had pleasure in unrighteousness" (2: 8-12, ASV). Notice how closely the themes of unrighteousness and falsehood are here connected. They not only rejected the truth, but they "had pleasure in unrighteousness." It was sin which kept them from believing the truth, or, as Paul says in a somewhat similar passage, they "hinder the truth in unrighteousness" (Rom. 1:18, ASV). Professor Alfred Plummer has excellently expressed it: "Just as the first coming of Christ caused a crisis, a separation of the lovers of light from the lovers of darkness (John 3:19), so this coming of the great adversary separates those who love the truth from those who take pleasure in unrighteousness. As Christ does mighty works and signs and wonders for the instruction and salvation of mankind, so also does he (the adversary) for their deception and ruin. As Christ came to seek and to save those who are lost, so this rival comes to complete the perdition of those who are perishing." A century ago the eminent Scotch exegete, John Eadie, remarked on these words: "This unparalleled hallucination indicates a mysterious state of mind and of society — anti-Christian, antitheistic, credulous, with a fatal facility of being imposed upon by hellish mystery and subtlety."

There is one clause here that must be further considered: "For this cause God sendeth them a working of error" (2:11; cf. Rom. 1:24, 25, where we read that God gave up men to vile passions). As Professor Findlay has said: "The result is inevitable, and comes about by what we now call a natural law. That persistent rejection of truth destroys the sense of truth, and results in fatal error, is an ethical principle and a fact of experience as certain as any in the world. Now, he who believes in God as the Moral Ruler of the universe knows that its laws are the expression of His will. Since this Satanic delusion is the moral consequence of previous and willful rejection of the truth, it is manifest that God is here at work; He makes Satan and the lawless one His instruments in punishing false-hearted men." In John's first epistle there is a striking phrase with reference to this same general deception: "We are of God: he that knoweth God heareth us; he who is not of God heareth us not. By this we know the *spirit of truth, and the spirit of error*" (4:6, ASV). One has a right to conclude from this verse that every human being will yield his mind and give his allegiance either to that which is taught by the spirit of truth, or that which is promoted by the spirit of error. Again in his second epistle, John reminds us that, ". . . many deceivers are gone forth into the world, even they that confess not that Jesus Christ cometh in the flesh" (v. 7, ASV; see also I John 2:18-23; 4:2,3). This archenemy of God does not deny that there was a person Jesus of Nazareth on this earth; that he would probably never be so foolish as to attempt; but he denies that Jesus is the Christ, the Son. That the earth looks for a Christ, that is, the Messiah, he would not deny; but that Jesus of Nazareth is the Messiah, the One to whom we may look for redemption, this he does deny.

In his wonderful volume of lectures on I John, Dr. Robert Candlish has said: "Neither what He is to us as our Jesus, nor what He is to God as His Son, can be otherwise known than by what He is anointed to do, and actually does, as the Christ. Set aside His being Christ, the anointed Sacrificer and the anointed Sacrifice, the anointed Priest and the anointed Victim — the Lamb of God, that taketh away the sin of the world; set aside His actual work for which He is anointed — the work of redeeming us by His obedience, and the shedding of His blood, or the giving of His life in our stead, and we have neither any Jesus fit to be our Saviour, nor any Son of God worth the owning."

Much that is taught today under the cognomen of Modernism or liberal Christianity is nothing but that which Antichrist himself will proclaim, and is therefore a preparation for the advent of this evil being.

WORLD-WIDE DECEPTION

All that has been said of the deceiving work of the devil, from the garden of Eden to the present hour, is summed up in one

startling clause, so contrary in the truth it expresses to what
our sophisticated and self-satisfied age believes and in which
the divinely-inspired Apostle John refers to Satan as "the deceiver of the whole world." Taking this statement at face
value, one is forced to conclude that, inasmuch as the whole
world lieth in the evil one, and the evil one is the arch deceiver and thus the deceiver of the whole world, all men outside of Christ and all men who reject and repudiate Christ, are
living, working and thinking under the spell of this spirit of
deception. I do not know any other way to read my Bible, nor
do I know any other way to account for the present world-wide
rejection of Jesus Christ and the fact that more people are
under the power of atheistic communism today than are under
the power of a crucified and risen Lord.

A CASE IN POINT

Having spoken in a general way of the deception of Satan
down through the ages, and the deepening of a world-wide
delusion at the end of this age, let us be specific in regard
to one area and one period of time — a century of European
literature from 1850 to 1950. Early in 1952, the New York
Times issued a fifty-page brochure entitled "A Century of Books,"
in which were brought together reviews of 113 notable volumes
that had been considered in the pages of that paper from 1851
to 1951. A careful study of this illuminating document reveals
that by far the greater majority of these authors were either anti-
Christian or specifically non-Christian in their attitude toward
Christ and the Scriptures; in fact, apart from Nathaniel Haw-
thorne, one could not recognize here any other writer, man
or woman, as a believing Christian, and not one book among
these more than one hundred famous and influential works
was written to honor the Lord Jesus, to expound the Word of
God, or to extol Christian virtues. The only title here that is
occupied with the person of Christ is Renan's Life of Jesus,
which, though brilliant, was really a caricature of the gospel
records of our Lord's life, and resulted in a wave of unbelief
in relation to these accounts throughout the western world.
Pursuing this matter in more detail, we might list those books

which were either written deliberately to attack the Christian faith, or those which resulted in the undermining of faith in Christian truths whether or not the authors meant such to be the result.

Charles Darwin: *On the Origin of Species,* 1859.
Thomas H. Huxley: *Evidence as to Man's Place in Nature,* 1863.
Karl Marx: *Capital.*
Works of Friedrich Nietzsche.
Sigmund Freud. *The Interpretation of Dreams,* 1913.
John Dewey: *Experience and Nature,* 1925.
Adolf Hitler: *My Battle,* 1933.
The Letters of Lenin, 1914.
George Bernard Shaw, 1898.
Bertrand Russell: *The Problems of Philosophy,* 1912.

A second group of authors, and a very large one, would be characterized as having looked at and rejected the claims of the Christian faith, the deity of the Lord Jesus Christ, and salvation through His atoning work; sometimes bitterly, violently, blasphemously, though not always in the books here mentioned.

M. Renan: *The Life of Jesus,* 1863.
Henry D. Thoreau: *Excursions,* 1863.
Walt Whitman: *Leaves of Grass,* 1866.
George Eliot: *Daniel Deronda.*
Ralph Waldo Emerson: *Natural History of Intellect.*
William James: *Varieties of Religious Experience,* 1902.
Henri Bergson: *Creative Evolution,* 1911.
Henry L. Mencken: *The American Language,* 1919.
Sinclair Lewis: *Main Street,* 1920.
Albert Einstein: *Relativity,* 1920.

Finally, we must include books of immoral standards, some of which were for years banned from import to this country. All of these set forth immoral practices of one kind or another in terms implying approval and commendation.

Charles Baudelaire: *Flowers of Evil,* 1871.
Theodore Dreiser: *The Financier,* 1912.
Anatole France: *The Gods are Thirsty,* 1912.
D. H. Lawrence: *Sons and Lovers,* 1913.
James Joyce: *Ulysses,* 1922.
Marcel Proust: *Swann's Way,* 1922.
Andre Gide: Various Works.

Ernest Hemingway: *The Sun Also Rises*, 1926.
Hervey Allen: *Anthony Adverse*, 1933.
John Steinbeck: *Grapes of Wrath*, 1939.

There is no question that these thirty-one volumes — to say noth
ing of the eighty-two additional works that found a place in thi
brochure — exercised more influence upon the thinking o
the western world than any fifty books written during that same
period of time to defend and interpret the Christian faith. Some
of these volumes still have enormous influence throughout the
world, e.g., *Capital* by Karl Marx.

Why have such immoral, anti-Christian, and in some case
atheistic writings taken such a powerful hold on the modern
mind? We need only turn to the words of the Apostle John
for our answer: "They are of the world: therefore speak they
of the world, and the world heareth them" (I John 4:5)
Upon the death of George Bernard Shaw, the *Saturday Review
of Literature* significantly entitled its extended obituary notice
"Schoolmaster to the World." This could be said of many o
these other writers. Actually, the Christian Church today doe
not have writers whose works are influencing the minds of men
throughout the world. The *world* is learning from those who
have rejected the truth as it is in Christ; from those who, being
deceived themselves, can only deceive others by their writings
One can think only of the closing words of Paul's first lette
to Timothy, which, in the vivid translation of the late Dr
Arthur S. Way, read as follows: "Shun always the irreverent
babble, the dialectic tricks of what misnames itself 'spiritua
illumination,' which some men are ever parading, and so ir
dealing with the faith have shot wide of the mark of truth'
(6:20, 21).

THE CHRISTIAN AND THE CONFLICT

We noted earlier in the discussion of this first prophetic
utterance (Gen. 3:15) that the conflict is waged by two sides
It is not merely an attack of Satan upon the woman and he
seed, but also a counterattack by the woman and her seed unti
the serpent is mortally wounded. What is our position in thi
conflict today? What can we do in this titanic struggle, in which

numbers, as well as much of the world's learning, art, and culture are on the other side? What can break through this heavy screen of deception? Only one thing: *the truth*. Ridicule, condemnation, repudiation and warning will not expose the falsehood of Satan. It is only the light of truth that can truly reveal the deceivable nature of this great mass of worldly thought and utterance. First of all, Christ Himself must be recognized as the truth: the truth about God; about redemption; about the ideals, ethics, and goals of life; about the way of victory, reconciliation with God, deliverance from the power of fear, the certainty of hell, the assurance and hope of glory. He is the truth, and He spoke the truth. One of His strongest statements about the truthfulness of His own utterances has to do with the deceivableness of Satan: "Why do ye not understand my speech? Even because ye cannot hear my word. Ye are of your father the devil, and the lusts of your father it is your will to do. He was a murderer from the beginning, and standeth not in the truth, because there is no truth in him. When he speaketh a lie, he speaketh of his own: for he is a liar, and the father thereof. But because I say the truth, ye believe me not. Which of you convicteth me of sin? If I say truth, why do ye not believe me?" (John 8:43-46, ASV). Standing before Pontius Pilate a few hours before His death, Jesus replied to the question as to whether he was king, "To this end have I been born, and to this end am I come into the world, that I should bear witness unto the truth. Every one that is of the truth heareth my voice" (John 18:37, ASV). Moreover, He has sent the Spirit of truth into our hearts, to teach us the truth, to illuminate our minds (John 14:17; 16:26). You and I are to present Christ as *the Truth* for which the human heart was made. We are to understand the truth by the power of the Spirit of truth, and we are to bear witness to this truth and to the truthfulness of the Word of God in this generation. Only the entrance of the Word of God brings light. When confidence in this Word is lost; when something other than this Word is preached; when other religious texts are assumed to be equal with this Word, then the spell of deception cannot be broken. These things in themselves are deception and only rivet more firmly the chains of delusion.

THE CONCLUSION OF THIS CONFLICT

The Book of Revelation is the prophetic unfolding of the final conflict between Christ and Antichrist, between light and darkness, between God and anti-God, between the armies of heaven and the armies of the kings of the earth who go out to make war with the Lamb. All this must be left for treatment at another time. Here we conclude simply by saying that at the end of this age, so clearly revealed in these pages, all the schemes of destruction and delusion that Satan has ever conceived and used will be employed in one final thrust. The result of this conflict is announced in the nineteenth chapter of the Apocalypse, in that name given to Christ, "King of Kings, and Lord of Lords." By Him the deceiver of this world is finally cast into hell forever, together with the beast, the false prophets, the false christs, all liars, and all who have deceived and have been deceived. Then will the truth reign, and a kingdom of righteousness, peace, equity and beauty will replace all the nations and empires which have stained this earth with blood and marred the pages of history with cruelty and selfishness. The great conflict in which we find ourselves today has thus been unfolded for us in these divinely-inspired pages. The Word of God, if believed, will deliver men from fear, from the power of sin, from the deceptions of Satan, from a judgment to come, and from all the disillusionments that have brought sorrow to those who have placed their faith and hope in anything or anyone but Jesus Christ and His righteousness.

7

CHRIST INCARNATE IN CONFLICT WITH SATAN

by Wilbur M. Smith, d.d.

It was inevitable that the most powerful attack of Satan should be upon the historical person of the Lord Jesus Christ, for Satan surely knew that one of the main purposes for which Christ came into the world, was to expose, defeat and mortally wound the Devil. "To this end," says the Apostle John, "was the Son of God manifested, that he might destroy the works of the devil" (I John 3:8, ASV). And the writer to the Hebrews adds, "Since then the children are sharers in flesh and blood, he also himself in like manner partook of the same; that through death he might bring to nought him that had the power of death, that is, the devil; and might deliver all them who through fear of death were all their lifetime subject to bondage" (2:14, 15, ASV). In the conflict between Satan and Christ, the enemy of mankind suffered a threefold defeat. Our Lord resisted all temptation, and was thus triumphant over sin, in which rests Satan's power. He, more than any other prophet sent from God, either in the Old Testament times or in the days of the apostles, exposed with utmost clarity and detail the true nature of the person of Satan and his work. Finally, by His death on the Cross, He provided a deliverance from Satan, and established in the world of lost humanity a magnet by which vast multitudes would continually be drawn out of the kingdom of darkness into the kingdom of the light of God's Son. From the first day of His infancy to the last hour on the Cross Christ lived wholly apart from, and victorious over sin. The subject of the sinlessness of Christ is one which, for our particular purpose,

need not be discussed in detail here. It will suffice for us to
be reminded of our Lord's one comprehensive verdict concerning
His personal relationship to Satan, "The prince of this world
cometh and hath nothing in me" (John 14:30).

Christ turned the light of His holiness and omniscience upon
the character and work of Satan in His parabolic teachings, in
His discussions with the unbelieving Jews of His day, and in
pronouncements He made to the disciples. Most significantly,
the first reference to the devil in the teachings of Jesus concerns the sowing of the Word of God in the hearts of men,
i.e., the preaching of the Gospel to men, which, if received,
will deliver them forever from the power of the evil one. "When
anyone heareth the word of the kingdom," said our Lord, "and
understandeth it not, then cometh the evil one and snatcheth
away that which hath been sown in his heart." How many
millions and millions of souls, hearing the Gospel, reading the
Bible, having the Word of God quoted to them, receive it only
with the ear and mind, and, failing to embrace it with the heart,
go into eternity without that eternal life which is communicated
by the Word. And what might be some of the methods by
which Satan snatches away this Word? First of all, this Word
of God has been taken from the hearts and minds of many
through the reading of books which attack and set about to
destroy faith in the authority of the Word. This can take place
even in a classroom of a theological seminary, and it has happened
over and over again in many of our universities. How many
parents have been grieved to see their sons and daughters lose
their once implicit faith in the Word of God under the constant attacks and sneers of unbelieving professors. It can be
snatched away by preoccupation with other matters such as
work, or pleasure; or, most effectively, by walking the path of
sin, so that ultimately the heart is calloused and the power of
the Word is no longer felt.

In the second parable of this series the same figure of
speech is used, but here it is "the sons of the kingdom" that
are sown. The sowing by the Son of man of those who are
faithful to Him and will bear witness for Him, with the whole
world as the field, is followed by the sowing of tares on the

part of the evil one. These tares are the sons of his realm, the servants of his vile program. It is in this parable that our Lord actually refers to Satan as "the enemy" (Matt. 13:24-30, 36-43; Luke 10:19). However, it is in the Fourth Gospel, the Gospel which reveals most pointedly and constantly the conflict between belief and unbelief, that we find Christ's most penetrating description of Satan: "He was a murderer from the beginning" (John 8:44). As the first parable referred to Satan in relation to the Word of God, so our Lord's words here reveal the relationship of Satan to the truth, which is ultimately the Word of God and the Son of God. Notice both the negative and positive aspects of this revelation: Negatively, Satan does not stand in the truth and there is no truth in him; positively, he speaks lies and thus is the father of falsehood. The next clause sets forth clearly the violent conflict that must follow, for Christ, speaking of Himself, says, "I say the truth . . . Which of you convicteth me of sin?" To show that the truth about which He is speaking here is that revealed in the Word of God, He adds, "He that is of God heareth the words of God."

I realize that this is not a popular idea, one often brushed aside by those who week by week stand in Christian pulpits and by some whose books have hosts of devoted readers; but it is certainly clear from the teaching of our Lord Himself that those who reject His message, who would weaken or actually repudiate some of the statements from His lips, are doing the work of Satan. Such a declaration as Christ makes here irrevocably contradicts the idea that God will receive those who attempt to come to Him in some other way than by the Lord Jesus Christ. The words of God are not in Buddha, they are not in Mohammed, they are not in the founders of modern cults. The written Word of God is in the Holy Scriptures, and the incarnate Word is in His only begotten Son. In His teaching regarding Himself as the Shepherd of the sheep, Jesus again warns the disciples of the true nature of His enemy, and ours: "The thief cometh not but that he may steal and kill and destroy: I came that they may have life and may have it abundantly" (John 10:10). Our Lord not only defeated Satan at every point of temptation and exposed him to the white light of His uncompromising truthfulness, but He was consistently victorious over those mysterious emissaries of Satan, evil spirits. From the very beginning of His ministry, these demon powers were aware of the greater power of the Son of man and of His determination to bring about their defeat: "And straightway there was in their synagogue a man with an unclean spirit; and he cried out, saying, What have we to do with thee, Jesus thou Nazarene? art thou come to destroy us? I know thee who thou art, the Holy One of God. And Jesus rebuked him, saying, Hold thy peace, and come out of him. And the unclean spirit, tearing him and crying with a loud voice, came out of him (Mark 1:23-26, ASV). While often resisting the exorcising power of Christ, sometimes tearing those whom they had been indwelling (Mark 9:26), these demons nevertheless did come forth at the command of the Lord. This power was exercised also by the seventy whom Christ sent out, causing Satan and his host to know that they were now being confronted with a power which they could not overcome: "And the seventy returned with joy, saying, Lord, even the demons are subject unto us in thy name" (Luke 10:17, ASV). This is what lies behind the famous statement of Christ, so widely discussed in recent eschatological literature, "But if I by the Spirit of God cast out demons, then is the kingdom of God come unto you" (Matt. 12:28, ASV). Note carefully where this occurs: in the famous passage where He speaks of Beelzebub, the prince of demons, of a kingdom divided against itself, of Satan casting out Satan, and of Satan's kingdom standing and falling.

SATAN'S ATTACKS ON CHRIST BEFORE THE CRUCIFIXION

How many different individuals Satan used in one way or another in his effort either to destroy Christ, or to lead Him away from the will of God and thus make impossible His mission of salvation, we do not know. The Gospel records tell of the following: Herod the Great, the Pharisees, the Herodians, the chief priests, the scribes, the elders, the principal men of the people, the rulers, Pontius Pilate, two of His own disciples — Peter and Judas and, of course, in one violent attack, Satan himself. The demons must also be included here. No sooner did Herod hear that one had been born king of the Jews, fulfilling a rumor current in that day that such an individual would supplant the Herodian family, than he dispatched soldiers with orders to slay every babe three years old and under found in Bethlehem. The plot is summed up by Matthew in the prophetic pronouncement of the angel, "Herod will seek the young child to destroy him." The scheme failed.

Satan's next major attack was in the threefold temptation in the wilderness. Here again we should observe that the conflict is really based on the relationship of Christ to the Word of God, as was the first temptation in the garden of Eden, except that here Satan dares to quote the Scriptures. While Satan perverts the meaning of the Word, Christ uses it as the sword of the Spirit and comes forth victorious from each of the three attempts to persuade Him to compromise in respect to the will of God and to worship the devil. The temptation of our Lord is too well known to require detailed treatment. I want to note only that it stands at the very threshold of His ministry, and that it is unique in its subtlety and violence. Luke's account of the temptation points up a fundamental factor which we shall find constantly emphasized in the Book of Revelation: the matter of *kingdom* and *authority*. Here Satan offers to Christ all the kingdoms of the world, and no doubt he had them to offer, and Christ knew it. If the whole encounter had been a thing of fiction, there would have been no temptation at all. Further, Satan says of these kingdoms, "To thee will I give all this authority, and the glory of them" (Luke 4:6, ASV).

It is this struggle for authority; this conflict between the authority of Satan, the prince of this world, and the authority of Jesus Christ, the prince of life, which will be decided in the fearful encounters set forth in the Book of Revelation; where all the hosts of evil on earth, under the earth, and above the earth, will be marshalled together to prevent the Lord of lords from becoming the ruler of the kings of the earth. Someone has said of the voice from heaven at the baptism, and of the wilderness temptation, that it was necessary for the

Lord first to have the approval of heaven upon His character, then to come face to face with the evil proceeding from hell, before He could triumphantly confront enslaved mankind.

In the first chapter, brief reference was made to the fact that all the ecclesiastical authorities in Israel at the time of Christ's advent were determined, some at one time and some at another, to *destroy* Him. We are told that at the beginning of His ministry, after the healing on the sabbath day, "The Pharisees went out, and straightway with the Herodians took counsel against him, how they might destroy him" (Mark 3:6, ASV; Matt. 12:14). On Tuesday of Holy Week, after Christ drove out the money changers, and those that trafficked in animals, from the temple, "The chief priests and the scribes and the principal men of the people sought to destroy him" (Luke 19: 47, ASV; cf. Mark 11:18). This determination becomes increasingly intense and contagious as the ministry of Christ proceeds and His fame spreads further abroad. In the days preceding the Lord's death, we are told that "the chief priests and the elders persuaded the multitudes that they should ask for Barabbas, and destroy Jesus" (Matt. 27:20, ASV).

The resolve on the part of both Gentile and Jewish rulers to destroy Christ is emphasized in the parables, and its prediction in the Old Testament is quoted by the apostles after His resurrection. In the parable of the wicked husbandmen, Jesus, foreseeing His own death, said that the Jewish leaders, the husbandmen of the vineyard, would say among themselves when the owner of the vineyard sent his own son to them, "This is the heir; come, let us kill him, and the inheritance shall be ours. And they took him, and killed him, and cast him forth out of the vineyard" (Mark 12:7,8). In telling this parable, Jesus quoted Psalm 118:22 as a prediction of this very tragedy, that the stone which God made the head of the corner would be rejected by the builders.

In the first persecution of the newly-formed Church soon after Pentecost, the priests and the captain of the temple, the Sadducees and the rulers, the scribes and the high priest, all participated in the imprisonment of some of the disciples, and in a more or less mock trial the following day. Released from this mild harassment, the disciples came together for prayer, and, after praising God for His omnipotence in creation, quoted the opening verses of the second Psalm, a prediction of the very events that had recently come to pass in the city of Jerusalem: "Who by the Holy Spirit, by the mouth of our father David thy servant, didst say, Why did the Gentiles rage, and the peoples imagine vain things? The kings of the earth set themselves in array, and the rulers were gathered together, against the Lord and against his Anointed" (Acts 4:25-28, ASV). Here Gentiles and Jews are depicted as being bound together in their purpose to rebel against the Lord and against His Christ. In their minds, this determination seemed to have ended in success, at least for a few days: This man Jesus who was disturbing Israel and exposing her sins; claiming to be their Messiah and winning people away from the binding traditions of the fathers; cleansing the temple, and healing on the Sabbath; had been insulted, condemned, beaten, crucified, and the populace watched as He died in agony. But they did not know that soon He would be coming forth from the grave and all Jerusalem would again be in an uproar, with this difference, that now the preaching of Christ crucified and risen from the dead would bring thousands of Israelites into the kingdom of the Son of God.

It is a strange fact that two of the disciples are identified with Satan's attempts to thwart the purposes of God in His beloved Son. On that memorable day when Peter, and the other disciples through him, confessed that Jesus was "the Christ, the Son of the living God" (Matt. 16:16); when Simon Peter was commended for his discernment and Christ acknowledged that God Himself had revealed this to him, and that on this very confession the Church would be built; this same disciple reacted to the Lord's announcement of His coming suffering and death with a rebuke, "Be it far from thee, Lord: this shall never be unto thee" (Matt. 16:22, ASV). Now, in words of terrible sternness, Christ, who presumably within the hour had rejoiced in Peter's confession and commended him for it, must say to the same disciple who now suggested that Messiah need not die, "Get thee behind me, Satan: thou art a stumblingblock unto me: for

over Satan revealed in Hebrews 2:14, 15, ASV: "Since then the children are sharers in flesh and blood, he also himself in like manner partook of the same; that through death he might bring to nought him that had the power of death, that is, the devil; and might deliver all them who through fear of death were all their lifetime subject to bondage." In a book rarely seen today, R. McCheyne Edgar's *The Philosophy of the Cross*, there is a remarkable comment upon these words, well worth quoting:

> *In view of the Cross, the occupation of the great calumniator, like the occupation of Othello, is gone, and man can defy the devil, and face king death without a fear.* In view of the Cross, any sinner, be he dying ignominiously, like the brigand by Christ's side, or dying naturally and quietly "in his nest," can lift himself above his agonies, and contemplate, instead of a judgment-seat with its terrors, a paradise of peace and joy, where those washed white in the blood of the Lamb shall walk with Christ before the Father, and be blessed for evermore! . . .

> *Christ's crucifixion, when properly regarded, sanctifies death and the grave* . . . What the art of man cannot accomplish has been done for us by our God. Instead of vanquishing Satan through removing all necessity of death, instead of changing in the twinkling of an eye a world of mortal men into a glorious company of immortals, He preferred to robe Himself in the mortality of His human children, and to lie down with them in the dust. And so the Saviour died upon the cross and tenanted a tomb, and thus robbed death of its repulsive associations. There are experiences which we enter with interest because of their associations with those we have learned to love. How we prize old scenes and habitations which have been consecrated for us by the living presence of those loved ones that have left us! And so is it with death and the grave . . .

> *Every captive, delivered from the fear of death through the cross, is a trophy of Christ's triumph over Satan and his hosts* . . . Death, so far as Satan is concerned, is the *worst* that he can do. In presence of death, we may say, as Macbeth did about Duncan, "Treason has done his worst"; it is the *chef-d'oeuvre* of the devil. Not of course that we are to limit the death induced by Satan to the mere death of the body. The other death is included, since it consists in isolation from God, who is "the fountain of life." But into the realm of isolation, into the kingdom of the dead, the Son

of God came. He submitted to a divine desolation, He submitted to bodily death, and burial; and so, by taking death upon Himself, He has taken its loneliness and its fear away, and spoiled Satan's work in death completely. "Where sin abounded, grace did much more abound: that as sin hath reigned unto death, even so might grace reign through righteousness unto eternal life by Jesus Christ our Lord." (Rom. 5:20, 21).

8

THE LORD'S RETURN IN PATRISTIC LITERATUR

by WILLIAM F. KERR, TH.D.

A cursory reading of the literature of the Church Fathe
will show that the doctrine of the Lord's Return received i
share of attention from those who were active in the Ear
Church. This, in itself, is a testimony to the interest whic
these men had in matters eschatological. However, a readir
of this same material will show that these writers were not a
ways in agreement as to the nature of direct and associate
events connected with the Lord's return from heaven. This
especially true of their teaching concerning the Millennium. *i*
a result, divergencies of opinion about the Millennial questic
have arisen among students of Patristic Literature.

The existing situation demands a cautious spirit from *z*
interpreter of this literature undertaking an analytic study
material bearing on eschatological matters. Therefore, befo
attempting to set forth any doctrinal teaching of the peri
under consideration, a few precautionary observations shou
be made:

1. There is a marked difference between the teaching of t
Bible and the teachings of the Church Fathers. One is a resu
of inspiration; the other is a result of interpretation. One
the Divine Revelation; the other is man's comprehension of
Thus, in the teachings of the Church Fathers there is a decid
drop in quality and clarity from the teaching of the inspir
and infallible Bible.

2. There are many instances in the literature of this peri
where the actual writings have been lost. For our knowled

their content we are therefore partly dependent upon those
ho opposed the teachings contained in the lost documents.
heir representations, not always of reliable accuracy, are at
est fragmentary. Conclusions drawn on this basis are thus
equently inferential, and cannot be made with certainty.

3. We must be careful not to read present-day viewpoints
nd interpretations into the writings of the Church Fathers.
.ather, we must let them speak for themselves as clearly as
ossible in the light of their own theological background and
nvironment.

4. This leads us to the final observation, that the Patristic
iterature cannot settle any doctrinal issue. It can only point
p the vicissitudes which certain Biblical teachings experienced
uring that period of the Church's history. The settling of
octrinal issues is the sole prerogative of the Bible. It must be
ecognized that the truth of a doctrine cannot be solely deter-
iined by its historical antiquity.

With these preliminary remarks helping us to a better per-
pective, let us approach our study of the Patristic Literature,
llowing only those conclusions to be drawn which are in
armony with the evidences.

To facilitate our study, we shall advance three further con-
iderations:

I. The Character of the Times

The interpretation of a Biblical doctrine in any era of the
istory of the Christian Church is considerably conditioned by
he cultural and theological environment of that period. The
octrine under discussion is no exception to this rule. It did
ot escape the theological tensions and cross-currents of the
eriod in the hands of the early Church Fathers. Three factors
specially had a significant bearing upon its interpretation:

A. *Judaism*

The charge has been leveled against both the New Testa-
nent writers and the Church Fathers that their eschatological
eachings were unduly colored by the Jewish eschatology of
heir day. The truth of this charge cannot and need not be
lenied. A cursory reading of the literature of the Fathers who

deal with the doctrine of Christ's Second Coming will sho
a certain relationship to the Jewish eschatological teachin
prevalent in the century before, and for some centuries afte
the first advent of Christ.

A brief summary, framed in general terms and not implyir
either a complete or uniform teaching among Jewish write
along these lines, will help us orient ourselves to the situatic
as it existed in those days. The general concepts were:

1. A time of tribulation;
2. Elijah the forerunner of the Messiah;
3. The coming of the Messiah and His destruction of tl
   hostile powers in a divine judgment;
4. The restoration of the dispersed Jews to their land, ar
   the restoration of Jerusalem along the lines prophesic
   in such Old Testament passages as Ezekiel 40-48;
5. A kingdom of glory (not all are agreed as to its duratior
   centered in Palestine and covering the entire world;
6. The final resurrection and judgment.

There are striking similarities between these teachings ar
those of a number of the early Fathers, and these similariti
are not accidental. They can be accounted for along three line
the common source of both in the Old Testament Scripture
the incorporation of some Jewish eschatological teachings in
the New Testament through the act of divine revelation; tl
definite influence upon the Church Fathers of Revelation 2
producing a clear concept of the one-thousand-year period
the earthly kingdom.

These Jewish teachings, so-called, invoked a reaction fro
some of the Church Fathers against what they thought was
materialistic and sensualistic concept of an earthly kingdo
This was true of Origen, Augustine and, apparently, also
Barnabas. But, however that may have been, it has to be reco
nized that Judaism and a reaction against it colored the thinki
of the earthly Church Fathers.

B. *Gnosticism*

In its incipient form, the heresy called Gnosticism arose ear
in the primitive Church. Both Colossians and the letters

hn intimate this. It continued to develop and make inroads
1 the Church until it reached alarming proportions. Marcion
as an exponent of it; Irenaeus wrote against it.

To be sure, Gnosticism gave a place in its system to Christ.
owever, in order to do so, it had to recast radically the New
estament picture of Him. To the Gnostics matter was evil;
ily the spirit was good. This involved a denial of the assump-
on of flesh and blood by Christ. According to them, He only
ppeared to assume it. Salvation was deliverance from the
iysical, ultimately from the body.

In such a system, of course, a bodily resurrection was inad-
issible. With its denial went also the denial of any redemp-
ve work of Christ embracing the physical realm. Thus the
jection of an earthly kingdom was inherent in the system.

This heresy, however, met with a strong literary reaction
om the early Church, and especially from Irenaeus, who wrote
work entitled "Against Heresies." In his eschatological re-
arks, he inveighed against any allegorization of the physical in
:ophecies concerning an earthly reign of Christ, and remarked:
f any endeavor to allegorize prophecies of this kind, they shall
ot be found consistent with themselves on all points, and shall
: confuted by the very expressions in question" ("Against
leresies," Chapter 35:1). This reaction against Gnosticism
:rengthened the point of view already held by Irenaeus, and
her Fathers who believed in an earthly Kingdom of God.

C. *Secularism*

A third factor which influenced eschatological interpretation
i this period was what might be termed *Secularism*. By this
e mean the secular, as contrasted to the Christian, environment
' that period. The Roman Empire in all its paganism and
uelty was a reality to the early Christians, and the pages of
atristic Literature are replete with references to it.

Persecution and martyrdom were familiar to the Christian
>mmunity. Many suffered death for their fidelity to the Saviour.
uch ideas as suffering under the coming Antichrist were cur-
nt among them. The prophecies relating to Antichrist and
is ultimate judgment by the Son of God frequently appear in
ose portions dealing with Christ's Second Coming.

Another feature is the place assigned to the Roman Empi
and its relation to the number of the beast. The Roman Empi
is seen to have been prophesied by Daniel. Irenaeus write
"In a still clearer light has John, in the Apocalypse, indicate
to the Lord's disciples what shall happen in the last times, ar
concerning the ten kings who shall then arise, among who
the empire which now rules the earth shall be partitione
(*Against Heresies,* Chapter 26:1). And he advances the nan
of the Roman Empire or people as a possible solution to t
problem of the number of the beast (666), and says, "Latein
answers to this number (*Against Heresies,* Chapter 30:3).

For the later Fathers, the change in the Roman Empir
attitude toward the Christian Church with the conversion
Constantine necessitated a modification and change in t
identification of many of the signs of the Lord's coming. D. I
Kromminga, writing concerning Constantine's adoption of Chr
tianity as the official religion of the Roman Empire, says:

> As a result, the traditional interpretation of the precursory sig
> of the coming of the Lord had to be altered. It was no long
> possible to identify the Roman government with the antichristi.
> power. The application of the Danielic and Apocalyptic visio
> of the last empire to Rome needed modification . . . (*The M
> lennium in the Church,* page 107).

This brief sketch of the character of the times leads
naturally into the concepts of interpretation advocated by t
various writers in that period. There is more than a mere c
incidence between them.

II. THE CONCEPTS OF INTERPRETATION HELD

Two concepts of interpretation were prominent in this perio
both of which are characteristic of our contemporary metho
of interpreting the prophetic promises of the Old Testament

A. *The Literalistic*

In the main, until the time of Origen, most of the Fathe
interpreted the promises associated with the Millennial Kin
dom in a literal sense. Although Irenaeus spiritualized the co
enant relations of the Jews and transferred them to the Churc
yet he reacted adamantly against allegorizing or spiritualizi

he prophetic promises concerning the earthly kingdom (*Against Heresies*, Chapter 35:2).

This adherence to the literalistic fulfillment of these promises characterized many of the early Fathers' interpretations of the Millennial Kingdom; it also confirmed them in the natural interpretation of Revelation 20 and made them premillennialists.

B. *The Spiritualistic*

Although many of the Church Fathers jealously guarded the reality of a Millennial Kingdom, this was not true of men like Origen and Augustine. They wholly spiritualized these promises, both in reference to the Jews and in reference to the Millennial Kingdom. Origen's method of interpretation was definitely affected by his background. He was influenced by Greek philosophy, as were the Fathers from Alexandria. While he emphasized three ways of interpreting Scripture, he asserted that the real meaning of Scripture was to be found in its pneumatic or speculative sense. The literal sense of Scripture, said he, concealed the spiritual sense. This was in order that there might not be the casting of "pearls before swine." Thus, to him, the spiritual meaning was decisive. As for Augustine, this method caused him to identify the Kingdom of God with the Church. Thus, for him, there could be no earthly kingdom.

In general, we may conclude that the practice of the early Fathers was to interpret Scripture allegorically, though those who were millennialists insisted upon a literal interpretation of Revelation 20, and many were dogmatic in their insistence upon a literal earthly kingdom.

With these background studies in the character of the times and concepts of interpretation, let us pass on to the content of the teachings of the Fathers in reference to the Lord's return.

III. THE CONTENT OF THE ESCHATOLOGICAL TEACHINGS

It is necessary to point out at the very outset that not all the Fathers have discussed the Lord's return thoroughly and completely. Many times one finds that it is incidental either to their exposition or defense of the Christian faith. It would seem that they had no reason to discuss it in relation to the Millennium. As to the Lord's return, they taught:

A. *Its Certainty*

The doctrine of the Lord's Return was a certainty to the Church Fathers. The period of the Apostolic Fathers especially was largely eschatological. They lived in an age which anticipated the immediate return of Christ. Two examples will suffice to demonstrate this fact:

The Epistle of Barnabas (Chapter 15):
> Therefore, my children, in six days, that is, in six thousand years, all things will be finished. "And He rested on the seventh day." This meaneth: When His Son, *coming again,* shall destroy the time of the wicked man, and judge the ungodly, and change the sun, and the moon, and the stars, then shall He truly rest on the seventh day.

The First Epistle of Clement (34:3):
> It is requisite, therefore, that we be prompt in the practice of well-doing; for of Him are all things. And thus He forewarns us: "Behold, the Lord cometh, and His reward is before His face, to render to every man according to his work."

The following are examples of the same truth from subsequent Church Fathers:

Justin Martyr, in his *First Apology* (Chapter 51), writes:
> And how also He should come again out of heaven with glory; hear what was spoken in reference to this by the prophet Jeremiah.

Cyprian, *On the Vanity of Idols* (14), makes this statement:
> Then in a cloud spread around Him, He was lifted up into heaven, that as a conqueror He might bring to the Father man whom He loved, whom He put on, whom He shielded from death; soon to come from heaven for the punishment of the devil and to the judgment of the human race . . .

Irenaeus, *Against Heresies* (30:4):
> But when this Antichrist shall have devastated all things in this world, he will reign for three years and six months, and sit in the temple at Jerusalem; and then the Lord will come from heaven in the clouds, in the glory of the Father . . .

Tertullian, *Against Marcion* (Book 3:25), quotes I Thessalonians 4:17 as his hope of the Second Coming:

For we shall, according to the Apostle, be caught up into the clouds to meet the Lord (even the Son of Man, who shall come in the clouds, according to Daniel), and so shall we ever be with the Lord . . .

These are but a few testimonies of that faith which was universal among the Church Fathers, that Christ would most certainly come a second time.

B. *Its Relationship to the Millennium*

The question of a millennial period was not discussed by every Church Father. As in the case of all doctrinal teachings, they wrote concerning those doctrines which were of prime interest to them at the time. Therefore in many discussions where the Lord's return is mentioned, its ramifications are not discussed and no views on the Millennium are expressed. However, in the Early Church prior to the time of Origen, whenever such views were expressed, excepting those of the Church Father Caius, they were usually in harmony with the millennial interpretation. The Early Church was definitely characterized by its premillennial outlook. After a survey of the period's literature, George E. Ladd, in his book, *Crucial Questions About the Kingdom of God* (page 159), says:

> We are led to conclude that while there is evidence that not all Christians were millenarians, yet opposition was limited, and the doctrine was very widespread. No other positive interpretation is to be found before the time of Augustine; and the spiritual interpretation, when it appears, seems to be a new position, and not the recovery of a teaching which had been lost for several centuries.

This Premillennialism was expressed in terms of a literal interpretation of Revelation 20. A number of quotations from the early Fathers will show this to be true:

We quote again from *The Epistle of Barnabas* (Chapter 15):

> Attend, my children, to the meaning of this expression, "He finished in six days." This implieth that the Lord will finish all things in six thousand years, for a day is with him a thousand years. And He Himself testifieth, saying, "Behold, today, will be as a thousand years."* "And He rested on the seventh day."

* An alternative reading states, "The day of the Lord shall be as a thousand years."

> This meaneth: when His Son, coming again, shall destroy the
> time of the wicked man, and judge the ungodly, and change the
> sun, and the moon, and the stars, then shall He truly rest on
> the seventh day.

The letter reveals the significance of this seventh day by
pointing to an eighth day, which is interpreted thus: "When
giving rest to all things, I shall make a beginning of the eighth
day, that is, the beginning of another world."

Papias, quoted by Irenaeus, also wrote about the earthly kingdom, in these words:

> The days will come in which vines shall grow, having each ten
> thousand branches, and in each branch ten thousand twigs, and
> in each true twig ten thousand shoots, and in every one of the
> shoots ten thousand clusters, and on every one of the clusters
> ten thousand grapes, and every grape when pressed will give five-
> and-twenty metretes of wine. And when any one of the saints
> shall lay hold of a cluster, another shall cry out, "I am a better
> cluster, take me; bless the Lord through me."

Irenaeus, after this quotation (*Against Heresies*, Book 5:33-
35), continues in the same vein:

> And it is right that when the creation is restored, all the ani-
> mals should obey and be in subjection to man, and revert to the
> food originally given by God (for they had been originally sub-
> jected in obedience to Adam), that is, the productions of the earth.

Justin Martyr, *Dialogue with Trypho*, assents to the sum-
marization of his teaching on the earthly kingdom made by
Trypho:

> And Trypho to this replied, "I remarked to you, Sir, that you
> are very anxious to be safe in all respects, since you cling to the
> Scriptures. But tell us, do you really admit that this place, Jeru-
> salem, shall be rebuilt; and do you expect your people to be
> gathered together, and made joyful with Christ and the patriarchs,
> and the prophets, both the men of our nation, and other proselytes
> who joined them before your Christ came? Or, have you given
> way, and admitted this in order to have the appearance of worst-
> ing us in the controversies?" Then I answered, "I am not so
> miserable a fellow, Trypho, as to say one thing and think an-

other. I admitted to you formerly that I and many others are of this opinion, and believe that such will take place, as you assuredly are aware . . ."

Tertullian, *Against Marcion* (Book 3:25), speaks along similar lines:

> But we do confess that a kingdom is promised to us upon the earth, although before heaven, only in another state of existence; inasmuch as it will be after the resurrection for a thousand years in the divinely-built city of Jerusalem . . .

Two other examples will suffice to illustrate our point:

Nepos, an Egyptian Bishop, held no uncertain views about the earthly kingdom. Dionysius of Alexandria, quoted by Eusebius in *Ecclesiastical History* (Book VII, Chapter 24), complains about the influence of his teaching on the Early Church:

> But since they bring forward a certain work of Nepos, on which they rely confidently, as if it proved beyond dispute that there will be a reign of Christ upon earth . . .

Dionysius then goes on to deny that John the Apostle wrote the book of Revelation, and states that though of value, it is beyond his comprehension, but admits "that there is a certain concealed and more wonderful meaning in every part" (Chapter 25).

Eusebius, in introducing the subject, states concerning Nepos, that he taught "that the promises to the holy men in the Divine Scriptures should be understood in a more Jewish manner, and that there would be a certain millennium of bodily luxury upon this earth . . ."

Lactantius, in his *Of a Happy Life* (Chapter XIV), notes:

> For the great day of God is limited by a circle of a thousand years, as the prophet shows who says: "In thy sight, O Lord, a thousand years are as one day." And as God labored during those six days in creating such great works, so His religion and truth must labor during these six thousand years, while wickedness prevails and bears rule. And again, since God, having finished His works, rested on the seventh day and blessed it, at the end of the six thousand years all wickedness must be abolished from the earth and righteousness reign for a thousand years.

These quotations evidence the widespread belief in an earthly millennial reign, and while they are not uniformly applicable to all the Fathers of the Church, they nevertheless do point up the fact that the Early Church was dominantly Premillennial.

C. *Its Relationship to Antichrist*

To the majority of the Fathers, the Antichrist was a reality. Many expressed themselves concerning the conflict between him and Christ. Also, there were some who held that Antichrist would come from the tribe of Dan. A statement representative of this view is found in Hippolytus' treatise on *Christ and Antichrist* (14-15):

> For as Christ springs from the tribe of Judah, so Antichrist is destined to spring from the tribe of Dan . . . It is in reality out of the tribe of Dan, then, that that tyrant and king, that dread judge, that son of the devil is destined to spring and arise...

D. *Its Relationship to the Rapture and the Tribulation*

There is no clear conception among the Fathers as to the relationship of the Second Coming to the Rapture and the Tribulation. Such quotations on the subject as can be found appear in a context void of any positive chronological differentiation between the two. Some quote I Thessalonians 4:17; others no more than mention the term tribulation.

Hippolytus, for instance, says in this same book, *Christ and Antichrist* (56, 60, 61):

> He then, having gathered to himself the unbelieving everywhere throughout the world, comes at their call to persecute the saints, their enemies and antagonists . . .
>
> Now, concerning the tribulation of the persecution which is to fall upon the Church from the adversary. . . . That refers to the one thousand two hundred and three score days (the half of the week) during which the tyrant is to reign and persecute the Church . . .

Irenaeus, *Against Heresies* (5:29), writes:

> And therefore, when in the end the Church shall be suddenly caught up from this, it is said, "There shall be tribulation such as has not been since the beginning, neither shall be." For this is the last contest of the righteous, in which, when they overcome, they are crowned with incorruption.

Tertullian, we note, draws upon I Thessalonians 4:17:

> For we shall according to the Apostle, be caught up into the
> clouds, to meet the Lord (even the Son of man, who shall come
> in the clouds, according to Daniel), and so shall we ever be with
> the Lord, so long as He remains both on the earth and in
> heaven . . .

No definite conclusion concerning the relative positions of
the Rapture and the Tribulation can be drawn from these quotations. Tertullian's teaching that the promises made to Israel
had been transferred to the Church only served to becloud the
issue.

This summary presentation of the doctrine of the Lord's return in Patristic Literature leads us to draw certain tentative
conclusions:

IV. THE CONCLUSIONS TO BE DRAWN

A. The distinction between Biblical revelation and man's interpretation of that revelation is nowhere more clearly seen than
in the Patristic Literature. All sorts of doctrinal interpretations
have crept in, many of them wholly foreign to the Bible. The
various approaches to the doctrine of the Lord's return, from
the literalism of an earthly kingdom found in Irenaeus, to a
spiritualism of that kingdom found in Augustine, clearly demonstrate the way in which interpretation varied and changed.

B. Belief in an earthly kingdom, and the Premillennial interpretation of the doctrine of the last things, were quite prevalent in the Early Church. As Justin Martyr pointed out (*Against
Trypho LXXX*), these views, though rejected by some, were
generally held by Christians of his day.

C. From the dawn of the second century and the accession
to the leadership of the Church of men trained in the Hellenic
tradition, the promises of God made to Israel came to be applied
more and more to the New Testament Ecclesia. There were
exceptions. Irenaeus, for instance, held literally to the promises
concerning an earthly kingdom. However, in germinal form,
this is where the concept of the transmission of the covenants
had its beginning. Even Paul, in his time, had to spar with
the shadows of it in the church at Rome, as is evident from

Romans 11:1, 26, 29. A brief study of the background of the early Patristic period should help us to see the forces which shaped the eschatological thinking of those days:

1. *The Church Fathers were too close to the critical days of the Apostolic period to see Israel in the light of the Scriptures.* The wounds inflicted by the Jewish authorities upon the nascent Christian movement were still festering, nor were the Jews of the Diaspora particularly helpful to the church in its conflict with intellectual paganism. The age of Gentile Christianity had set in. What was to the original followers of the Messiah a tragedy to be redeemed, became to the disciples of the post-Apostolic times a hostility to be requited. The Epistle of Barnabas is permeated with this kind of anti-Judaic bias, denying the Jews the benefit of the Old Testament promises, or any further consideration from the Father because of their rejection of the Son. Proximity, in this case, did not make for perspicuity.

2. *The Judaism of the period, and its teachings, had a decidedly eschatological coloring.* Evidences of this are to be found in the Midrashim, Targumim, and sections of the Talmud. Some of the Church Fathers, like Papias and Irenaeus, were not uninfluenced by it, seeing that many of the Old Testament promises pointed directly to such New Testament prophesies as Revelation 20. Irenaeus found these promises of an earthly kingdom useful in combating the heresy of Gnosticism, but in other respects his method of interpretation was far from consistent. Some promises he accepted literally; others he spiritualized.

D. The history of Christian doctrine proves that there is a difference between a bare statement of facts and the intellectual definition of the same facts; and then we must not forget that in the days of the early Church Fathers the science of Biblical interpretation was in its infancy. So, when we find them confusing the term "saints" as found in Daniel 7 with the general use of the same term in the New Testament, or failing to distinguish between tribulation and *the Tribulation,* we must remember that they did not have the advantage of the centuries of Biblical research which have been vouchsafed to us, and that, until the establishment of Christianity in the Roman Empire, they knew tribulation as a daily experience.

E. Since these men were a product of their times, subject to the continual interaction between Judaism and anti-Judaism, between Gnosticism and anti-Gnosticism, one cannot be severe in criticism of them. However, the fact must be emphasized again that the Church Fathers cannot settle any issues in the realm of doctrine. To appeal to history for the final word on any doctrine is to incur the risk of capitulating to Roman Catholicism.

9

TRIBULATION FOR THE CHURCH — BUT NOT *THE TRIBULATION*

by William F. Kerr, th.d.

The question of the relationship of the Christian to the Tribulation period has taken on an aspect of acuteness in evangelical circles today. It is therefore of vital importance that we give it consideration in this Prophetic Congress.

The subject before us includes the Church's relationship to *suffering* in general, and also to that period of suffering called *the Tribulation* in particular. We propose to discuss it under three main heads:

I. Defining Terms

In the Greek New Testament there are two words translated "tribulation" in our Authorized Version of the Scriptures. These are the words *orge* and *thlipsis*. In English translation, however, they are also given the meaning of "wrath," "anger," "persecution," "affliction," "suffering." The word *orge* is frequently translated "wrath," while the word *thlipsis* is generally translated "suffering" or "tribulation."

To be quite exact in our treatment of these words and their specific relationship to the problem before us, let us note the ways in which the Spirit of God uses these words in Holy Writ.

A. *The Usage of the Words*

1. Defining the word *thlipsis* we note that it occurs forty-five times in the New Testament and is used in the following meanings:

98

a. To designate the *period of Tribulation* which is to come before the establishment of the Millennium. One passage of Scripture will suffice to demonstrate this. In Matthew 24:9, 21, 29 we read:

> Then shall they deliver you up to be afflicted, and shall kill you: and ye shall be hated of all nations for my name's sake.
>
> For then shall be great tribulation, such as was not since the beginning of the world to this time, no, nor ever shall be.
>
> Immediately after the tribulation of those days shall the sun be darkened, and the moon shall not give her light, and the stars shall fall from heaven, and the powers shall be shaken.

b. In other passages of Scripture, it is used to set forth the idea of *suffering, anguish, pain,* or *persecution.* In Matthew 13:21 we note:

> Yet hath he not root in himself, but dureth for a while: for when tribulation or persecution ariseth because of the word, by and by he is offended.

2. Turning now to the word *orge,* we find that it is used thirty-five times in the Word of God, and the meanings given to it are as follows:

a. To designate *Divine wrath.* It is used in this way in Matthew 3:7—

> But when he saw many of the Pharisees and Sadducees come to his baptism, he said unto them, O generation of vipers, who hath warned you to flee from the wrath to come.

b. To set forth *human anger.* Romans 13:4, 5—

> For he is the minister of God to thee for good. But if thou do that which is evil, be afraid; for he beareth not the sword in vain: for he is the minister of God, a revenger to execute wrath upon him that doeth evil.
>
> Wherefore ye must needs be subject, not only for wrath, but also for conscience sake.

c. A clear reference of its use to designate the *period of the Tribulation* is found in Luke 21:23—

> But woe unto them that are with child, and to them that give suck, in those days! for there shall be great distress in the land, and wrath upon this people.

B. *The Meaning of the Words*

The brief references given above detail for us some of the ways in which these words are used. And, since the meaning of the words is established by their usage, we shall now endeavor to find out if *these* words have any doctrinal significance that would throw light on the Church's relationship to *the Tribulation* as contrasted with suffering per se.

1. A full and close examination of the Scriptural use of the word *thlipsis* will reveal that its primary meaning is "suffering." This can be seen from its association with suffering in various experiences of life, such as the suffering of child-birth (John 16:21), the suffering of religious persecution (Acts 11:19), the suffering of domestic trouble (I Cor. 7:28). And, strange as it may seem, when the word is used to describe such experiences, more frequently than not the persons involved are Christian believers. Thus the word tells us nothing specific about Tribulation as the outpouring of God's wrath. Its emphasis is rather upon the idea of suffering, pointing up the conclusion that suffering, whenever and by whomever endured, produces the same human reactions. In fact, Paul tells us that we are appointed unto suffering and suffering alone. Note I Thessalonians 3:3 —

> That no man should be moved by these afflictions: for yourselves know that we are appointed thereunto.

As we examine the meaning of *orge*, we find that its usage in Scriptures justifies the following conclusions:

2. In its characteristic general meaning the word refers to wrath or anger which either proceeds against sin or is the result of the sinful nature. As such it is used in connection with divine wrath or judgment (John 3:36); human anger (James 1:19); the period of Tribulation (Rev. 6:16, 17).

3. The specific meaning of the word is *God's reaction against sin.* The International Standard Bible Encyclopaedia defines it —

> as the natural expression of the Divine nature, which is absolute holiness, manifesting itself against the wilful, high-handed, deliberate, inexcusable sin and iniquity of mankind. God's wrath is always regarded in the Scripture as the just, proper, and natural expression of His holiness and righteousness which must always under all circumstances, and at all costs be maintained.

By its usage in Scripture we are led to believe that the word signifies God's judgment against sin, and that those always referred to in the New Testament as the objects of God's wrath are the unbelievers or sinners. It is in this sense that it is used in connection with *the Tribulation*. And we are reminded by Paul that we, Christian believers, are *not* appointed unto wrath or judgment. In I Thessalonians 5:9 we read:

> For God hath not appointed us to wrath, but to obtain salvation by our Lord Jesus Christ.

From Revelation 6:16, 17 we learn that the period of Tribulation is defined as the wrath of the Lamb. This same word *orge* is used here. The passage reads:

> And said to the mountains and rocks, Fall on us, and hide us from the face of him that sitteth on the throne, and from the *wrath* of the Lamb. For the great day of his *wrath* is come; and who shall be able to stand?

4. Summing up our definition of these two words, *thlipsis* and *orge*, we see that *thlipsis* simply means "suffering" and has no special bearing on the Church's relationship to the period of Tribulation. We do recognize, however, that the word *orge* is definitely related to the *Tribulation*, because this is the time of God's wrath or judgment, termed the *orge* of the Lamb (Rev. 6:16, 17). To this time and judgment, Paul definitely states, the Church is *not appointed* (I Thess. 5:9).

II. DISTINGUISHING RELATIONSHIPS

Now that we have defined the usage and meaning of New Testament terms which shed light on the Tribulation problem, we must proceed to a discussion of the relationships to God sustained by those who are either to be involved in or saved from this awful period of judgment.

In the study of eschatology, especially that phase of it which covers the period of the Tribulation, three fundamental distinctions are absolutely essential.

A. *The Church and Israel*

The Church is revealed in the Scriptures in a threefold way:
1. *It is a new relationship*. The initial history of the Church

is found in the Book of Acts, chapter 2. It began with the coming of the Holy Spirit on the day of Pentecost in an unprecedented way to baptize the disciples who waited in the upper room. Ever since that day the Holy Spirit regenerates all who believe on the Lord Jesus Christ (John 3:6-8; 16:7-14), and baptizes them into the one body (I Cor. 12:13), thus making us members of the Body of Christ. The Church is distinctly an entity of New Testament revelation, uniquely and fully related to the work of the Holy Spirit.

2. *It performs a new function.* The function of the Church is to gather itself together in local assemblies, and to carry out, through its various ministries, the proclamation of the Gospel and edification of the believers. This also is a unique function empowered and directed by the Holy Spirit, distinctly New Testament in nature.

3. *It possesses a new kind of future.* A study of the Scriptures will show that the future of the Church, unique in its revelation, is assured by the ministry of the Holy Spirit. In fact, the whole ministry of the Holy Spirit is irrevocably interrelated with the origin, the course, and the consummation of the Church. In its future there is the *promise* of the Rapture (I Thess. 4: 13-17), and the *time* of its consummation is predicted (II Thess. 2:6,7). This last portion dealing with the phrase "only he who now letteth, will let, until he be taken out of the way" has had many and various interpretations, but the most logical of them is that the phrase refers to the Holy Spirit. If this is so, and I believe it can be adequately defended, then we know that the Church will be raptured before the revelation of the Antichrist and the period of Tribulation.

By contrast, the people of Israel had their origin with Abraham (Gen. 12:1,2). Membership in Israel is obtained through a twofold relationship: natural generation, and religious affiliation with the beliefs, rituals, and practices of Judaism. For the present Israel is a "mystery" people (Rom. 11:25), in that their history has been interrupted and they, as a people, partially and temporarily, have been blinded (Matt. 23:37-39). However, covenants unconditional and irrevocable are being held in reserve for them (cf. Gen. 17:1-8; II Sam. 7:12-16; Jer. 33:14-17; Rom. 11:25-27).

The Scriptures differentiate very clearly between the Church and Israel, and God's ways of dealing with both. For instance, the Church's present and future can be summed up in the words of I John 3:2 — "Beloved, now are we the sons of God, and it doth not yet appear what we shall be: but we know that, when he shall appear, we shall be like him; for we shall see him as he is." Israel's present is conditioned by the Saviour's pronouncement in Matthew 23:39 — "For I say unto you, Ye shall not see me henceforth, till ye shall say, Blessed is he that cometh in the name of the Lord," and the nation's future is a composite of tribulation and blessing, the latter arrived at only by way of the former (cf. Zech. 12:10; 14:1-5).

The Church is not of this world (John 17:16), and her destiny is heavenly, wholly independent of the element of sight (I Pet. 1:3-9). Israel, on the other hand, is chosen for an earthly mission, to which the nation can attain only by *looking* upon the Messiah whom they once pierced (Matt. 23:39; Zech. 12:10).

Israel's God-appointed destiny must be worked out on the loom of earth's history. This is made especially clear in Daniel 9:26, 27, where we see God's program for Israel's "remnant of days":

> And after threescore and two weeks shall Messiah be cut off, but not for himself: and the people of the prince that shall come shall destroy the city and the sanctuary; and the end thereof shall be with a flood, and unto the end of the war desolations are determined.
>
> And he shall confirm the covenant with many for one week: and in the midst of the week he shall cause the sacrifice and the oblation to cease, and for the overspreading of abominations he shall make it desolate, even until the consummation, and that determined shall be poured upon the desolate.

Let us note carefully that the Church has no place in this prophecy. The seventy weeks of Daniel's prophecy is Israel's Messianic calendar, and the last of the seventy sevens, reckoned in years, is Israel's time of travail or Tribulation.

> Seventy weeks are determined upon thy people and upon thy holy city, to finish the transgression, and to make an end of sins,

and to make reconciliation for iniquity, and to bring in everlasting righteousness, and to seal up the vision and prophecy, and to anoint the most Holy (Dan. 9:24).

Alas! for that day is great, so that none is like it: it is even the time of Jacob's trouble; but he shall be saved out of it (Jer. 30:7). The day of the Lord is darkness, and not light (Amos 5:18b).

B. *The Types of Punishment*

The Scriptures also differentiate between remedial and penal punishment.

In Hebrews 12:5-7 we read about punishment in the form of scourging. This punishment is obviously used by God in order that the believer, here designated a son, may learn to abide in fellowship with the Father and "live soberly, righteously, and godly in this present world." This is because God loves His own and chastises them to remedy their lives. This, however, is remedial and not judicial or penal punishment. It must not be confused with the wrath of God, which is judicial and penal.

In I Thessalonians 5:9 judicial or penal punishment is set forth. This has no reference to the believer, but is always the outpouring of God's wrath upon the unbelieving and upon human sin. Paul tells us here, as we have noted before, that "God hath not appointed us to *wrath*, but to obtain *salvation* by our Lord Jesus Christ." There is no condemnation to those who are *in* Christ Jesus (Rom. 8:1; John 5:24).

Yet the Bible is equally clear in its teaching that Israel *will* undergo judicial punishment. Ezekiel 20:33-38 reads in part:

> As I live, saith the Lord God, surely with a mighty hand, and with a stretched out arm, and with fury poured out, will I rule over you: And I will bring you out from the people, and will gather you out of the countries wherein ye are scattered, with a mighty hand, and with a stretched out arm, and with fury poured out. . . . And I will cause you to pass under the rod, and I will bring you into the bond of the covenant.

C. *The Purposes of the Punishment*

One question to which I have never seen an answer in print is: "What is the purpose of the punishment during the period of the Tribulation?" As far as the Church is concerned the categorical answer can be only, None whatsoever! For the Church to pass through the Tribulation and be punished serves no purpose in God's program, and God does nothing without a purpose.

But it is different in the case of Israel. Here, the Scriptures reveal at least two purposes for the Tribulation: (1) To punish past unbelief and sin; (2) To spur the remnant to turn to God and accept the Crucified Saviour as their Messiah and King (Ezek. 20:33-38; Rom. 11:26).

We now come to our final consideration:

III. Defining Duration

The duration of the Tribulation has been fairly well established in Scripture. However, since some insist that it is only three and one-half years in length, it may be helpful to consider this question again.

The problem here seems to be the intensity of judgment during this period. Those who believe that the Tribulation lasts only three and one-half years do so mainly because, from their point of view, the breaking of the covenant by the Antichrist and the sacrifice of the abomination of desolation (Dan. 9:27; Matt. 24:15) is the occasion for the outpouring of God's terrible judgments. However, judgment need not be confined to this intensified form alone. For while there may be a difference in the *degrees* of God's judgment, there is no difference in the *kind* of God's judgment. The whole of the seventieth week of Daniel is the period of God's wrath. God can and does judge by the withdrawal of Himself and the unique ministry of the Holy Spirit. This withdrawal takes place when the Church is raptured. At that moment, because of the removal of the restraining power of the Holy Spirit, the powers of hell are unleashed on the earth. It is the wrath of the Antichrist against Israel that begins in the middle of the week.

Another reason for believing that the Tribulation and the seventieth week of Daniel are coincidental is to be found in the fact that the Church is not mentioned in chapters 4 to 18 of Revelation, chapters which speak of the period of judgment. Of course, some hold that the argument from silence is not valid. However, its validity depends upon whether or not, in given circumstances, a particular event, person, or group, should have been mentioned, and was not. For instance, if someone reported that I and my family attended a certain gathering, and yet only my wife, myself, and four of our sons were mentioned by name, it would then be safe to argue from the lack of mention that my fifth son was not present. The same logic supports the validity of the argument from silence.

The Church is prominent in chapters 1 through 3, but is treated with silence in chapters 4 to 18. Why? Obviously because the Church already is in heaven and not involved in the events described.

Finally, to restate for further emphasis what has been noted before, the Church is also not mentioned in Daniel 9:25-27, which is a prophecy relating to the people of Israel. This is in keeping with the divine logic of Scripture. Since the Church is not mentioned in the first sixty-nine weeks, why should she be brought into the seventieth week? The Scriptural distinction between the Church and Israel would not allow such an introduction. We believe that a review of all the reasons advanced will show that, while the Church will experience tribulation (suffering), she will not pass through *the* Tribulation.

10

THE PROPHETS SPEAK TO THE TWENTIETH CENTURY

by RICHARD A. ELVEE, ED.D.

But now we see *not yet* all things put under him" (Heb. 2:8).

There is a deathless urge in the heart of humanity for a better world. Sometimes it glows with faith. Sometimes it finds expression in the song of a poet. Sometimes there is with it the dull pain of disappointed expectations, and a voice in the darkness cries out, "How long, O Lord, how long?" Panaceas for earth's ills have been tried and have failed. Yet the belief persists that there must be for humanity on this earth a life — a corporate, ordered life; a life not for the few powerful and fortunate, but for all a life that shall be rich in truth, justice, power and love. No centuries of lies, injustice, weakness and hate have been able to extinguish this hope in the heart of humanity.

Plato writes his "Republic," Campanella, his "City of the Sun," Sir Thomas More, his "Utopia." But time counts out the days and years, and they are still as before years of war, years of the ruthless reign of the strong over the weak, years filled with the delusions of shallow optimism.

There are those who would save us from these evils, but evil in all forms is as old as the race. The oldest brick dug from a Mesopotamian mound bears record of ambitions, pride and greed such as are making history today. Forms of government from despotism to democracy have been tried. Education, legislation, and even religion, have left the world factors unchanged and we are at the end of our resources. The song of the angels at the birth of Christ, "Glory to God in the highest, and on earth peace, good will toward men" has little meaning unless there is a divine plan to bring order out of the chaos.

ISRAEL GOD'S OBJECT LESSON

When we turn to the Bible, we find that there is a divine plan in history. Upwards of four thousand years, amid all climes and civilizations, under all circumstances and governments, God has been working out this plan in the life of one distinct people, using them as His experimental laboratory, and as an object lesson for all the nations of the earth. The golden age of this people was at its zenith long before the balmy days of Greece and Rome. Before Herodotus wrote history, Socrates philosophy, or Homer the "Iliad," Israel was a well organized and civilized nation.

The preservation of this people is the miracle of history. They were called to be a witness to the unity of God in the midst of universal idolatry. Deuteronomy 6:4 says: "Hear, O Israel: The Lord our God is one Lord." And Isaiah 43:10, 11 again refers to the unity of God: "Ye are my witnesses, saith the Lord, and my servant whom I have chosen: that ye may know and believe me, and understand that I am he: before me there was no God formed, neither shall there be after me. I, even I, am the Lord; and beside me there is no saviour."

They were to demonstrate to the nations the blessedness of that people whose God is Jehovah. In Deuteronomy 33:26-29 we find the remarkable and wonderful statement, indicating that God wanted to give the nations of the world a living example of the blessedness of the people who own Him as Lord: "There is none like unto the God of Jeshurun, who rideth upon the heaven in thy help, and in his excellency on the sky. The eternal God is thy refuge, and underneath are the everlasting arms: and he shall thrust out the enemy from before thee; and shall say, Destroy them. Israel then shall dwell in safety alone: the fountain of Jacob shall be upon a land of corn and wine; also his heaven shall drop down dew. Happy art thou, O Israel: who is like unto thee, O people saved by the Lord, the shield of thy help, and who is the sword of thy excellency! and thine enemies shall be found liars unto thee; and thou shalt tread upon their high places." Israel was to receive and transmit the divine statutes and oracles, so that the peoples of the world would say, "Surely this great nation is a wise and understanding people" (Deut. 4:6). The people of Israel were to be a blessing to all the nations of the earth, for God had said to their father, Abraham: "In thee and in thy seed shall all the families of the earth be blessed" (Gen. 28:14).

This great purpose for the nation of Israel has as yet not been fully realized. The delay gave rise to the prophets, whose ministry in relation to the covenant people and the divine program was both immediate and future.

MILLENNIUM NOT THE ETERNAL STATE

The prophets, speaking to our twentieth century, would say to us that within the divine plan there is yet to be another age; an age of peace and security. Note the words of the prophet Isaiah:

> And there shall come forth a rod out of the stem of Jesse, and a Branch shall grow out of his roots: and the spirit of the Lord shall rest upon him, the spirit of wisdom and understanding, the spirit of counsel and might, the spirit of knowledge and of the fear of the Lord; and shall make him of quick understanding in the fear of the Lord: and he shall not judge after the sight of his eyes, neither reprove after the hearing of his ears: but with righteousness shall he judge the poor, and reprove with equity for the meek of the earth: and he shall smite the earth with the rod of his mouth, and with the breath of his lips shall he slay the wicked. And righteousness shall be the girdle of his loins, and faithfulness the girdle of his reins. The wolf also shall dwell with the lamb, and the leopard shall lie down with the kid; and the calf, and the young lion and the fatling together, and a little child shall lead them. And the cow and the bear shall feed; their young ones shall lie down together: and the lion shall eat straw like the ox. And the suckling child shall play on the hole of the asp, and the weaned child shall put his hand on the cockatrice' den. They shall not hurt nor destroy in all my holy mountain: for the earth shall be full of the knowledge of the Lord, as the waters cover the sea (Isa. 11:1-9).

It will be an age of equality and social justice. The prophet Micah, declares: "But they shall sit every man under his vine and under his fig tree; and none shall make them afraid: for the mouth of the Lord of hosts hath spoken it" (4:4).

It will be a time of universal peace. Isaiah 2:4 states: "And he shall judge among the nations, and shall rebuke many people: and they shall beat their swords into plowshares, and their spears into pruninghooks: nation shall not lift up sword against nation, neither shall they learn war any more."

The prophets describe this golden age as an experience on earth, and not in the eternal state. Here are a few illustrations of this truth: "There shall be no more thence an infant of days, for the child shall die an hundred years old" (Isa. 65:20). "Thus saith the Lord of hosts, There shall yet old men and old women dwell in the streets of Jerusalem, and every man with his staff in his hand for very age" (Zech. 8:4). But regarding the eternal state we read: "The children of this world marry, and are given in marriage: but they which shall be accounted worthy to obtain that world, and the resurrection from the dead, neither marry nor are given in marriage" (Luke 20:34, 35).

The prophet Isaiah, speaking about this golden age which is to come here on earth tells us: "Moreover the light of the moon shall be as the light of the sun" (30:26). But in the glorious description of the eternal state found in Revelation 21, we read: "The city had no need of the sun, neither of the moon, to shine in it: for the glory of God did lighten it, and the Lamb is the light thereof" (v. 23).

The prophet Ezekiel gives a tremendous description of the temple of the Lord as it shall appear in the golden age (chapters 40 to 48). But when it comes to the eternal state, the Book of Revelation tells us: "And I saw no temple therein: for the Lord God Almighty and the Lamb are the temple of it" (21:22).

Speaking to our twentieth century, the prophets tell us of a covenant people. As we look back, Moses, one of the early prophets, speaking to his people, declared:

> And it shall come to pass, if thou shalt hearken diligently unto the voice of the Lord thy God, to observe and to do all his commandments which I command thee this day, that the Lord thy God will set thee on high above all nations of the earth: and all these blessings shall come on thee, and overtake thee, if thou

shalt hearken unto the voice of the Lord thy God. Blessed shalt thou be in the city, and blessed shalt thou be in the field. Blessed shall be the fruit of thy body, and the fruit of thy ground, and the fruit of thy cattle, the increase of thy kine, and the flocks of thy sheep. Blessed shall be thy basket and thy store. Blessed shalt thou be when thou comest in, and blessed shalt thou be when thou goest out. The Lord shall cause thine enemies that rise up against thee to be smitten before thy face: they shall come out against thee one way, and flee before thee seven ways. The Lord shall command the blessing upon thee in thy storehouses, and in all that thou settest thine hand unto; and he shall bless thee in the land which the Lord thy God giveth thee. The Lord shall establish thee an holy people unto himself, as he hath sworn unto thee, if thou shalt keep the commandments of the Lord thy God, and walk in his ways. And all people of the earth shall see that thou art called by the name of the Lord; and they shall be afraid of thee (Deut. 28:1-10).

The prophet Moses also said:

But it shall come to pass, if thou wilt not hearken unto the voice of the Lord thy God, to observe to do all his commandments and his statutes which I command thee this day; that all these curses shall come upon thee, and overtake thee: cursed shalt thou be in the city, and cursed shalt thou be in the field. Cursed shall be thy basket and thy store. Cursed shall be the fruit of thy body, and the fruit of thy land, the increase of thy kine, and the flocks of thy sheep. Cursed shalt thou be when thou comest in, and cursed shalt thou be when thou goest out. The Lord shall send upon thee cursing, vexation, and rebuke, in all that thou settest thine hand for to do, until thou be destroyed, and until thou perish quickly; because of wickedness of thy doings, whereby thou hast forsaken me (Deut. 28:15-20).

On through that twenty-eighth chapter Moses continues to prophesy what will befall these people, the people of whom God once said that they were the apple of His eye:

And the Lord shall scatter thee among all people, from the one end of the earth even unto the other; and there thou shalt serve other gods, which neither thou nor thy fathers have known, even wood and stone. And among these nations shalt thou find no ease, neither shall the sole of thy foot have rest: but the Lord shall give thee there a trembling heart, and failing of eyes, and sorrow of mind: and thy life shall hang in doubt before thee; and thou shalt fear day and night, and shalt have none assurance

of thy life: in the morning thou shalt say, Would God it were
even! and at even thou shalt say, Would God it were morning
for the fear of thine heart wherewith thou shalt fear, and for
the sight of thine eyes which thou shalt see. And the Lord shall
bring thee into Egypt again with ships, by the way whereof I
spake unto thee, Thou shalt see it no more again: and there ye
shall be sold unto your enemies for bondmen and bondwomen,
and no man shall buy you (Deut. 28:64-68).

[But] it shall come to pass, when all these things are come upon
thee, the blessing and the curse, which I have set before thee, and
thou shalt call them to mind among all the nations, whither the
Lord thy God hath driven thee; and shalt return unto the Lord
thy God, and shalt obey His voice according to all that I command thee this day, thou and thy children, with all thine heart,
and with all thy soul; that then the Lord thy God will turn thy
captivity, and have compassion upon thee, and will return and
gather thee from all the nations, whither the Lord thy God hath
scattered thee. If any of thine be driven out unto the outmost
parts of heaven, from thence will the Lord thy God gather thee,
and from thence will he fetch thee: and the Lord thy God will
bring thee into the land which thy fathers possessed, and thou
shalt possess it; and he will do thee good, and multiply thee above
thy fathers. And the Lord thy God will circumcise thine heart,
and the heart of thy seed, to love the Lord thy God with all
thine heart, and with all thy soul, that thou mayest live. And the
Lord thy God will put all these curses upon thine enemies, and
on them that hate thee, which persecuted thee. And thou shalt
return and obey the voice of the Lord, and do all his commandments which I command thee this day. And the Lord thy God
will make thee plenteous in every work of thine hand, in the
fruit of thy body, and in the fruit of thy cattle, and in the fruit
of thy land, for good: for the Lord will again rejoice over thee
for good, as he rejoiced over thy fathers: if thou shalt hearken
unto the voice of the Lord thy God, to keep his commandments
and his statutes which are written in this book of the law, and
if thou turn unto the Lord thy God with all thine heart, and
with all thy soul (Deut. 30:1-10).

The prophets would say to us as did Zechariah:

Thus saith the Lord of hosts; It shall yet come to pass, that
there shall come people, and the inhabitants of many cities: and
the inhabitants of one city shall go to another, saying, Let us go
speedily to pray before the Lord, and to seek the Lord of hosts

I will go also. Yea, many people and strong nations shall come to seek the Lord of hosts in Jerusalem, and to pray before the Lord. Thus saith the Lord of hosts; In those days it shall come to pass, that ten men shall take hold out of all languages of the nations, even shall take hold of the skirt of him that is a Jew, saying, We will go with you: for we have heard that God is with you (Zech. 8:20-23).

The prophet Jeremiah declared:

Behold, the days come, saith the Lord, that I will make a new covenant with the house of Israel, and with the house of Judah: not according to the covenant that I made with their fathers in the day that I took them by the hand to bring them out of the land of Egypt; which my covenant they brake, although I was an husband unto them, saith the Lord: but this shall be the covenant that I will make with the house of Israel; After those days, saith the Lord, I will put my law in their inward parts, and write it in their hearts; and will be their God, and they shall be my people. And they shall teach no more every man his neighbour, and every man his brother, saying, Know the Lord; for they shall all know me, from the least of them unto the greatest of them, saith the Lord; for I will forgive their iniquity, and I will remember their sin no more. Thus saith the Lord, which giveth the sun for a light by day, and the ordinance of the moon and of the stars for a light by night, which divideth the sea when the waves thereof roar; The Lord of hosts is his name: if those ordinances depart from before me, saith the Lord, then the seed of Israel also shall cease from being a nation before me for ever. Thus saith the Lord; If heaven above can be measured, and the foundations of the earth searched out beneath, I will cast off all the seed of Israel for all that they have done, saith the Lord (Jer. 31:31-37).

The prophets speak to the twentieth century, and they would have us realize that the final form of government this earth shall see will be a theocracy. Out of Israel shall come the divine rule and the royal Person.

One night I was with a friend of mine, a rabbi. The Friday evening service had come to a conclusion. Both of us were sitting in the last seat of the temple. The lights were dim, with the exception of those in the front of the auditorium which shone on a symbol. There was the symbol of a lamb and a lion. I turned to him and said, "Friend, if you and I tonight could

agree on that symbol, we could be united. The lamb speaks
to me of 'the Lamb of God which taketh away the sin of the
world.' The lion represents to me 'the Lion of the tribe of Judah,'
who comes again to reign."

The prophet Jeremiah said: "Behold, the days come, saith
the Lord, that I will raise unto David a righteous Branch, and
a King shall reign and prosper, and shall execute judgment
and justice in the earth" (23:5).

And Isaiah cried out: "For unto us a child is born, unto us
a son is given: and the government shall be upon his shoulder:
and his name shall be called Wonderful, Counsellor, The mighty
God, The everlasting Father, the Prince of Peace. Of the
increase of his government and peace there shall be no end, upon
the throne of David, and upon his kingdom, to order it, and
to establish it with judgment and with justice from henceforth
even for ever. The zeal of the Lord of hosts will perform this"
(9:6,7).

Government will no longer be built on the sword, cemented by
blood, throbbing with hate, pulsing with fear, and ruled by
oppression; but a government of God, administered by the
hands of a righteous and benevolent person who is the fullness
of light, knowledge and understanding.

The devil will be chained. Someone has truly said that it is
impossible to conceive what heights of spiritual, intellectual and
physical perfection will be attained in earth's golden age.

The prophets speak to us about another age in the divine
plan. The prophets speak of a covenant people whom God has
not forsaken. The prophets tell us that a theocracy will yet be
God's government upon earth.

The Apostle Paul accurately describes all of this, and the
meaning of it, in the Epistle to the Romans. Here he speaks
of Israel, saying:

> I also am an Israelite, of the seed of Abraham, of the tribe
> of Benjamin. . . . Boast not against the branches. But if thou
> boast, thou bearest not the root, but the root thee. Thou wilt say
> then, The branches were broken off, that I might be graffed in
> Well; because of unbelief they were broken off, and thou stand
> est by faith. Be not highminded, but fear: for if God spared
> not the natural branches, take heed lest he also spare not thee

Behold therefore the goodness and severity of God: on them which fell, severity; but toward thee, goodness, if thou continue in his goodness: otherwise thou also shalt be cut off. And they also, if they abide not still in unbelief, shall be graffed in: for God is able to graff them in again. For if thou wert cut out of the olive tree which is wild by nature, and wert graffed contrary to nature into a good olive tree: how much more shall these, which be the natural branches, be graffed into their own olive tree? For I would not, brethren, that ye should be ignorant of this mystery, lest ye should be wise in your own conceits; that blindness in part is happened to Israel, until the fulness of the Gentiles be come in. And so all Israel shall be saved: as it is written, There shall come out of Sion the Deliverer, and shall turn away ungodliness from Jacob: for this is my covenant unto them, when I shall take away their sins. As concerning the gospel, they are enemies for your sakes: but as touching the election, they are beloved for the fathers' sakes. For the gifts and calling of God are without repentance (Rom. 11: 1, 18-28).

The Apostle Paul then pleads: "I beseech you therefore, brethren, by the mercies of God, that ye present your bodies a living sacrifice, holy, acceptable unto God, which is your reasonable service. And be not conformed to this world: but be ye transformed by the renewing of your mind, that ye may prove what is that good and acceptable, and perfect, will of God" (Rom. 12:1).

The prophets speak to the twentieth century, and in speaking they tell us that God's judgment is just, but that God's mercy is great; that God is faithful to His own divinely revealed plan, to the people whom He had called out of the loins of Abraham, and to His Son who will surely be King of kings and Lord of lords.

11

THE TIMES OF THE GENTILES

by JOHN F. WALVOORD, TH.D.

THE TIMES OF THE GENTILES is one of the great time programs of God. The exact expression is found in Luke 21:24. There, after predicting that the inhabitants of Jerusalem would "fall by the edge of the sword," Christ further prophesies, "And Jerusalem shall be trodden down of the Gentiles, until the times of the Gentiles be fulfilled."

DEFINITION OF THE TERM

The term, "times of the Gentiles," is understood by most evangelical students of Scripture as referring to that period of time which began about 600 B.C., when Nebuchadnezzar, the king of the mighty empire of Babylon, subdued Jerusalem through the force of arms. Our Lord predicts that this condition will continue until the times of the Gentiles are fulfilled. Today ancient Jerusalem is still in the hands of Gentiles. Israel has conquered the area around Jerusalem and built it up into new city, but the historic Jerusalem is still in the hands of non-Jews.

CONTRASTING DIVINE PROGRAMS

To comprehend the great significance of this period as it is unfolded in Scripture, it will be necessary to contrast it at the outset to some of the other important programs of God. In addition to the times of the Gentiles, another tremendous program was predicted by Daniel the prophet, in chapter 9, verse 24-27, where the seventy weeks, or the seventy sevens of Israel's history is unfolded. Fulfillment of all except the last seven years of this period proves the units to be years. God's program for Israel did not begin with the times of the Gentiles, but about 150 years later, circa 450 B.C. Its terminus, however, is the same as that of the times of the Gentiles. It will end when Christ comes back to establish His millennial kingdom.

There is a third program known as the kingdom in mystery form, revealed in Matthew 13. This time periods spans the first and the second comings of Christ. The Old Testament contains no revelation concerning this period. The times of the Gentiles did not include it. Israel's program as revealed to Daniel did not predict it. This phase of the kingdom of God now present in mystery form is to be distinguished from that future kingdom which Christ will set up when He comes back to reign over the earth for one thousand years.

In addition to this kingdom of heaven, or kingdom of God in mystery form, which occupies the entire interadvent period, including the Tribulation time, there is another period known as *the Church Age*. This began with the formation of the Church by the baptism of the Spirit on the Day of Pentecost, is now in progress, and will terminate when Christ comes back. At that time the dead in Christ will be raised and the living Christians translated.

The four major programs of Scripture, therefore, are *the times of the Gentiles, the seventy sevens of Israel, the kingdom in mystery form,* and *the Church* or the body of Christ. Culminating and following all these programs will be the final and last period before eternity, that is, *the millennial age.* Scripture gives us an outline of history in advance, together with an intelligent interpretation of history from the divine viewpoint. This helps us to understand past history, current events, and to project ourselves into the revealed future.

THE REVELATION TO DANIEL

The times of the Gentiles are the subject of several major sections of the Book of Daniel, the first of which is the second chapter. King Nebuchadnezzar, the head of one of the greatest empires in the world up to that time, had a dream. This dream having apparently gone from him, he called in his wise men to tell him the dream and to interpret it. To this they protested,

"There is not a man upon the earth that can shew the king's matter: therefore there is no king, lord, nor ruler, that asked such things at any magician, or astrologer, or Chaldean. And it is a rare thing that the king requireth, and there is none other that can shew it before the king, except the gods, whose dwelling is not with flesh" (Dan. 2:10, 11).

The king in his anger then issued an order that all the wise men should be put to death; and Daniel and his companions, captive Jewish youths classified as wise men, were collected along with the others to be put to death. When Daniel learned of the matter, he asked for time. He and his companions gave themselves to prayer, and in response God revealed the dream to Daniel in a night vision. Daniel then went to the king and told him the dream in these words: "Thou, O king, sawest, and behold a great image. This great image, whose brightness was excellent, stood before thee; and the form thereof was terrible. The image's head was of fine gold, his breast and his arms of silver, his belly and his thighs of brass, his legs of iron, his feet part of iron and part of clay. Thou sawest till that a stone was cut out without hands, which smote the image upon his feet that were of iron and clay, and brake them to pieces. Then was the iron, the clay, the brass, the silver, and the gold, broken to pieces together, and became like the chaff of the summer thresh-ing floors; and the wind carried them away, that no place was found for them: and the stone that smote the image became a great mountain, and filled the whole earth" (Dan. 2:31-35).

The tremendous dream thus unfolded was then given divine interpretation. Daniel said to King Nebuchadnezzar: "Thou, O king, art a king of kings: for the God of heaven hath given thee a kingdom, power, and strength, and glory. And whereso-ever the children of men dwell, the beasts of the field and the fowls of the heaven hath he given into thine hand, and hath made thee ruler over them all. Thou art this head of gold. And after thee shall arise another kingdom inferior to thee, and another third kingdom of brass, which shall bear rule over all the earth. And the fourth kingdom shall be strong as iron" (Dan. 2:37-40).

THE FOUR EMPIRES OF PROPHECY

This prophetic vision as unfolded in the Book of Daniel, becomes very clear. The first kingdom is Babylon. It was historically followed by the kingdom of the Medes and Persians. Daniel 5 records how the Medes and the Persians led by Darius captured the supposedly unconquerable city of Babylon in one night. Following the Medes and Persians arose a third empire, the kingdom of Greece, as indicated in Daniel 8:21. The fourth kingdom, not named by Daniel, is Rome.

In the seventh chapter these same empires are represented by beasts. Babylon is represented by a lion with eagle's wings. Medo-Persia, the kingdom of silver, is shown as a bear (Dan. 7:5). Greece, the kingdom of brass, is portrayed as the leopard (7:6). The second and third kingdoms are also mentioned by name in Daniel 8:20,21, "The ram which thou sawest having two horns are the kings of Media and Persia. And the rough goat is the king of Grecia: and the great horn that is between his eyes is the first king." The important point for us is that the first three kingdoms are named in the Book of Daniel.

The fourth kingdom, described as a terrible beast (Dan. 7:7,8), is not named. However, practically all evangelical scholars agree that the fourth kingdom is Rome, which historically picked up the remnant of the Grecian Empire in its last stages and welded it together into a mighty empire. While it is not possible to go into the details of these four empires, God's prophetic program is readily seen in majestic progression, one empire following another, until the fourth kingdom is destroyed.

The destruction of the fourth kingdom, as Daniel saw it in the vision, was accomplished by a stone cut out of a mountain without hands: "Forasmuch as thou sawest that the stone was cut out of the mountain without hands, and that it brake in pieces the iron, the brass, the clay, the silver, and the gold; the great God hath made known to the king what shall come to pass hereafter: and the dream is certain, and the interpretation thereof sure" (Dan. 2:45). There has been a great deal of discussion concerning this stone. What is it that destroyed the Roman Empire?

In history to the present there is nothing that would cor respond to this event. The Roman Empire went on for hun dreds of years after our Lord was crucified; and, due to the in herent immorality, corruption, decay, and especially the military pressure of the barbarian hordes of the north, the Roman Em pire finally fell. The obvious fact is that while the Scripture was literally fulfilled in every detail right up to the time of the first coming of our Lord, the climax which Daniel's prophecy predicted never took place. The best explanation for this is that the prophecies of Daniel both in regard to Israel's seventy weeks as well as the times of the Gentiles have been interrupted by the ushering in of the present Church Age, and will be re sumed after the Church is caught up to be with the Lord. The last seven years of Israel's program, and the destruction of the image by the stone cut out without hands, are yet future.

When our Lord, in Luke 21:24, mentioned that Jerusalem should be trodden under the feet of Gentiles until the times of the Gentiles are fulfilled, He disclosed what Daniel did no know, that during the present age there would be no fulfillmen of Daniel's program, no deliverance from Gentile domination Jerusalem would be under control of the Gentiles throughou the entire interadvent period and until Christ comes back to set up His kingdom.

TIMES OF THE GENTILES AND OTHER DIVINE PROGRAMS

Question may be raised concerning the times of the Gentile in relationship to other divine programs. Where does the Church and Israel, and the mystery form of the kingdom, fit into the picture? The answer is plain. The times of the Gentiles begar in 600 B.C., and they will have their ultimate termination whet Christ returns to establish His kingdom.

The program for Israel began about 450 B.C., 150 years later and ran its course right up to the time of the crucifixion of Christ. The first sixty-nine sevens were literally fulfilled on schedule. Sir Robert Anderson has demonstrated in his chron ology how the sixty-nine sevens, or 483 years, terminated per haps the week before the crucifixion of Christ, but that fulfill ment of the last seven years was indefinitely postponed. Whil

Israel's program runs concurrently with the times of the Gentiles, there is no progress for the former in the present age.

In the meantime two other divine programs hold the stage of history: The one is the kingdom in mystery form, revealed in Matthew 13; the rule of God while the king is absent, not foreseen in the Old Testament. It extends from the first coming of Christ to His return to establish His earthly kingdom. The other is the Church, which for the most part runs concurrently with the kingdom in mystery form, except that its beginning and terminus are more definite. The Church program began specifically with the baptism of the Spirit on the Day of Pentecost, and it will end at the Rapture. The Church will be taken to heaven first. Then the times of the Gentiles and the last seven years of Israel's program will run their course and culminate in the return of our Lord and Saviour Jesus Christ to earth.

CHARACTERISTICS OF THE TIMES OF THE GENTILES

The times of the Gentiles constitute one of the major programs of God revealed in Scripture and have four principal characteristics. First of all, the image revealed to Daniel shows that as the times of the Gentiles progress there is a deterioration of glory and an increase in strength. The gold, the silver, the brass, and the iron are progressively lighter metals, less valuable and less glorious. But by the same token they seem to increase in strength, so that the glory of Babylon is followed by the Medes and the Persians, a lesser glory but a stronger government. The Medes and the Persians in turn are followed by the Grecian Empire represented by the brass. Finally comes the rule of iron typifying the Roman Empire, a well organized and model government in many respects, from which we have learned much in the realm of political science. History has literally fulfilled much that has been anticipated in this image. The very nature of the image makes it top-heavy. Gold is much heavier than silver and brass is heavier than iron. This anticipates the sudden fall of Gentile power when it is succeeded by the fifth kingdom — the millennial rule of Christ.

The second characteristic feature of the times of the Gentiles is rebellion against God. This is indicated in the way Nebuchad-nezzar erects his golden image. He apparently did not like the idea that his empire would fall, so he built an image all of gold, as if he were the sole embodiment of imperial government. He demanded the worship of everyone, and as a result of this Daniel's three companions, who refused to worship the image, were cast into the fiery furnace. Rebellion against God has been the religious characteristic of the Gentile world from that day to this. Except for individual Gentiles saved in the Old Testament or New Testament times, Gentile world dominion as such has been essentially pagan.

The third important characteristic of Gentile times is the deification of man. Nebuchadnezzar wanted people to worship him. Down through human history great world leaders have asked and received the worship of men. In the twelfth chapter of Acts, Herod received the worship of men. You will recall that, according to the prophetic word, the last world dictator to dominate the political scene at the time when Christ comes back will demand the worship of the entire world. Some say that we have grown too advanced in our thinking to deify man. But have we? What is the philosophy of humanism but the deification of man — man declaring his independence of and insubordination to an almighty and sovereign Creator? There is something in the unregenerate human heart that refuses to bow and worship the God and Father of our Lord and Saviour Jesus Christ.

The fourth obvious characteristic demonstrated in the times of the Gentiles, the one to which our Lord expressly calls our attention in Luke 21:24, is the oppression of Israel. From the time of Nebuchadnezzar to the present day the sad prophecies of Moses have been enacted by pagan world powers. In our own generation, under the regime of Hitler, the most fearful persecution and slaughter of Israelites the world has ever known took place, and the Scriptures predict still another time of trouble in the period of great tribulation. According to Zechariah 13:8, two-thirds of all the Israelites in the land will perish under the awful persecution instigated by the Antichrist and the nations under his leadership.

Fulfillment of the Times of the Gentiles

But what is the end of it all? The Word of God leads us to believe that the major part of the times of the Gentiles has already been fulfilled. The climactic stage will be literally fulfilled after the Church is caught up to be with the Lord. Then will follow a rapid sequence of events predicted in the Word of God. The seven-year program for Israel will run its course, and simultaneously with it the last segment of the times of the Gentiles. In the first part of that seven-year period there will be a revival of the ancient Roman Empire. Politically, the Mediterranean world will resume its importance to approximately the same extent as in the time of our Lord. The states about the Mediterranean which formerly were included in the Roman Empire will be banded together in a confederacy or league of nations. After the destruction of the Russian army, as predicted in Ezekiel 38 and 39, the head of the revived Roman Empire will be placed in a position to declare himself the dictator of the entire world. This will take place approximately in the middle of the period, and as soon as he obtains supreme political power, he will follow the pattern of those who preceded him by declaring himself god. He will then break the covenant with Israel, and the Jews will come under his terrible disfavor. At the same time, and by the same token, there will be Satanic persecution of those who will have come to trust in Jesus Christ during the first three and one-half year period after the Church has been raptured. There will also be a multitude which no man can number out of the various nations of the world who will turn to Christ in that day. They too will at once become the object of terrible persecution and will have the choice of worshiping the beast or paying for refusal to do so with their blood. During all this time, Jerusalem will be trodden under the feet of Gentiles.

Some years ago when Israel was fighting the Arabs to gain possession of Palestine, they occupied Mount Zion. In the ordinary course of events, because of superior military position, they would have been able to conquer the ancient city of Jerusalem in a few days. At that precise moment, however, the armistice was declared, other boundaries were fixed, and Israel fell short of gaining possession of Old Jerusalem. Christ had said that Jerusalem would be trodden under the feet of Gentiles until the times of the Gentiles are fulfilled. But one of these days, just as surely as God's program has been fulfilled to the present hour, will come the day when the returning Christ will destroy Gentile power and deliver Jerusalem from Gentile domination.

WHILE IT IS CALLED TODAY

For us who live today the main issue is our relationship to the Lord Jesus Christ. Are we His? Are we ready for Him? The very next event in history is the end of the present day of grace, this day of opportunity when the pierced hands of our Saviour are outstretched to welcome everyone who will come to Him. Jew and Gentile alike may be saved through simple faith in Jesus Christ as Saviour and Lord.

One of these days, and it may be sooner than anyone imagines, the program for the Church will be brought to its consummation. In that hour the supreme question will be: Do I know Jesus Christ as my Saviour and my Lord? We can settle that question now if we will put our faith in the One who loved us, the One who died for us, the One who said, "Him that cometh to me I will in no wise cast out." May our answer be in the words of the hymn, "O Lamb of God, I come, I come."

12

WILL THE CHURCH GO THROUGH THE TRIBULATION?

by JOHN F. WALVOORD, TH.D.

DIFFERENT VIEWS ON THE LORD'S RETURN

The subject before us is obviously controversial. All who read the Bible and have faith in the Lord Jesus Christ do not have the same opinion as to whether the Church will go through the coming Tribulation. As far as I know, all the speakers at the present Congress on Prophecy hold the pretribulational point of view. By this we mean that Jesus Christ is coming before the Tribulation to meet the Church in the air. The dead in Christ will be raised and living Christians will be translated to be forever with the Lord. Following the great Tribulation, Christ will come back from heaven with His Church, to establish His millennial kingdom. This is the pretribulational position.

Opposed to this belief are several other points of view, the most popular of which is the posttribulational. Adherents of this position hold that when Christ comes for His Church He will at the same time establish His millennial kingdom. Therefore, His coming for the Church will be after the Tribulation, requiring the Church to pass through the Tribulation before it meets Christ in the air. They visualize Christ's coming to establish the millennial kingdom and His coming for the Church as one and the same event.

Still another position is the midtribulational. Those who hold this teaching believe that Christ will come for His Church in the middle of that seven-year period, at the beginning of the

Great Tribulation. The Church will go to heaven with the Lord at the middle of Daniel's seventieth week, and return when He comes to establish His kingdom.

There is still another position, held by only a few, known as the partial Rapture. Followers of this teaching hold that when Christ comes for His Church only the spiritual ones, those who are looking for His coming, will be raptured, and that all other Christians will pass through the Tribulation.

For the purpose of our study here, this theme will be approached from the exegetical point of view. Instead of listing formal arguments, the Scriptures will be allowed to speak for themselves. Passages in the Word of God revealing His coming to establish His millennial kingdom, and passages which deal with His coming for the translation of the Church, will be examined to see what they actually say.

No Translation at Establishment of Millennial Kingdom

In the study of these Scriptures it soon becomes apparent that there is not one passage referring to Christ's coming to establish His millennial kingdom which reveals anything about a translation. On the other hand, there is clear evidence that when He comes to translate His Church, He leaves the world unchanged, and no kingdom is founded.

In support of these conclusions, the important Scriptures that deal with the subject can be cited. In Matthew 25:31 this description of His Second Coming is given: "When the Son of man shall come in his glory, and all the holy angels with him, then shall he sit upon the throne of his glory: and before him shall be gathered all nations: and he shall separate them one from another, as a shepherd divideth his sheep from the goats." In this familiar portion of Scripture there appear some very obvious facts: (1) the Son of Man comes in His glory accompanied by His holy angels; (2) He comes to the earth where both saved and unsaved are living; (3) before Him while He is on the earth are gathered the nations or, as it is better translated, the Gentiles; (4) He sets up His throne; (5) He separates the sheep from the goats, or the righteous from the unrighteous. Why is that order so important? Because it is apparent that if one accepts this chronology he cannot believe the posttribulational point of view. According to the posttribulational teaching, the following order must be fulfilled: (1) Christ comes back in the air; (2) all the living saints are caught up to meet Christ in the air; (3) He comes to the earth; (4) He sets up His throne; (5) He judges the wicked, the separation of the righteous from the unrighteous taking place before Christ ever touches the earth. Actually, however, Matthew 25:31 is silent on the subject of translation. The sheep are not translated at all, but go into the millennium in their natural bodies. This imposes the conclusion that there is no translation when Christ comes to establish His millennial kingdom.

In Jude 14, 15 another picture is given of the coming of Christ to establish His kingdom: "And Enoch, also, the seventh from Adam, prophesied of these, saying, Behold, the Lord cometh with ten thousands of his saints, to execute judgment upon all, and to convince all that are ungodly among them of all their ungodly deeds which they have ungodly committed, and of all their hard speeches which ungodly sinners have spoken against him." Once again in this major passage on the Second Coming of Christ no mention whatever is made of translation.

The great classic passage on the Second Coming is found in Revelation 19, where a sequence of events is described as immediately following. Beginning in verse 11, John in his vision "saw heaven opened, and behold a white horse; and he that sat upon him was called Faithful and True, and in righteousness he doth judge and make war. His eyes were as a flame of fire, and on his head were many crowns; and he had a name written, that no man knew, but he himself." The name is given to us in verse 16, "KING OF KINGS, AND LORD OF LORDS." Obviously, this is a picture of Jesus Christ coming back to establish His millennial kingdom. In verses 17-21 the awful destruction of the wicked is described. The beast and the false prophet are cast alive into the lake of fire burning with brimstone, and the rest are slain.

In Revelation 20 Satan is bound for a thousand years so that he no longer deceives the nations. In verse 4 we read of "the souls of them that were beheaded for the witness of Jesus, and for the word of God, and which had not worshipped the beast, neither his image, neither had received his mark upon their forehead, or in their hands; and they lived and reigned with Christ a thousand years." In other words, mention is made here of the resurrection of the Tribulation saints who were martyred. The passage then tells of the first resurrection as in contrast to the second death, and how the thousand years are going to run their course and end in the judgment of the Great White Throne. A careful reading of this major Scripture on the coming of Christ to establish His kingdom will reveal that not one word is said here about the translation. Ardent post-tribulationists sometimes challenge anyone to find one Scripture that teaches a pretribulation rapture of the Church. There are many, as we shall see. But I should like to reverse that question. Can anyone find one passage in the Bible where the Church is translated at the coming of Christ to establish His millennial kingdom?

TRANSLATION BEFORE THE TRIBULATION

The first mention of the translation is found in the fourteenth chapter of John. These wonderful words of Christ were addressed to the disciples in the upper room the night before He was to be crucified: "Let not your heart be troubled: ye believe in God, believe also in me. In my Father's house are many mansions: if it were not so, I would have told you. I go to prepare a place for you. And if I go and prepare a place for you, I will come again, and receive you unto myself; that where I am, there ye may be also." This must have been a most astounding revelation to the disciples. They were expecting Christ to establish His millennial kingdom in connection with His first advent. As they studied the Old Testament which mingles the first and second advents of Christ, they anticipated that Christ would at His first coming establish His kingdom, free Israel from their oppressors, and bring in the glorious period of righteousness and peace in which they would have a share. They did not know, though it is well known to us today, that between the first and second advents of Christ there is a long, unmeasured period of time which the Old Testament did not reveal. They did not understand that His Second Coming rather than the first would introduce the millennial kingdom. For that reason, they could not understand the prophecy that He would take them to heaven. They expected to stay on the earth and share the glories of the millennial kingdom.

This is the first clear revelation concerning the coming of Christ for His own in this present age. Accordingly, when Christ comes for His disciples, they will go from earth to heaven, to the Father's house, where Christ is now preparing a place for them. When Christ comes to set up His kingdom on the earth, just the opposite will occur. Then they will be coming from heaven to earth. If Christ's coming has as its purpose to take the saints from earth to heaven, then it is foolish to say that He is going to come for the saints on the way down to the earth to establish His millennial kingdom. The two events are decidedly different.

A second important Scripture is found in I Corinthians 15: 51, 52: "Behold, I shew you a mystery; We shall not all sleep, but we shall all be changed, in a moment, in the twinkling of an eye, at the last trump; for the trumpet shall sound, and the dead shall be raised incorruptible, and we shall be changed." The context of this Scripture should be recalled. The earlier part of this chapter undertakes to proclaim first of all the Gospel, the certainty of the death of Christ for our sin, and then unfolds the proof of it in the doctrine of resurrection. Paul cites as evidence the many witnesses who saw Him, including five hundred at once. The doctrine of resurrection is proclaimed as essential to the Christian faith. In the discussion which follows, the necessity of resurrection is expounded. The main thesis is this: these mortal bodies of ours are not suited for eternity and therefore, when they die, they are resurrected as a different kind of body. Having established this pattern of death and resurrection as normal, Paul says there is one exception to the rule, caused by the last trump, when Christ will come and the living will be changed into resurrection-type bodies without experiencing death in a physical way.

This teaching is quite plain, but a significant point should not be overlooked. This truth is declared to be a mystery, and, according to Colossians 1:26, a mystery is a truth "which hath been hid from ages and from generations, but now is made manifest to his saints." There are two essentials to a mystery: first, it must not have been revealed in the Old Testament; second, it must be revealed in the New Testament. That is what the Bible teaches. Now there is no revelation of a translation of the saints in the Old Testament, except possibly by example as in the case of Enoch and Elijah. Until the New Testament there is no prophetic declaration that Christ is coming for the living saints. Paul declares this mystery in the following words: "We shall not all sleep, but we shall all be changed." The fact that there will be some living at the coming of Christ is no mystery. In relation to the Lord's coming for His millennial kingdom, the Old Testament fully anticipates that there will be multitudes of people living in the world at that time. As in the judgment of the sheep and the goats, a separation will then take place and Christ will set up His millennial kingdom. The idea of living saints is not a mystery. The exact content of the mystery is that all the true believers will be translated, changed in a moment, in the twinkling of an eye, at the last trump. "For the trumpet shall sound, and the dead shall be raised incorruptible, and we shall be changed."

Right here is one of the most positive evidences for the pretribulation rapture. It demonstrates that there must be a period of time between His coming for His Church and His coming to establish His millennial kingdom. The reason for it is that there must be a whole generation of righteous raised up after the Church is taken out of the world, to populate the millennial earth.

Proof of this is found in Isaiah 65:20 ff. In the preceding context the subject of the new heaven and the new earth is discussed in verse 17. In the passage which follows, however, the millennial earth is in view: "There shall be no more thence an infant of days, nor an old man that hath not filled his days:

for the child shall die an hundred years old; but the sinner being an hundred years old shall be accursed. And they shall build houses and inhabit them; and they shall plant vineyards, and eat the fruit of them. They shall not build, and another inhabit; they shall not plant and another eat: for as the days of a tree are the days of my people, and mine elect shall long enjoy the work of their hands. They shall not labour in vain, nor bring forth for trouble; for they are the seed of the blessed of the Lord, and their offspring with them." These statements could not be made of people resurrected or translated. In the millennial earth those who in the Tribulation trust in Christ will retain their natural bodies. They will go into the Millennium in their natural bodies and live out their span of life.

A similar portion is found in Zechariah 8:5, "And the streets of the city shall be full of boys and girls playing in the streets thereof." This is a picture of children born in the millennial time of parents who were natural parents who went through the Tribulation, or were born subsequent to it, now living out their appointed span of life. In consideration of these Scriptural facts, there must be a period of time between the translation of the Church and the coming of Christ to establish His kingdom during which a new generation of kingdom believers will be raised up.

Some have attempted to dispute pretribulationism on the basis of the reference to *the last trump* found in I Corinthians 15:52. This trump of God has no reference to the angelic trumpets of Revelation. It is evidently a trump of resurrection and translation. The trumpets of Revelation have to do with the judgment of unbelievers and are described in a totally different context. There are many trumpets in Scripture, and it is foolishness to put all the trumpets together as relating to one event. The "last trump" concludes the Church Age and signals resurrection and translation.

Another major portion of Scripture bearing on the subject is I Thessalonians 4:13-18. The Thessalonians were young Christians who, nevertheless, were instructed in prophetic truth. They had written Paul concerning a fine point in doctrine. The question was: When Christ comes for us and we are caught

up to be with the Lord, will our loved ones in Christ who have
died be raised at that time, or will they be raised later? They
believed in the resurrection of the dead and that there was
a time of trouble ahead. They apparently believed that Christ
was coming for them before that time of trouble, but their question was about their loved ones who had died.

Paul answered them simply and assuringly that their loved
ones would be raised from the dead at the same time that they
themselves would be translated. In fact, it would occur a moment before their translation. He writes in verses 15-17: "We
which are alive and remain unto the coming of the Lord shall
not prevent them which are asleep. For the Lord himself shall
descend from heaven with a shout, with the voice of the
archangel, and with the trump of God: and the dead in Christ
shall rise first: then we which are alive and remain shall be
caught up together with them in the clouds, to meet the Lord
in the air: and so shall we ever be with the Lord."

This is a rich passage of Scripture and it certainly teaches
that the coming of the Lord is a blessed hope. Of special interest
in our present study is the exhortation which concludes this
passage, "Therefore comfort one another with these words"
(v. 18). The doctrine of the coming of the Lord for His Church
was intended to be a comfort to those who had lost loved
ones in Christ through death. Consider for a moment the incongruity of this exhortation if Paul were a posttribulationist.
How could he have extended this comfort to the Thessalonians
if they had first to pass through the Tribulation?

Usually posttribulationists recognize this difficulty and minimize the Tribulation until it become equivalent to the ordinary
troubles of life. If Paul believed the Thessalonians had to pass
through such a literal Tribulation, it would be unthinkable for
him to extend the hope of the Lord's coming to them as an
immediate comfort.

Another important passage follows in I Thessalonians 5:1-11.
It discusses, specifically in verse 1, the very question we have
here before us, i.e., the times and the seasons when the Lord
will come. Paul writes: "But of the times and seasons, brethren,
ye have no need that I write unto you. For yourselves know

erfectly that the day of the Lord cometh as a thief in the night."
This passage has created some differences of opinion. There are
worthy Bible teachers, especially in the last generation, who
share with us our hope of the pretribulation coming of the
Lord for His Church, but they say the "day of the Lord" begins with the Millennium. Over against this view, others believe the day of the Lord begins immediately after the translation
of the Church. We believe the day of the Lord includes the
Tribulation, the Second Coming, and the whole thousand-year
reign of Christ. Today we are in what we call *the day of grace,*
the day which will end when Christ comes for His Church.
This term does not mean that grace will terminate completely
at the Rapture, but that this present age, when grace is su-
premely revealed and manifested, will end. Just as soon as the
day of grace ends, the day of the Lord begins. In this period
God punishes sin, and pours out immediate judgment upon rebellion and unbelief. In the Millennium Christ will exercise
absolute rule over the earth.

When the Millennium ends and the new heaven and new
earth begin, the fulfillment of Peter's "day of God" (II Pet. 3:12)
will take place. This is simply another expression for eternity.
While none of these terms define themselves, they can be defined according to the context in which they are found in Scripture. We have, then, these three periods: the day of grace,
the day of Jehovah, and the day of eternity or the day of God.
Just as soon as the translation of the Church occurs, the day of
the Lord begins. Some of the events in the day of the Lord
do not necessarily begin at once, however. An ordinary day begins at midnight, while the events of the day may not begin
until after daybreak. So with the day of Jehovah. The day
begins with the translation of the saints, and the other events
take place in order as the day progresses.

The Thessalonians were asking, When is the Lord coming?
When will we see our loved ones again? The discussion turns
from the Rapture to the day of the Lord without any break.
Why? Because the Rapture, by its very nature, brings one day
to its close (the day of grace), and begins another (the day of
the Lord). Concerning "the times and seasons," however, says

Paul, he did not need to write, because there are no signs. Th
day of the Lord will come as a thief in the night, that i
it will be unexpected. By contrast, the coming of Christ to b
gin His kingdom rule over the earth has many signs in Matthe
24, and there are more in Revelation 4-19. But in connectio
with the Rapture not a sign is given. "When they shall sa
Peace and safety; then sudden destruction cometh upon then
as travail upon a woman with child; and they shall not escape
that is, the unbelievers will not escape. Of the believers h
writes, "But ye, brethren, are not in darkness, that that da
should overtake you as a thief. Ye are all the children of ligh
and the children of the day: we are not of the night, nor of dar
ness." Then Paul concludes by exhorting the Christians not t
sleep as the others, not to be drunken, but to watch and to b
sober: "But let us, who are of the day, be sober, putting on th
breastplate of faith and love; and for an helmet, the hope c
salvation." This hope is based on certain deliverance from th
wrath of God. As he states in verse 9, "For God hath not aj
pointed us unto wrath, but to obtain salvation by our Lor
Jesus Christ."

Posttribulationists who deal with this portion of Scriptur
say the Church will go through the Tribulation, but it wil
not experience the wrath of the Tribulation. This sounds plaus
ible until one starts studying the Tribulation. What are th
judgments of the Tribulation? They are earthquakes, war, fam
ine, destruction poured out from heaven. Perhaps atomic bomb
will be used. When such methods of destruction are visite
upon a civilized world, do they single out any special class? Th
very nature of this wrath is such that none will escape it. In
deed, the Scriptures tell us that those who come to Christ i
that day, and refuse to worship the beast, will be put to deatl
by the thousands. If any survive, they will be the exceptio
rather than the rule. But the Thessalonians are told not to fea
this day of wrath. This is not their appointment. It will no
overtake them as a thief. Why not? Because they will hav
been previously caught up to meet the Lord in the air togethe
with their loved ones. We who are the Lord's will be witl
Him when these tremendous events take place on the earth.

13

THE MYSTERY OF GODLINESS

by Roy L. Laurin, D.D.

Christians are expected to be "stewards of the mysteries of God." These mysteries mark the current Church Age, and include the mystery of the divine indwelling referred to in Colossians 1:26, 27: "Even the mystery which hath been hid from ages and from generations, but now is made manifest to his saints: To whom God would make known what is the riches of the glory of this mystery among the Gentiles; which is Christ in you, the hope of glory."

Besides this mystery relating to the Christian experience, the New Testament speaks of two contrasting mysteries: namely, the mystery of iniquity which is Antichrist (II Thess. 2:7-9), and the mystery of godliness which is Jesus Christ (I Tim. 3:16). "And without controversy great is the mystery of godliness; God was manifest in the flesh, justified in the Spirit, seen of angels, preached unto the Gentiles, believed on in the world, received up into glory." In the mystery of godliness, Jesus Christ is the central figure and the prime expectation of prophecy. We are not looking for Antichrist's appearance or for the Tribulation, but for the Rapture of the Church and the reign of the sovereign Christ.

When we think of Jesus Christ, there are no normal words, descriptive of people generally, that are applicable to Him. Neither are there human standards appropriate to men which can be properly applied to Jesus Christ. There is only one word which can adequately sum up the significance and importance of the person, the coming, the career, and the coming again of Christ. It is the word "incomparable," for Jesus Christ is not merely a superlative and stupendous character; He is super natural, and the supernatural is beyond compare. I speak, then of the mystery of godliness which is the incomparable Christ The field of Christological truth reveals eight phases of this mystery of godliness.

THE MYSTERY OF PRE-EXISTENCE

Jesus Christ appears upon the human scene as a historical miracle. He is the only historical person who lived before He was born, and who, after He died, continued to live in the same form in which He had lived after He was born.

Jesus Christ antedates His birth at Bethlehem. If this is not so, He was the world's most irresponsible claimant, for He said to His contemporaries, "Before Abraham was, I am." This is not a reference to His relationship to time, as if He had lived in some theophanic form prior to His incarnation. He had in mind eternity, for He spoke of His preincarnate glory. "In the beginning was the Word, and the Word was with God, and the Word was God . . . and the Word was made flesh" (John 1:1, 14). Of whom could this be said? Not of a godlike or godly man! Only of the One who is co-equal with the sovereign God of the universe — Jesus Christ.

The continuity of Christ's dominance of history remains un broken to the present moment. He is affirmed to be "the same yesterday, and today, and for ever" (Heb. 13:8). Thus He is our greatest contemporary, the same in our generation as He was in His own. His massive proportions surmount all the great men of all the ages, for none can approach the miracle which is Christ. It is this *One* who is the theme of the prophets and the expectation of the Church.

No one who witnessed the televised tumultuous return of General Douglas MacArthur to this country will ever forget that moving and memorable spectacle. He was seen on film arriving in Honolulu. He was seen by television arriving in San Fran cisco. Then he arrived in Washington where he addressed Con gress in joint session. His peroration referred to a barracks ballad which said, "Old Soldiers never die; they only fade away.' But there has been no fading away of the Captain or "file leader" of our salvation. He is the same, today, tomorrow, forever.

THE MYSTERY OF INCARNATION

The birth of Christ was a biological miracle, since it involved the virgin birth. It is impossible to account for the incomparable personality of Jesus Christ apart from His virgin birth. All of the exaltation which men give to Him must have supernatural origin for its source. Whence came His words, His wisdom, and His powers? Were they found in the carpenter shop? Did He get them from Mary? Were they found in the temple? Did He receive them from the rabbis? We ask, where did they come from except from a divine nature processed by a divine birth which linked Him with the eternal God?

The thirty-three years of Jesus' life were an interlude in flesh, spent in the arena of human experience; that, being tempted as we are, He might be "touched with the feelings of our infirmities," and might prove to be a faithful and merciful High Priest.

THE MYSTERY OF LEARNING

The mastery of Jesus Christ in the field of learning and language was a philological miracle. It was said of Him as it could be said of no other person — "never man spake like this man." The background of this estimate takes us back to Jerusalem, where the priests conceived the arrest of Jesus as a seditious person and sent the Sanhedrin officers to apprehend Him. They found Him speaking to the people, and, listening at the fringes of the throng, they were captivated and conquered by what He was saying, Having come to arrest Him, these officers of the Sanhedrin were arrested by His dynamic speech, and forgetting their official duty, they returned to their superiors without Him. When asked why they had not brought Him with them, they said, "Never man spake like this man." They were rendered powerless in the hearing of His words of power and wisdom.

Learning springs from wisdom, and Jesus Christ was possessed of a wisdom beyond human proportions. Those who were His contemporaries asked, "Whence hath this man this wisdom, and these mighty works? Is not this the carpenter's son? Is not his mother called Mary? and his brethren . . . and his sisters, are they not all with us? Whence then hath this man all these things?" (Matt. 13:54-56). They could not explain Christ's philology on the basis of His being the carpenter's son. It could only be explained because He was God's Son in the unique sense of the mystery of godliness. Christ, the incomparable!

A modern writer is recorded as saying, "The historical Christ was an ignorant man." The basis of his judgment is what we know today, against what they knew in Jesus' day. He assumes that Jesus had no idea of the existence of the new world; that He had the most crude knowledge of the properties and functions of the human body; that He had an ignorance of the heavens and earth which would seem abysmal to a modern schoolboy. And then this detractor of Jesus Christ goes on to make this patronizing remark: "It is well to bear in mind that the really arresting thing is not that He was ignorant, but that He escaped in the most remarkable manner the results of His ignorance." It is only an abysmally ignorant man who would say this about the Saviour whose knowledge of the human body was so complete that as the Great Physician He could control its functions and repair its disorders. His knowledge extended also to human nature, so that He knew what was in the mind of man, and could discover men's secret thoughts.

Whatever lack of knowledge Jesus seemed to have by our standards, and whatever limitations He was subject to in His age, these were self-imposed and voluntarily assumed. "Who being in the form of God, [He] thought it not robbery to be equal with God: but made himself of no reputation, and took upon him the form of a servant, and was made in the likeness of men" (Phil. 2:6,7). This reveals the kenotic act of self-limitation by which, as a member of the Godhead, Christ voluntarily surrendered the independent employment of His divine powers, and became obedient to God in every act and word. This limitation was His own, by will and not by nature, for He was by nature omniscient and omnipotent.

THE MYSTERY OF PERSONALITY

There is about Jesus Christ all the evidence of a psychological miracle as seen in those things which characterized Him both as the Son of God and the Son of Man. He was one person, yet He possessed two natures, the divine and the human. He was both man and God; truly man, and truly God. He was so human that He could succumb to weariness; yet so divine that He could say, "Come unto me, all ye that labour and are heavy laden, and I will give you rest." He was human enough to become thirsty, yet so divine that He could say, "Whosoever drinketh of the water that I shall give him shall never thirst; but the water that I shall give him shall be in him a well of water springing up into everlasting life." He was so human that He *grew* in wisdom and stature, yet so divine that His wisdom and stature were the proportions of God.

Jesus came with the hands, the face, the voice and the heart of a carpenter's son, yet "He was the hand of God, reaching down to take man by the hand. He was the face of God, looking into man's face. He was the voice of God, speaking to man. He was the heart of God, throbbing out love to man's heart!"

THE MYSTERY OF TRUTH

By the miracle of His message, Jesus Christ has won the loyalty of millions upon millions of every age, of every locale, of every race, of every culture, and of every level of understanding. He was, and is, a philosophical miracle.

A modern Jewish writer, in desperation to minimize the influence of Jesus, said, "For us he [Jesus] offers no leadership that we do not or did not already possess." Does he mean that Jesus was not greater than Abraham, or Moses, or any modern Jew? If so, let it be proved by preaching, and let them do what Jesus did. When Jesus preached, it was reputed by the Jews themselves that "all the world is gone after Him." Has any modern Jew commanded the world after him? Has any healed the sick or raised the dead? Has any Jewish leader walked out of his own grave? How then can anyone honestly say that Jesus offers no leadership the Jews do not already possess? Of whom will it ever be said, except of Jesus, that at His name "every knee should bow . . . and that every tongue should confess that [He] is Lord"? Who dares such presumption save

He who can rightfully claim these honors as the divine Son of God?

THE MYSTERY OF SERVICE

The social service activities of the Son of God constitute a philanthropic miracle. Confronted with skeptics, who being devoid of works contested with words, Jesus had for them the one kind of proof that is incontrovertible. He said, to those who disputed His divine claims, "Believe me for my works' sake."

What works gave proof of Jesus' incomparable stature? He performed a surgical miracle when He restored Malchus' severed ear. He performed a medical miracle by using dust and spittle to heal a man of congenital blindness. He performed a chemical miracle when He multiplied the loaves and fishes of a lad's lunch to feed a multitude of hungry people. He performed the biological miracle of resuscitation three times: once by raising a dead child at Capernaum; once by raising a dead youth at Nain; and once by raising the dead Lazarus at Bethany. Here was death in three ages: a child, a youth, and an adult. Here also was death in three stages: on the death bed, in the burial procession, and in the corruption of the grave.

THE MYSTERY OF SALVATION

An Army officer made this observation: "Unless there is some force in the world that can change the heart of man, the world is doomed." This force is represented in the soteriologic nature of Jesus' mission to men. None but God can offer salvation, and the Scriptures declare that "God was in Christ, reconciling the world unto himself" (II Cor. 5:19). The focal points of salvation are in Jesus' incarnation and crucifixion. By His incarnation He became what we were, and by His crucifixion we become what He is, for "He [God] hath made him to be sin for us, who knew no sin; that we might be made the righteousness of God in him" (II Cor. 5:21). By incarnation He became our sin; by crucifixion we become His righteousness. His death made it possible for us to share His life, which we receive by an act of faith in Him.

THE MYSTERY OF HIS RETURN

In the prophetic plan of God, Jesus Christ will be an eschatological miracle by His return to this world and His reign upon earth. The redemptive ministry of Jesus Christ will not be finished until salvation is succeeded by sovereignty, redemption is followed by rulership, and grace is followed by government.

To the unbelieving world, the Second Coming of Christ is as much of a mystery as the first coming. Few understand the Saviour's coming to suffer. Only a handful of people are waiting with anticipation for His regal return. Even His disciples misjudged His earthly mission. It is not surprising if men today are saying, "Where is the promise of his coming? for since the fathers fell asleep, all things continue as they were from the beginning of the creation" (II Pet. 3:4).

When He comes in the Rapture, there will be the mystery of the Church's disappearance. Men will wonder and speculate, and assign all sorts of reasons to the eschatological wonder.

One day Jesus shook the wood shavings from His tunic, stamped the dust from His sandals, turned the key for the last time in the door of Joseph's carpenter shop, and walked down Nazareth's dusty street to His mother's cottage. For a few moments He held His mother in His arms; then, kissing His sisters, and bidding farewell to His brothers, He stepped out of the door to face the world. He walked to the edge of the village, over the brow of the hill, and crossing the plains of Esdraelon He finally came to the Jordan. From its waters of baptism He set out upon the path which had been mapped out for Him "in the volume of the book," until at last He came to Golgotha, there to purchase our salvation with His own blood.

Another day will come, perhaps sooner than we think, when Jesus Christ will shake the stardust from His royal robes, unlock the gates of heaven, and come back to earth to claim it as His own. He will rule and reign. He will cleanse and purify. He will deliver and change the earth, so that it will once more be the possession of God and the pleasure of His people. We, assembled in this prophetic congress, lift heart and voice to Him in petition, "Even so come, Lord Jesus."

14

CURRENT TRENDS IN ESCHATOLOGICAL BELIEFS

by HERMAN A. HOYT, TH.D.

The subtleties of Satan and of the carnal heart are many. Sometimes they are so imperceptible that only a mind steeped in the Word of God and a heart quickened by the Spirit of God can detect them. These subtleties are aimed principally at one thing, namely, the relation of the Son of God to a world which He came to save.

The salvation which He came to bring is not to be measured by the narrow theological lines which some men have drawn, but by the broad lines of theology which are recorded in the written revelation, the Bible. This salvation includes not only what conservative theologians preach in abundance — a deliverance from the penalty of sin in the past, wrought at Calvary and made effective in the sinner at the moment of faith; and a deliverance from the power and pollution of sin in the present, made progressively effective in the believer by the operation of the Spirit of God and the Word of God; but also a deliverance in the future from the very presence of sin in the believer and its effects in his environment by the immediate presence of Christ in the earth.

This last, in the narrowest sense, is the aspect of Christ's ministry which theologians label "Eschatology." However, in a larger sense, and I believe in a more completely Biblical sense, eschatology covers the entire sweep of God's dealings with the world from the moment of Christ's first coming right on through to the establishing of the eternal state. It is my conviction that the failure, almost universal, to see this picture whole has opened the way for Satan's attacks upon this truth. If possible, I would like to establish this by presenting four propositions and discussing them briefly.

I. ESCHATOLOGY COVERS THAT AREA OF BIBLICAL TRUTH KNOWN AS THE LAST THINGS WHICH OCCUR IN THE LAST DAYS

To reiterate, in the larger and more completely Biblical sense eschatology covers the entire sweep of God's dealings with a lost world from the first coming of Christ to the ushering in of the New Heavens and the New Earth. The reading of several passages from the Bible will confirm this.

Christ's first coming was in the last days. "God, who at sundry times and in divers manners spake in times past unto the fathers by the prophets, hath in these last days spoken unto us by his Son" (Heb. 1:1, 2).

Christ's atoning death occurred in the end of the age. "For then must he often have suffered since the foundation of the world: but now once in the end of the world (Greek, age) hath he appeared to put away sin by the sacrifice of himself" (Heb. 9:26).

The descent of the Holy Spirit at Pentecost was in the last days. "And it shall come to pass in the last days, saith God, I will pour out of my Spirit upon all flesh" (Acts 2:17). Someone may insist that the complete fulfillment of this prophecy is at the ushering in of the kingdom. And this is true. But both occur in the last days.

The entire sweep of the Church is in the ends of the age. "Now all these things happened unto them for ensamples: and they are written for our admonition, upon whom the ends of the world (Greek, age) are come" (I Cor. 10:11). This was written to the church in Corinth. And if that congregation was living in the ends of the age, then surely the Church of this day is living in the ends of the ends of the age.

Scoffers, it was prophesied, would come in the last days; and they did come, and are still coming. "Knowing this first, that there shall come in the last days scoffers, walking after their own lusts, and saying, Where is the promise of his coming?"

(II Pet. 3:3, 4). Several years later, Jude declared that they were here. "These are murmurers, complainers, walking after their own lusts. . . . But, beloved, remember ye the words which were spoken before of the apostles of our Lord Jesus Christ; how that they told you there should be mockers in the last time, who should walk after their own ungodly lusts" (Jude 16, 17).

The Apostle John did not hesitate to declare that it was the last time. This he affirmed of the period in which he lived, now almost 1900 years ago. "Little children, it is the last time: and as ye have heard that antichrist shall come, even now are there many antichrists; whereby we know that it is the last time" (I John 2:18).

The mediatorial kingdom is to be established in the earth in the last days. It is to run its course during the last days. "And it shall come to pass in the last days, that the mountain of the Lord's house shall be established in the top of the mountains, and shall be exalted above the hills; and all nations shall flow unto it" (Isa. 2:2).

When the period of transition has run its course, and the thousand years of millennial blessedness have drawn to a close, the eternal state with its new heavens and new earth will be ushered in. "We, according to His promise, look for new heavens and a new earth, wherein dwelleth righteousness" (II Pet. 3:13).

The history of the resurrection as given in I Corinthians ties together the beginning and the end of the vast period known as the last days. In Christ every man experiences resurrection, "But every man in his own order; Christ the firstfruits; afterward they that are Christ's at his coming. Then cometh the end" (I Cor. 15:23, 24). The resurrection of Christ marks the beginning of the last days and the end of the age. When He comes the second time there will be the resurrection of the righteous dead. After a period of a thousand years, at the end of the millennial kingdom, there will be the end-resurrection, which is the resurrection of the wicked dead. It is then that Christ shall deliver the kingdom up to the Father and the eternal state will be ushered in (I Cor. 15:24).

After reviewing this amazing set of passages, one is led to

conclude that the Bible is almost completely given over to the discussion of eschatology.

II. SATAN'S ATTACK HAS ALWAYS BEEN AIMED AT THE LORD'S PROGRAM FOR THE EARTH

This is the message of the Holy Spirit to the Church through the Apostle John. "Beloved, believe not every spirit, but try the spirits whether they are of God: because many false prophets are gone out into the world. Hereby know ye the Spirit of God: Every spirit that confesseth that Jesus Christ is come in the flesh is of God: and every spirit that confesseth not that Jesus Christ is come in the flesh, is not of God: and this is that spirit of antichrist, whereof ye have heard that it should come; and even now already is it in the world" (I John 4:1-3).

"Jesus Christ is come in the flesh." This states an amazing fact that covers the ministry of Christ from its inception at His incarnation until it is complete at the ushering in of the eternal state. The verb is in the perfect tense and could well be rendered in English by the phrase "has come." It underlines the fact that all of Christ's ministry for a lost world, from its very beginning to the end, is performed in the garb of human flesh.

This, it will be seen, is the point of Satan's persistent attack. From whatever vantage point Christ's ministry in the flesh seemed to be most vulnerable, at that point, and at the most strategic moment, Satan has launched his attack against it. This attack has taken various forms through the centuries, first one important bulwark of the faith, and then another has been assailed. We find it today in the general trends of modernism and liberalism.

It has been aimed at the revelation of God in the flesh. In the early centuries it took the form of "Docetism," the teaching that Christ only *appeared* to be a man. Today we meet the same thing in Christian Science and its denial of material existence.

It has been aimed at the propitiation of God in flesh. Now we see the reverberations of it in Seventh Day Adventism with

its legalism and consequent denial of the sufficiency of Christ's
sacrifice.

It has been aimed at the resurrection of God in flesh. Though
we meet this everywhere in the denial of the bodily resurrection of Christ, it is most subtle in the doctrine of "Jehovah's
Witnesses," who insist that death is annihilation. If Christ was
annihilated at death, then there could be no resurrection.

It has been aimed at the mediation of God in flesh. This form
of attack, having run its course through the Christian centuries,
is gaining new ground today in the various eschatological movements within the professing Church. It gathers about the discussion of the mediatorial or millennial kingdom, its initiation,
its course, and its consummation. Subtle casuistry in certain
areas of theological thought has introduced intricacies of interpretation whose logical end can be nothing but a complete
denial of Christ Incarnate ushering in a kingdom here on the
earth and ruling over it as God's mediator.

III. Satan's Attack Has Been Aimed Specifically at the Fact of a Coming Crisis

The Apostle Peter faced this attack in the course of his
ministry, and under the direction of the Spirit of God he warned
the Church of its peril. "Knowing this first, that there shall
come in the last days scoffers, walking after their own lusts, and
saying, Where is the promise of his coming? for since the fathers
fell asleep, all things *continue* as they were from the beginning
of the creation" (II Pet. 3:3, 4).

A crisis is a period of transition, when a current order passes
away and a new order is ushered in. This is precisely the teaching of the Bible concerning the return of the Lord Jesus Christ.
The hopes of true believers depend upon the passing of this
order and the coming of the new. The prospects of sinners depend upon the *continuation* of the present order of things. If
this order passes, they must pass with it, for they have no hope
beyond this life.

Scoffers arose very early in the Christian era, and their tribe
is increasing today. They deny with seemingly plausible reasoning the possibility of a crisis, basing their argument on the

experience of the fathers. Then, having established that nothing startling has happened in a relatively recent period, they super-impose this upon the entire period from the creation of the world to the present time and insist that conditions will *continue* without change right on into the unlimited future. This is the meaning on the verb "continue" in the original of the above passage.

Now with respect to the past such reasoning is absolutely fallacious, as Peter points out in verses 5 and 6 of the same chapter. There was at least one, and possibly two floods that destroyed world orders of ages past (Gen. 1:2 and Gen. 6). And it is noteworthy that the same Word of God which re-cords these crises also predicts another to come in the future (II Pet. 3:7).

Those who deny the possibility of a divine revelation con-cerning the future facetiously suggest that there might be wis-dom in dealing with one world at a time. Believers are painted by them as people indulging in other-worldliness, a thing al-together impractical. But it is remarkable how this pseudo-philosophical attitude, when it meets the resistance of a vital faith, soon degenerates from scoffing to hatred, and successively to threatening and violence. When the wise men told Herod that the King of the Jews had been born, Herod with all Jerusalem was troubled, for it meant the passing of his king-dom; and so he straightway planned and executed the massacre of Bethlehem's infants to prevent it (Matt. 2:1-4, 12, 16).

Opposing arguments cannot remove the fact of a coming crisis, but subtle reasoning against it can shatter the hope of many, and spurious eschatological theories will tend to weaken the force of the clear teaching of God's Word.

IV. THE ATTACK OF SATAN HAS BEEN AIMED MOST SPECIFICALLY AT THE SECOND COMING OF CHRIST

This has been clearly affirmed by John in his second epistle. "For many deceivers are entered into the world, who confess not that Jesus Christ is come in the flesh" (II John 7).

The verb "is come" here is not in the perfect tense as in I John 4:2. In this passage the verb is in the present tense and is best translated into English by the phrase "is coming." This is what may be called the futuristic present, and two things are clearly suggested by the use of this tense in relation to a future event. First, it indicates that the future is near; and second, it marks the fact that this event may occur at any moment. Thus it is the nearness and the imminency of the Second Coming of Christ that is here seen as under attack by Satan.

The Second Coming of Christ is a highly complex event consisting of several phases, periods of development, and many details. Let us not imagine that it is possible to touch any aspect of this great event without eventually affecting all the rest. Whenever and wherever it is attacked, even in what seems the most harmless fashion, the real reason lies in the fact that the Second Coming of Christ ushers the crises into full motion. It is this phase of the work of the Son of God that we call in the strictest sense eschatology, and it is this phase that has suffered much at the hands of interpreters, many of whom are its avowed enemies.

The attacks upon this great area of Christian truth have come from two quarters. They have differed in degree, although not in kind. I believe that they form two stages in the development of the one attack.

The first stage of the attack comes from the conservative or orthodox quarter. The atmosphere of man's thinking often initiates trends that are not in keeping with the divine plan. This was true of Peter when he responded as he did to the prophecy of Christ concerning His coming death (Matt. 16:21-23), and it explains why serious blows are dealt to the doctrine of the Second Coming by its avowed friends.

Careful examination of the various interpretations reveals a progressive trend downward, once there has been a change from the level to the inclined plane. First, a question is raised about the immediacy of the crisis. To put it in other words, the imminency of Christ's return for the Church is held up to question. This appears today under the label of the "mid-tribulation rapture." Though it may not at first be realized, this is unquestionably a move to set a date for the return of Christ. No period of time in Scripture is so well measured as the Tribulation. Its duration can be counted by days, months, years; and therefore to declare that the Rapture will be in the middle of this period is to set a specific date. The Church is then robbed of the blessed hope, and in its place the prospect of the coming of Antichrist and Tribulation is substituted.

Upon this presupposition is based the conclusion that the Church is on earth during the Tribulation, and once this assumption is made, terminology must inevitably be explained. So the term "saints," used of some who will be on earth during the Tribulation, is made to mean Church-saints, and the name "Israel" is applied to the Church.

The next step down the inclined plane is to place the crisis of Christ's coming at the end of the Tribulation period. This is known as the "posttribulation rapture." In looking over the prophecy notes of a teacher in one of this country's prominent schools, it was interesting to note the proportion of argument employed to support the midtribulation and the posttribulation views of the Rapture. For the midtribulation view there was one page of supporting material; for the posttribulation view there were nine pages of argument. It was quite evident that the midtribulation view had little to commend it, and the only safe position seemed to be a retreat to the posttribulation view.

The third movement in the trend is to delay the crisis for a thousand years. This is called the "a-millennial" view of the coming of Christ. Basically this view denies that there will be a literal thousand-year kingdom, at least here on the earth. Nothing is too clear about some of the amillennial affirmations concerning the kingdom. It is referred to as a spiritual kingdom, and the thousand years is just an ideal number to mark the lapse of time between the first and the second coming of Christ, but the presuppositions of the midtribulation and the posttribulation rapture advocates are retained. The saints are still the Church-saints, and Israel is again the Church. There is a Tribulation before the Second Coming of Christ, through which the Church must pass, and then comes the general judgment and the ushering in of the eternal state. The average person, trying to understand what is being affirmed, finds himself bewildered by the hopeless confusion of terminology and the twisting and turning of interpretations.

Finally there is the "postmillennial" view of the coming of Christ. Acceptance of the amillennial method of spiritualizing terms and declarations sooner or later leads to one conclusion, namely, that this system cannot stand by itself. To be consistent, one must take the next step down the inclined plane, agree to a complete denial of the crisis, and go the whole way to postmillennialism. This school insists that the Church, by its own efforts, brings in the kingdom. The idea is that, by the preaching of the Gospel, the moral and spiritual atmosphere keeps getting better and better until the kingdom is ushered in and runs its course of a thousand years. At the end of this time the Lord comes back, the general judgment takes place, and the eternal state begins. By this method of interpretation the clear teaching of the Word of God concerning the coming crisis is completely nullified, and it goes without saying that the sanctifying value of the blessed hope is thus completely set at naught.

The second and final stage of the attack upon the eschatology of the Bible comes from the liberal quarter. It carries on the same essential denials, and its utter disregard of the teaching of the Word of God climaxes the trend which we have had under examination.

A volume on "The Social Gospel," recently authored by a professor of the department of religion in one of the famous universities, carries this amazing first sentence: "No thinking Christian believes in the eschatology of Jesus." Thus with one sweep of the pen the Bible is completely divested of its entire eschatological teaching. But the professor did not stop there. With this as a premise, he drove his logic to its ultimate and disastrous end by saying that since this eschatology must be set aside, then all that is left is the doctrine of the grace of God. But since the Church has had the doctrine of grace for 1900 years and it has not done the world any good, it is now necessary to reinterpret the doctrine of grace and apply it to our times. It must be made to produce results in society. The Church must get into community and civic interests, join the community chest, get into local, national and international politics. In short, the Gospel must be translated in the terms of a social and economic panacea.

Thus, when an attack upon the eschatology of the Bible is launched, the pursuit of the bitter end can only result in the complete negation of the entire message of the Bible. Our Lord can be wounded in the houses of His friends as well as of His enemies.

With such trends as a background, how refreshing, how reassuring, how stimulating it is to hear from the lips of our Lord: "I will come again, and receive you unto myself" (John 14:3). "And what I say unto you, I say unto all, Watch" (Mark 13:37). "For in such an hour as ye think not, the Son of man cometh" (Matt. 24:44). The Gospel of the grace of God will transform the lives of men, and the Gospel of the Second Coming will transform the world for them to live in.

15

THE BLESSED HOPE AND HOLINESS OF LIFE

by CLAUDE A. RIES, TH.D.

When a man learns to plow he has two points clearly before him, the starting point and the distant one. As he plows directly from the one to the other, he makes a straight furrow.

A city-bred lad learning to plow was told to choose a distant mark and plow toward it. He chose a cow. The result was inevitable. Not only must a distant object be kept in mind if one is to plow a straight course, but that object must furnish the directive. These truths apply not only on the farm, but also in everyday life. No greater incentive for a Christ-like character can be set before man than a living expectancy of the imminent return of our Lord.

BELOVED COMMUNITY EXHORTED

The Apostle Peter, in his last message to the Church, as recorded in II Peter 3, strongly emphasizes that fact. Four times he addresses the people as "beloved," and each time he gives a new exhortation centering in the soon coming of our Lord. In verses 1 and 2, he says, "Beloved . . . be mindful." In verse 8, "Beloved, be not ignorant." In verse 14, "Beloved, be diligent." And in verse 17, "Beloved . . . beware."

In substance, the Apostle says in the first four verses, "Be mindful of God's words given by the prophets and apostles concerning the Second Coming of Christ. Men will scoff at it, but be assured Christ is coming and will bring judgment on ungodly men." In verses 8 through 13, he admonishes, "Be not ignorant of the fact that one day is as a thousand years with the Lord, and though the Lord may seem to delay His coming, He will surely come, and with cataclysmic power. Knowing this, live accordingly a righteous and holy life." We turn to the fourteenth verse, and the Apostle again urges, "Beloved, be diligent." Knowing the certainty of His coming and the attendant circumstances, be diligent to be found in Him in peace, without spot and blameless at His coming." In verses 17 and 18, he cautions, "Beloved, beware lest you fall into the same error of the wicked, but grow in grace and in knowledge of our Lord Jesus Christ." In these ways the beloved in Christ are admonished to live daily under the shaping influence of our Lord's return.

The Apostle John likewise strongly emphasizes the same moulding influence: "Beloved, now are we the sons of God, and it doth not yet appear what we shall be: but we know that, when he shall appear, we shall be like him; for we shall see him as he is. And every man that hath this hope in him purifieth himself, even as he is pure" (I John 3:2, 3). In other words, the Christian's expectancy of Christ's coming at any time is the greatest deterrent to indulgence in any form of impurity, and the strongest incentive to holy living. As the *American Standard Version* words it, "Every one that hath this hope set upon him, purifieth himself, even as he is pure." This hope leads to a "radical and thorough self purification" under the empowerment of the Holy Spirit.

THREE KINDS OF CHRISTIANS

Bible-believing Christians may be divided into three groups according to the attitude they take toward the coming of Christ:

There are those who believe the "glorious appearing of the great God, even our Saviour Jesus Christ" to be a cardinal doctrine of our evangelical faith, but such believing *works no change* in their lives.

Then there are those who not only profess to believe in the imminent return of our Lord, but they say they are looking for Him. As evidence of the fact, they speak frequently of His coming, they read magazines on prophecy, and much of their summer vacation is spent in attending prophetic conferences. They are keen to learn all the latest details about the Second

Coming. Such persons are to be commended. We would praise God for all who are watching the signs of the times, even as Christ expects us to do. But is it not true that such persons may become so enamored with Second Coming details that they lose sight of the Person who is coming, and their own relationship to Him in view of His coming? It is possible to look for His *coming*, rather than for *His* coming; to be interested in the coming of the Lord rather than in the Lord who is coming; to know all about the time table and yet miss the train.

That brings us up to the third class, namely, those who "love His appearing" (II Tim. 4:8) even as a bride loves the appearing of the bridegroom. The Christian who does not love the appearing of Christ is not passionately in love with Him. Surely all our plans and ambitions should center in Him. "Wherefore," says the Apostle John, "be diligent that ye may be found of him in peace, without spot and blameless." Live daily under the shaping and purifying influence of our Lord's imminent return! Let its searching, separating and expulsive power dominate your daily living! That is the incisive admonition of the Scriptures.

GREAT CLOUD OF WITNESSES

The churches of the New Testament were powerfully moved by the truth of the imminent coming of the Lord Jesus. It was the driving power back of their daily living and service. As a result they were characterized as "these are they who turned the world upside down." Though they were small in numbers when compared with the nations, pagan rulers had to reckon with them. Men and women of every stratum of society were challenged by them. The truth of the Coming of Christ possessed them so that they lived holy, bold and fruitful lives.

Down through the centuries the truth of the Second Coming of Christ has been an article of faith in the Church. Our hymnology breathes the hope of His return, from Thomas of Celano's Latin hymn written in 1200 A.D., to the beautiful hymn of Frances Havergal, "Thou Art Coming, O My King."

Thou art coming! Thou art coming!
We shall meet Thee on Thy way!
Thou art coming! We shall see Thee
And be like Thee on that day.

What Manner of Persons Ought We To Be

The hope of the soon coming of our Lord is a call to inner heart purity. The expression "purifieth himself" does not imply a self-achieved holiness. It points rather to the human side of a great transaction, when by a definite will to have it so in my life, Christ in truth becomes "my sanctification," as I Corinthians 1:30 assures us. By faith I accept Him as the Purifier of all the inner drives of life. He, the triumphant Christ, becomes pre-eminent in my life. Walking on this plane I have fellowship with Him, and the blood of Jesus Christ keeps cleansing me from all sin.

In II Corinthians 6:17, 18, the Apostle beautifully depicts a born-again soul. Life attitude is shown in separation from the world; life relationship is seen in that God becomes our Father and we His sons and daughters. Thus we enter that God-honored company — the "dearly beloved." Then in 7:1, he follows this with the exhortation: "Having therefore these promises, dearly beloved, let us cleanse ourselves from all filthiness of the flesh and spirit." This is a coming to grips with the inward motives of life as they affect the activity of flesh and spirit. Now the Holy Spirit would not have inspired the Apostle to exhort saved people to purify themselves from all filthiness of flesh and spirit if such purification were not possible. It is not only the privilege, but the responsibility of every saved soul to bring to the light of a full confession to God these inner defilements of flesh and spirit which mar our own peace of soul, hurt our fellowmen, grieve the Holy Spirit, and keep us from being what we ought to be at His coming.

In All Holy Conversation

In Ephesians 4:30-32, we are exhorted, "Grieve not the Holy Spirit of God, whereby ye are sealed unto the day of redemption." Then the Apostle gives two practical ways in which we can keep from grieving the Holy Spirit. Dr. G. Campbell Morgan designates these as an abandonment to purity and an abandonment to service. The first, an abandonment to purity, is commanded in verse 31. Paul is speaking to saved people. "Let all bitterness, and wrath, and anger, and clamour, and evil speak-

ing, be put away from you, with all malice." Notice the ex
pression "Be put away." It is in the aorist tense, which denotes
something definite. Dr. A. T. Robertson, the great Greek scholar
translates it, "Make a clean sweep of them." This is the practical
carrying out of the exhortation, "He that hath this hope in
him, purifieth himself even as He is pure."

The second, an abandonment to service, is presented in verse
32: "And be ye kind one to another." The Greek word for "kind"
means *useful*. Hence the literal meaning would be: "Be ye
created useful to one another, tenderhearted, forgiving one an
other, even as God for Christ's sake hath forgiven you."

THE GRACE OF SELF JUDGMENT

Oh, what a responsibility rests upon saved people! — the re
sponsibility to face before God the envy that eats as a canker
the pride that swells with selfish ambition; the self-will that
refuses a whole-hearted abandonment to the whole will of God
the temper that flies off upon provocation, like that of Miles
Standish, whom Longfellow described as a "little chimney heated
red hot in a minute." These defilements can all be cleansed
God has a glorious remedy. When Jesus said on Calvary, "It
is finished," He completed a full redemption for man, giving
man a deliverance from the power and also the condemnation
of sin. Through the Holy Spirit "your whole spirit and soul
and body [can] be preserved blameless unto the coming of our
Lord Jesus Christ. Faithful is he that calleth you, who also
will do it" (I Thess. 5:23, 24). In the words of Paul S. Rees
"Christ's power waits on your willing consent."

THE CALL OF A GREAT HOPE

The hope of the soon return of our Lord is a blessed hope
"For the grace of God that bringeth salvation hath appeared to
all men, teaching us that, denying ungodliness and worldly lusts
we should live soberly, righteously, and godly, in this present
world; looking for that blessed hope, and the glorious appear
ing of the great God and our Saviour Jesus Christ; who gave
himself for us, that he might redeem us from all iniquity, and
purify unto himself a peculiar people, zealous of good works"
(Titus 2:11-14). Yes, it is a blessed hope. It blesses all who

"love his appearing" with a present Christlikeness of disposition. It provides incentive for the command, "Have this *disposition* in you which was also in Christ Jesus" (Phil. 2:5, ASV). The Bible is replete with passages portraying the blessedness of Christlikeness now, in view of the Second Coming of Christ.

The soon coming of our Lord calls for a life of sincerity and genuineness: "That ye may be sincere and without offence till the day of Christ" (Phil. 1:10).

It calls for considerateness: "Let your moderation be known unto all men. The Lord is at hand" (Phil. 4:5). Matthew Arnold paraphrases the word moderation as "sweet reasonableness." This is frequently a lacking virtue in the body of Christ.

It calls for patience: "Be ye also patient; stablish your hearts: for the coming of the Lord draweth nigh" (James 5:8).

It calls for faithfulness: "I charge thee therefore before God, and the Lord Jesus Christ, who shall judge the quick and the dead *at his appearing* and his kingdom; preach the word, be instant in season, out of season; reprove, rebuke, exhort with all longsuffering and doctrine" (II Tim. 4:1, 2).

It calls for watchfulness and prayerfulness: "But the end of all things is at hand: be ye therefore sober, and watch unto prayer. And above all things have fervent charity among yourselves" (I Pet. 4:7, 8).

It calls for a people who are peculiar in their zealousness for God's cause: "Looking for that blessed hope and the glorious appearing of the great God and our Saviour Jesus Christ; who gave himself for us, that he might redeem . . . and purify unto himself a peculiar people, zealous of good works" (Titus 2:13, 14). Zealousness means "burning out." It has been said that the great task of the Church today is not only to get sinners to heaven, but also to get saints out of bed. Those who are really looking for His coming are peculiar in the tirelessness of their zeal for God and His cause.

The Challenge of a Great Hope

Need I remind you that the Second Coming calls for purity of life? "When Christ who is our life shall appear, then shall ye also appear with him in glory. Mortify therefore your members which are upon the earth: fornication, uncleanness, inordinate affection, evil concupiscence, and covetousness, which is idolatry" (Col. 3:4, 5). It is plain that the Apostle is here emphasizing bodily purity. At the time of the flood gross lewdness and wickedness were rampant, but the Scriptures declare that Noah was perfect. The word "perfect" here is *tamim,* which essentially means physical purity. That is, in the midst of universal physical corruption, Noah and his family kept the physical strain pure. The Word of God expressly says that the days prior to the Second Coming will be like those of Noah. This is a day of gross immorality, and we must not fail to sound from our pulpits the stern call to purity.

The Second Coming calls for a dynamic faith: "That the trial of your faith being much more precious than of gold that perisheth, might be found unto praise and honour and glory at the appearing of Jesus Christ" (I Pet. 1:7). How we need to keep His soon coming before us, lest our faith grow dim! The Scriptures raise the pertinent question, "When the Son of man cometh, shall he find faith on the earth?"

The Second Coming calls for living with an eternal perspective: "But thou, O man of God, flee these things [desire of earthly riches], and follow after righteousness, godliness, faith, love, patience, meekness. Fight the good fight of faith, lay hold on eternal life, whereunto thou art called. . . . I give thee charge in the sight of God . . . and before Christ Jesus . . . that thou keep this commandment without spot, unrebukeable, until the appearing of our Lord Jesus Christ" (I Tim. 6:11-14).

The truth of the Second Coming of our Lord constantly reminds us that this earth is not our permanent dwelling place, that we are pilgrims here, and that we "look for a city which hath foundations, whose builder and maker is God." Therefore we must hold lightly the things of this world, and all of earth's activities should be carried on with the eternal viewpoint ever in mind.

As we live amid the babel voices of our rushing age, thronged about by the unnecessary and trivial, how glorious is the up-calling of the Lord Jesus Christ to those who love Him: "I will come back. Be ye also ready."

16

ESCHATOLOGY ACCORDING TO CHRIST

by S. Maxwell Coder, d.d.

The Olivet Discourse is the major prophetic section of the New Testament, and the longest apart from the Revelation, of which it is almost an index. It forms the bridge between what the Old Testament prophets and the New Testament apostles wrote about the divine program of the ages. It is the background against which later prophecy is drawn. If the space devoted to it were made the criterion, we would have to admit that our Lord's message on prophecy is more important than the Sermon on the Mount, the ratio being 166 verses in three Gospels to 139 verses in two Gospels. Yet there are many books on the Sermon on the Mount; few on the Olivet revelation. Sermonic literature often develops the one, almost never the other.

The greatest concentration of references to the time of the end and the coming of Christ anywhere in the New Testament appears on these pages. There are fifteen specific mentions of the end, or of His coming, in Matthew 24 and 25 alone. More time words and definite signs are given here than anywhere else within the same space. This should put us on our guard against the common error of assuming that the Olivet Discourse speaks of the days in which we live.

It is not given unto us to know the times or the seasons (Acts 1:7). No signs are given to the Church by which to calculate the date when her great commission will end and she will be gathered to meet her risen Head (I Thess. 4:16, 17). It may be soon, or it may be in the distant future. Inevitable disappointment awaits the reader who assumes that the Olivet Discourse was intended to serve as a guide for the Church in her

last days on the earth. Its many time words have to do with
the closing days of Israel's history, which does not resume its
course until the Church is safe at home with the Lord. Its
several signs have not yet been seen.

Before we develop these themes which form the fabric of the
Olivet Discourse, let me point out that the language used by
our Lord is remarkably clear and free from metaphor. It is
evidently intended to be easily understood. In fact, the key
to the entire passage is found in the simple truth that it means
what it says, and says what it means. Let us then approach
our exposition of Matthew 24 and 25 believing that all of Christ's
words are literally true. It is astonishing how such an attitude
of simple trust opens to us the riches of what is regarded as a
difficult and complex prophecy.

Omitting the three parables of the servants, the virgins and
the talents, because of the limited time available, we now come
to the five natural divisions of the Olivet Discourse:

1. The beginning of sorrows, and its signs   Matthew 24: 4-8
2. The end of the age, and its sign   24: 9-14
3. The Great Tribulation, and its sign   24:15-28
4. After the Tribulation, a new sign   24:29-42
5. The dawn of the kingdom, and its sign   25:31-46

1. *The beginning of sorrows, and its signs,* Matthew 24:4-8.

At the outset we are faced with the question, Where in the
prophetic program did our Lord place the false Christs, wars
famines, pestilences, earthquakes, mentioned in verses 6-8? But
this is solved beyond question in Luke 21:12, where, for our
guidance in this matter, we have been given one of the Lord's
important time words, "before all these." In the Luke record
the Lord's answer to the disciples' question is obviously in the
conversational style, and as often happens in a conversation
one thought runs ahead of another, and it becomes necessary to
stop and say, "now let us go back for a moment."

The phrase "before all these" points us directly back to Luke
21:6, where the Lord begins His prophecy about the destruc
tion of the temple with the words, "As for *these things* which
ye behold"; then to verse 7, where the disciples use the same
words in framing their question, "Master, but when shall these

hings be?"; and finally to verse 12, where our Lord uses "But
efore *all these*" as an interpolation in completing His answer
） the "when" and "what sign" of the disciples' question.

An examination of the Olivet Discourse record in the synop-
ɔc Gospels would reveal the fact that all the Evangelists present
 substantially identical sequence of predicted events: first, false
Christs, rumors of wars, national uprisings; next, persecution,
nprisonment, betrayal, martyrdom, hatred; third, the siege of
erusalem, days of vengeance, mass carnage, captivity, the end
f the times of the Gentiles and the deliverance of Jerusalem.
ınd it is noteworthy that Luke emphasizes the futuristic char-
ɔcter of the Discourse (21:24), linking it with Daniel's seventieth
veek, the fact that some A.D. 70 events followed the same
attern notwithstanding.

In studying the Olivet Discourse we must not make the com-
ıon mistake of supposing that wars and rumors of wars are
igns of the imminent return of Christ. Even though the in-
ɔrvening centuries have been filled with false Christs, wars,
ımines, pestilences and earthquakes, the Book of Revelation
ıakes it clear that these five evils are to culminate in a series
f terrible manifestations at the beginning of *the time of sorrows*.

The opening of the seals by the Lamb in Revelation 6 may
e regarded as a divinely given commentary on these verses
f Matthew 24. As the first seal is opened and a rider on a
vhite horse comes into view, the false christs of the centuries
nd their embodiment in the Antichrist. As the second seal is
roken and a red horse appears, wars break out all over the
ɔrth. When the third seal brings forth a black horse, famine
veeps the earth. The fourth seal and its pale horse introduce
vhat students and artists alike have always understood as pesti-
ɔnce, bringing death and hell in its wake. The next two seals
ring martyrdom and "a great earthquake."

The placing of these sore judgments at the very beginning
f the fifteen chapters of Revelation which describe the sorrows
ıat are yet to come upon the earth indicates that Christ's "be-
inning of sorrows" refers primarily to the last days of Israel's
letermined" period (Dan. 9:24), rather than to the last days
f the Church on earth. The Greek word used here means

"death throes" or "birth pangs." The end of the one age and the beginning of another are before us here.

2. *The end of the age, and its sign,* Matthew 24:9-14.

Another time word introduces this section of the Olivet Dis course, *"Then* shall they deliver you up to be afflicted." The question that naturally suggests itself as we read these words is "When?" To arrive at the correct answer, we must notice carefully the disciples' question. It was, "What shall be the sign . . . of the consummation of the age?" When they asked this they were living in the age when Israel still had its temple and sacrifices at the holy place chosen by God. The age of the Church, at that time still a "mystery . . . hid in God" (Eph 3:9), was not to begin until Pentecost. The immediate concern of the disciples was the announced destruction of their temple and the consummation of the age of which it was the symbol

It is of course true that in the Luke 21 record the disciples asked only about the destruction of the temple and the events that would lead up to it, but this is not to be construed to mean that Luke 21 and Matthew 24 deal with different periods of history. The extended question with which they came to the Master on the Mount of Olives (Matt. 24:3), asking now for information also about His return, and about the end of the age, was undoubtedly provoked by our Lord's reference in His previous answer to the fate of Israel following the destruc tion of the temple, and to the subjugation of Jerusalem to Gentile domination *until* the times of the Gentiles reached their fullness (Luke 21:24).

The whole Olivet Discourse breathes the spirit of infinite patience and sympathy with which our Lord was leading the bewildered disciples into an understanding of the shape of things to come. He had just told them that the world they had known and loved was soon to pass away—the world which, until His coming, had represented all of God to them. Who would not be bewildered under conditions like these? And in addition they were *so* limited in understanding. We can well assume that this was one of the "many things" He had to say to them which, for the time being, they were incapable of receiving (John 16:12). When the Spirit of Truth came, these things would

tand out in bold relief, as was the case with the puzzled apostles
n Jerusalem (Acts 15:6-17), when the Holy Spirit opened the
understanding of James to see that God's unprecedented visita-
ion of the Gentiles had been spoken of beforehand by the
prophets. But this much the disciples saw clearly: the "until"
of Israel's scattering and Jerusalem's humiliation (Luke 21:24),
nd the "until" of Israel's blindness concerning the Messiahship
of Jesus (Matt. 23:39), were intimately related, and both de-
imited by His return to earth and the consummation of the
age. Obviously, these events were still in the womb of the
unborn future; hence their return to the previously voiced dual
question, "when" and "what sign?"

However brave and insistent the protestations that Matthew
24 and 25 apply to the Church, the prophecy as a whole, taken
in its own context, makes such an interpretation untenable. For
instance, the concluding three verses of Matthew 23, which
form a natural introduction to the Olivet Discourse, certainly
have Israel only as their subject. Israel's house is to be left
desolate. Israel will not see the Messiah until the latter part
of verse 39 is fulfilled. The abomination of desolation of verse
15, taken from Daniel 12, is a sign given only to Israel. Those
who in verse 16 are warned to flee are residents of Judea, and
hey are counseled to pray that their flight shall not be on the
Sabbath day, a prayer that would sound strange on the lips
of a Christian. The tribes of verse 30, mourning at Christ's
return, seem to be the tribes of Israel (Zech. 12:10-14).

What generation in the history of Israel is referred to in the
words, "Then shall they deliver you up to be afflicted"? There
can be no doubt that verse 9 speaks not of the disciples to whom
he Discourse was addressed, but rather of that generation of
God's elect mentioned in verse 22. They are the faithful "remnant" of Israel in the last days.

The use of the pronoun "you" should cause no one any difficulty. Frequently in the Scriptures we find a similar form of
expression. In Numbers 15:2, God addressed the generation
hen living as though they were going to enter the promised
and, although He had previously announced that they would
die in the wilderness (14:35). Again, in I Thessalonians 4:17

there appears the statement, "We which are alive and remain shall be caught up." Many generations have read this passage without failing to understand that the words obviously refer to the generation which will be on earth when Christ returns for His Church.

After the "beginning of sorrows" is past, *then* an elect company from within Israel, convinced by the rapture that Jesus is the Messiah, will be delivered up to affliction, martyrdom, hatred by the nations. Doubtless this event coincides with the signing of a covenant between the nation Israel and Antichrist, referred to in Daniel 9:27 and in Isaiah 28:18. As in Old Testament days, these servants of God will have to contend with false prophets (v. 11), and with their own brethren.

At the close of this period of persecution, the sign of the end of the age will be fulfilled, the age which was interrupted at Calvary, so that God could gather out of the Gentiles a people for His name. The Gospel of the kingdom will be preached by this company in all the world as a witness to all nations, "and then shall the end come." If we can forget the popular interpretation of these words and confine ourselves to the logical sequence of the Word of God, it will become crystal clear what our Lord actually said.

The expression "the gospel of the kingdom" means literally "the good news concerning the kingdom." It appears first in Matthew 4:23, where "Jesus went about all Galilee, teaching in their synagogues, and preaching the gospel of the kingdom." What He preached is found in Matthew 4:17, "From that time Jesus began to preach, and to say, Repent: for the kingdom of heaven is at hand." In Matthew 10:6, 7, the Lord instructed His disciples, "Go rather to the lost sheep of the house of Israel. And as ye go, preach, saying, The kingdom of heaven is at hand." They were expressly told on that occasion, "Go not into the way of the Gentiles" (v. 5). And in verse 22, our Lord used some of the very words which appear in Matthew 24:9, 13. Thus we have a clear link between the two parts of Israel's age; and into the gap between these the Church was placed as a divine parenthesis.

The Gospel of the kingdom is a message calling on men to

repent because the kingdom is at hand. To read the Church and its glad tidings of salvation through Christ into this prophecy is to confuse things that differ. The very witness of the Church throughout its history is against such an interpretation. We do not proclaim the message once preached to Israel at the command of Israel's King, "Repent, for the kingdom of heaven is at hand." The kingdom was rejected, and the king has gone away until *they* shall say, "Blessed is he that cometh in the name of the Lord" (Matt. 23:39). Instead, the message preached for the past 1900 years has been, "Believe on the Lord Jesus Christ, and thou shalt be saved" (Acts 16:31). This message had already been given "in all the world," "to every creature which is under heaven" (Col. 1:6, 23), but it did not bring the end of which the Lord spoke. Thank God, it is again today reaching out into the world, but when every last tribe has been evangelized, it will still not be the fulfillment of Matthew 24:14, even though in a secondary sense we may apply this, and other verses, to our own age.

The sign of the end is therefore the worldwide announcement by a hated company of faithful Jews (the 144,000 of Revelation 7:1-8) that the kingdom of heaven, once before heralded but rejected, is once more at hand. And there is a very good reason why this worldwide preaching is to be "for a witness to all nations." Without it the judgment of Matthew 25:32 would be difficult to understand, because the nations are to be judged later on the basis of their treatment of these brethren of Christ.

3. *The Great Tribulation, and its sign,* Matthew 24:15-26.

A large part of the prophetic Word is devoted to the tremendous events which will take place throughout the world during those terrible days when the good news of the coming kingdom will be proclaimed. A beast is to arise. All the concentrated hatred of the ages against the Jews is to be summed up in this evil being. Tribulation is to break over Israel. And so now our Lord turns to the sign by which His followers are to be made aware that the Great Tribulation, "the time of Jacob's trouble" (Jer. 30:7), has come.

To understand Matthew 24:15, as our Lord commands us to do, we must examine what Daniel the prophet actually wrote.

of the Tribulation cast their shadows before, then any religious movement of our time claiming to show signs and wonders is immediately suspect. In both Matthew 24:24 and Revelation 13:13 such things attest the work of Christ's enemies rather than that of His friends.

4. *After the Tribulation, a new sign*, Matthew 24:27-42.

Not a few students have overlooked the importance of the *time words* in the Olivet Discourse. Our Lord used so many of them as to make His prophecy unique in this respect: words like "before," "the beginning," "when," "the end," "then," "immediately after." Attempts have often been made to identify the Great Tribulation of Matthew 24 with the destruction of Jerusalem in A.D. 70, but they all founder on our Lord's words in Matthew 24:29, "immediately after the tribulation of those days." If the Tribulation is past already, so is the coming of the Son of Man, the gathering of His elect, and the judgment of the nations. But these things have not happened. The Great Tribulation is yet future.

In *this* Discourse, with divine clarity, Christ declares that His coming is to be as public, as instantaneous, as shining and shocking as a lightning flash (v. 27). This whole passage (vv. 23-30) does two things. First, it disposes of every claim that He *has* come as ascetic, hiding in some desert place, or that He has come as a mystic to some secret sanctuary; and in the second place, it lends contrast to the appearing for which we are waiting according to I Thessalonians 4:16, when "the Lord himself shall descend from heaven with a shout."

There is another statement in the Discourse that has been regarded as highly puzzling: "For wheresoever the carcase is, there will the eagles (or vultures) be gathered together" (v. 28). Among the curious suggestions to be found on this point in the commentaries, the most common is that the carcase is the nation Israel, and the vultures are heavenly messengers of judgment. But the Scriptural explanation of this reference to vultures and dead bodies is found in Revelation 19, a passage parallel to this one in Matthew. It depicts the Lord's return in judgment (v. 11) and the destruction of the armies of the beast, whose image is the abomination of Matthew (v. 19). In between there is a call to

"all the fowls that fly in the midst of heaven," to gather themselves together to eat the flesh of the vast host which has fought
against the Lord at His coming. The Olivet Discourse, key to
later prophecy, merely touches upon this event, while Revelation
develops it with an amazing picture of the heavens darkened by
"ravenous birds of every sort" to which God has given the flesh
of the enemies of His Son (Ezek. 39:4). Job wrote of the eagle,
"where the slain are, there is she" (39:30). These Scriptures
point to the literal interpretation of our text.

Although the time at our disposal does not permit us to look
at every phase of this great Discourse, we must call attention
to the fact that there is no reason whatsoever for spiritualizing
the references in verse 29 to the sun, moon, stars, and the powers
of heaven. If these are to be understood to mean exactly what
they do in the common language of mankind, we should expect
the shaking of these powers to affect the earth, and this is just
what we find in Luke 21:25, "the sea and waves roaring," causing men's hearts to fail them for fear, and for looking after
those things which are coming on the earth.

Our Lord has not been pleased to reveal just what is "the
sign of the Son of man in heaven" (v. 30). We think that it
is the Shekinah glory of Old Testament days again. When He
came to Bethlehem, that glory illumined the heavens (Luke 2:9).
But whatever it is, it results in the fulfillment of Zechariah 12:10,
"they shall look upon me whom they have pierced, and they
shall mourn for him, as one mourneth for his only son." Then
shall the tribes of the land, the people of Israel, mourn, and they
shall see the Son of Man coming in the clouds of heaven with
power and great glory.

We can only touch briefly upon the remainder of Matthew 24.
Of whom was Christ speaking in verses 33 and 34? Certainly
not the generation then living. There is only one satisfactory
explanation of these statements. He is here referring to that generation which shall "see all these things." Luke 21:28 exhorts,
"When these things begin to come to pass, then look up, and
lift up your heads; for your redemption draweth nigh." The
generation which sees the beginning will see the end. "This
generation shall not pass, till all be fulfilled" (v. 32).

What is the meaning of the reference to one being taken, and the other left, at the coming of the Son of Man (Luke 21: 40, 41)? The context of the entire Discourse obliges us to conclude that these are taken away in judgment. There is no warrant for assuming that the rapture of the Church has suddenly been introduced here, and that some are taken to heaven for blessing while others are left behind for judgment.

Those who endure to the end of the age, in verse 13 are saved. They remain on earth for the blessings of the kingdom. Those who flee Judea do so to escape death so that they may remain on earth for the Lord's return. The shortening of the days in the Tribulation is for the elect's sake, because blessing is ahead for them if their lives are preserved. Those who were taken away by the flood (Luke 21:39) were taken in judgment, while those who remained entered the blessing of the cleansed earth and a new age. Finally, those who "go away" in Matthew 25:46 go into everlasting punishment, while those who remain enter the kingdom prepared for them from the foundation of the world.

In view of the fact that the subject of the judgment of the nations is to be treated by another speaker, and this message of mine has already reached larger proportion than at first anticipated, I shall conclude without making any reference to the latter part of Matthew 25.

With such a picture as the Scriptures have painted for us, it is a most solemnizing thing to read the words which immediately follow the Olivet Discourse: "When Jesus had finished all these sayings, he said unto his disciples, Ye know that after two days is the feast of the passover, and the Son of man is betrayed to be crucified" (Matt. 26:1, 2).

His death on Calvary divides men today, no less than His royal decree will divide them at His coming. Those who have received Him as Saviour will escape these terrible things which are coming on the earth. Those who have rejected Him will enter the darkest days the world has ever known. We determine our destiny by our attitude toward the Cross. He that believeth not is condemned already, but he that believeth hath everlasting life, and shall not come into judgment, but is passed from death unto life.

17

THE MARRIAGE SUPPER OF THE LAMB

by ROBERT T. KETCHAM, D.D

Blessed are they which are called unto the marriage supper of the Lamb. (Rev. 19:9).

In this message I am not particularly interested in the marriage supper. And for the moment I am not especially interested in the Bride. The Groom is going to occupy our attention.

The thing which particularly interests me about the Groom here is the title He wears on this occasion. Why does He come to His wedding as the Lamb? Why not under one of the other 700 or more titles ascribed to Him in the Scriptures? Also, since in the marriage contract the bride takes the name of the groom, why does our Lord want the bride to be forever known as the Lamb's Wife? There must be something in this particular title which caused our Lord to select it as the one to be used in the contracting of His eternal marriage. May the Spirit of God assist us as we endeavor to find out why.

With this as our objective, I want to organize our thinking around the Bridegroom, and especially the significance of His title as He enters into everlasting holy wedlock with His Bride. The declaration of the text is that this is the marriage supper of the "Lamb."

This wedding announcement could have read, "Blessed are they which are called unto the marriage supper of the Creator," for in every sense of the word He is that. He who now approaches the marriage altar of the ages, about to be united to His Bride, is the Creator. Multiplied centuries ago, when this thing that is now a universe was nothing but empty, limitless space, inhabited only by a triune personality known as Father,

171

Son and Holy Ghost, this same Individual whom we now see coming into the picture rose from the bosom of deity, spake, and it was done; commanded, and it stood fast; and the result was a throbbing universe. He flung worlds from His fingertips, sprinkled the stardust across the sky, set a compass upon the seas, molded the hills and valleys, and painted the deserts with a riot of colors.

But there was another day when this same blessed, eternal Individual wrought another work of creation. That was the day when the blueprint handed Him by the Father did not have upon it flowing rivers, crystal lakes, snow-capped peaks, flower-decked plains, and star-studded skies; but instead, as He unfolded that blueprint, there stared Him in the face a grim, drear, awful Cross, with Himself, encased in sinless humanity, nailed upon it. And why was He there? To bring into being *another* creation — a creation that so far outshines, and in significance and glory so outstrips the old creation as to be beyond comparison. When Jesus Christ brought this world into existence, He had only to whisper, and the delicate tint of the flower was there; He had only to speak, and the sun and moon began to shine. Now, however, a new creation was to be brought into existence, and in order to accomplish this He must speak again, but this time through the jagged, gaping, bloody lips of five wounds in His blessed body! He had only to *speak* to accomplish the first, but He had to *die* to bring about the second. And now, in the day of consummation, here is the Creator of heaven and earth about to be married to His blood-bought and blood-washed Bride, and she is none other than His new creation. Yes, this passage could very correctly have been made to read, "Blessed are they which are called unto the marriage supper of the Creator," for here stands the crown and climax of all His creative power, now arrayed in fine linen — the righteousness of the saints; but it doesn't read that way. It says, "Blessed are they which are called unto the marriage supper of *the Lamb*."

Again, this announcement could have been properly worded, "Blessed are they which are called unto the marriage supper of the Lord," for here is His Bride, chosen from every tribe, tongue and nation, who, after owning His Lordship through all the ages past, is now at last to be united with Him for all ages to come. But it doesn't say that it is the marriage supper of the Lord. It is, pronouncedly, the marriage supper of *the Lamb*.

And yet again, this announcement could have been appropriately worded, "Blessed are they which are called unto the marriage supper of the King," for this event described in Revelation 19 is indeed the marriage of a king—the King Eternal, taking to Himself the Queen eternal, who is to sit at His side and reign with Him forever. But as we look at it again, the simple announcement reads, "Blessed are they which are called unto the marriage supper of *the Lamb*."

The title that adorns the brow of the heavenly Bridegroom in the hour of His great glory and joy; the title that rides above all the splendor when His new creation comes to His side as His submissive Bride and takes her place with Him upon His throne; it is not the great, shining, glimmering title of Creator, or Lord of lords, or King of kings. It is rather the most wonderful title that has ever been given to the matchless Son of God—the title of *Lamb!* It is the title over all other titles, for whatever these are, they mean absolutely nothing unless and until this one title surmounts them all!

I remember my friend Anthony Zeoli coming into my study in Waterloo, Iowa, one day and handing me his then new book "727 Titles of Jesus." I didn't even open the book, but, making a gesture as if to return it to him, I said, "Anthony, do you have the *one title* in there? If you haven't, the other 726 mean nothing to me." He said, "What title do you mean?" I said, "Jesus, the Lamb of God." Yes, it was there, Anthony wouldn't leave *it* out.

It is true that Jesus Christ carries the title "Creator." It was He who flung worlds into space, and among them this earth of ours and all that is in it. But something else is also true. One day the black hand of Satan reached up, took this vast creation out of His hand, and hurled it with all the fury of hell upon the rocks of sin and ruin, so that tonight all of this mighty creation lies shattered, groaning and travailing in pain. Now unless this Creator can find some way, by an act wholly His own, to gather up the broken fragments of His creation and put them together so that they will once again sing forth His praise, what good is this title "Creator"? Who would want a title like that?

It is true that Jesus Christ is called the "Lord of lords." But what good is that title if there be not found anywhere in this universe a soul that bows before Him and owns Him as Lord? For has not a usurper come and stolen the allegiance of the human beings over whom He was supposed to be Lord, so that every one of them is a walking enemy with a heart gangrenous with the putrefaction of sin? What if men insolently turn their faces to God and laugh, retaining no thought of Him in their minds? If this is the Lord of lords, and this is a picture of His subjects, who would want to wear a title like that? Unless . . . unless this Lord of lords can find some way, by an act of His own, wholly within Himself, to bring back these same human beings, so that they will bow before Him and love Him and His everlasting Lordship.

It is true that Jesus Christ is "King of kings." But if a usurper is occupying the throne of the kingdoms of the earth, and the likelihood is that they will always continue to be under the sway of the prince of the power of the air — the god of this age, what good is that title? Unless by an act of His own, wholly within Himself, without the aid of any outside agent, the King of kings can find a way to regain the kingdoms of this world and make them the kingdoms of Himself and of His God, that title "King of kings" is just so much tinsel and meaningless decoration.

But bless God, He *did* find a way — and a way wholly within Himself, without the aid of another. The Creator *did* find a way to put His broken creation together again. The Lord *did* find a way to break men's rebellious hearts and make of them His willing servants. The King *did* find a way whereby the kingdoms of this world shall become His. And what was that way? It was when He who is *the Way* — the Creator, the Lord, the King, became a Lamb! It was when the Creator died for man's sin. It was when the Lord broke rebel hearts with His own loving heart. It was when the King became a subject. And the wonder of it is that the Saviour did it all alone. There on Calvary the eye of faith rests upon the lonely *Worker,* as in one mighty act He gives value and eternality to all His titles.

I shall never forget those ten short months when five precious ones were snatched from my side in death. The light went out, darkness had settled, and my agonizing soul was crying, "Why? Why? Why?" I would lock myself in my room by night, and shut myself in my study by day, crying out in the awful state of loneliness and confusion, wondering what it all meant. I couldn't see. But oh, blessed be God! In those dark hours when I couldn't see and couldn't feel, again and again I sensed a presence and smelled the fragrance of the Rose of Sharon and the Lily of the Valley. You ask, "Why was the fragrance there?" It was because my Creator and King and Lord, having offered Himself as the Lamb of God, found a way to conquer sin and death; and there He was, my Risen Saviour, to fulfill His promise, "Lo, I am with you alway . . ." And unless you have a Saviour like that, you are basing your hope on a broken lily and a drooping rose. Therefore, I say again, that unless across the skies of time, from eternity past through all the eternities to come, there rides one great and glorious title — "the Lamb of God" — showering its light and significance upon all the other titles of Jesus, you can take them all away, for they will mean nothing to me.

The title "Lamb of God" has adorned the brow of Jesus Christ from before the foundation of the world. He was the Lamb of God before He was the Creator! Back yonder, before ever there were seas, twinkling stars, shimmering moons, shining suns, and azure heavens, Jesus was already the Lamb of God. "Lamb of God" is the title given Him by the Holy Spirit in the first typical picture we have of Him in the Bible.

Back in the Old Testament types, the first picture the Holy Spirit drew of Jesus Christ was that of a lamb. You remember the incident. Here was God's glorious creation, perfect as it could be, coming from the hand of a perfect Creator. Then a man by the name of Adam, and a woman by the name of Eve, decided to mess it up. So, like Samson, they reached out their arms of determination and self-will around the pillars of God's mighty temple of creation and pulled the whole structure down upon themselves, but by the same act also upon all of us. So all this beautiful perfection was utterly wrecked on account of a willful man and a willful woman. Now the slug is in the apple, the thorn is in the rose, the roar is in the throat of the ferocious beast, and God's wonderful creation is a mass of discord and disharmony.

Now God comes into the garden in the cool of the day. You would expect Him to come as a flame of fire, demanding in tones of thunder and judgment, "Adam, where art thou?" You could expect Him to pierce them through with His flashing sword of judgment, and He would have the right to do just that. But instead, what do we see? At the feet of that sinning pair lies a little innocent victim with its throat cut and its knees buckling, and the God of infinite grace takes the skin of the animal and makes of it coats to cover the nakedness of the guilty pair. You ask, "Is this a literal, historical event?" Yes, but it is not recorded for mere historic purposes. It is recorded that the typical index finger might be lifted from that bleeding, dying lamb and pointed down the archway of the skies to Jesus, the Lamb of God. His hands and feet were torn that, as His blood was shed, God in heaven might take His righteousness and weave it into a garment to cover the unrighteousness of a guilty sinner called Bob Ketcham! The Lamb of God! Yes, "Lamb of God" is His title.

"Lamb of God" was His title in Abraham's day, when on the side of Mount Moriah Isaac asked the question, "Where is the lamb?" And for old Abraham (I can see him turning his back to the sloping mountain as he shades his tear-dimmed eyes with a shaky hand and looks into the future) God pulled back the veil and permitted him to behold a sight down the vistas of the years. There outside the city's gate he saw a Cross uplifted, and someone on that Cross. That vision enabled him to turn to his questioning son and say, "Fear not, my son. God will provide Himself a (as the) lamb."

"Lamb of God" was His title in Egypt's dark night of doom, when God said, "When I see the blood, I will pass over you."

There were some strangely designated homes in Egypt that night, where the sideposts and the lintels of the doors were marked with blood. I am not a Hebrew scholar, but I believe that the word passover comes from the same Hebrew root as the word translated "hover over." Oh, how much that means to me! If the Hebrew scholars are correct, what a picture we have here. God's messenger of judgment was abroad in Egypt that night, moving sovereignly across that mighty nation, but God hovered over every blood-marked home and kept the first-born of the family from threatened death, all because he could see the blood. The blood of what? The blood of a lamb of course! Centuries later Paul gave us the full meaning of what transpired that night, when he wrote, "Even (so) Christ, our Passover, is sacrificed for us."

"Lamb of God" is the title given to our Lord in Isaiah's prophecy. As the prophet leads us down the corridor of that great 53rd chapter, its white marble walls and high-vaulted ceiling reaching up into the eternities of God, we hear him intone the solemn words of confession, "All we like sheep have gone astray . . . but the Lord hath laid on Him the iniquity of us all," and immediately there rises up before us the vision of an altar and a sacrificial lamb laid upon it. But since we are no longer living among the types and shadows of the past, the mind persists in asking, "Who is it that took upon Himself our guilt, so that by His stripes we might be healed?" And Isaiah, with bated breath, answers our inquiry by saying, "It is He, the one despised and rejected of men; the Man of Sorrows and acquainted with grief. It is Jesus!"

> There was none other good enough to pay the price of sin;
> He only could unlock the gates of heaven and let us in.

Coming to the New Testament, "Jesus, the Lamb of God" is His title when John the Baptist introduces Him at Bethabara beyond Jordan. Peter gives Him the same title when reminding the saints of the Diaspora that they were redeemed in no other way than by the precious blood of Christ. And "Jesus, the Lamb of God" is still His title when, at the beginning of the Apocalypse, John raises a paean of praise "Unto Him who loved us, and washed us from our sins in His own blood."

Thus we have followed the Lamb of God from Genesis to Revelation, and in the very nature of things it would seem that here we should have to bid the Lamb farewell, for in the book of Revelation there can hardly be room for so mild a creature. In this great drama we have the consummation of the ages; here all the battles of time and eternity are joined and the roar of heaven's artillery is let loose. Surely, says someone, there is no place for a lamb where stars are falling, where blood is flowing to the horses' bridles, where vials of wrath are being poured out, where wars sweep across the earth like mighty tidal waves, where heaven and hell are locked in one final gigantic contest for universal dominion.

No place for a lamb here? But what a mistaken notion! Let me call your attention to the fact that in this book Jesus Christ is called "Lamb of God" more times than in all the rest of the Bible. In chapter five we find John weeping because no one is found worthy enough to take the book and open its seals. But suddenly one of the elders cries out, "Oh yes, there is someone worthy! The Lion of the tribe of Judah hath prevailed to open the book and to loose the seals thereof." And John says, "I looked [you can almost hear him say, "I looked to see a lion"], and behold a lamb as it had been slain standing in the midst." In the sixth chapter we see men crying for the rocks and mountains to fall upon them and hide them from the face of God, but also from the wrath of the Lamb. Then, when we come to the last chapter but one, we read, "And the city had no need of the sun, neither of the moon to shine in it, because the glory of God did lighten it, and the Lamb is the light thereof."

You see, gladly acknowledging that Jesus is the Creator, the King of kings, the great Teacher, the Light of the World, and all the rest, I have tried to demonstrate that to be our Saviour He must nevertheless be the Lamb of God. Leave me Jesus with this title alone, and I have Someone upon whom this poor sinful soul of mine can rest itself. "Lamb of God" is the title He bears regardless of what His function is at any given time, and it lends glow and glory to His every word and act.

And now Jesus comes as the Lamb to His wedding. Why? Because it was the Lamb you fell in love with. You didn't fall in love with a Creator, or a King, or a Lord. Think back and you will recall that those were the very things that drove you in fear from Him. But it was different when at last you came to see Him as the Saviour who shed His blood for you.

I shall never forget that night forty years ago in the little Galeton Baptist Church when David Scott arose to sing "What Will You Do with Jesus?" Somewhere between the first verse and the middle of the next a boy rose from his seat with the purpose of running from the service. I tried to get away from the God who, in utter justice and judgment, was going to cast me in hell. Driven by the frenzy and fear in my soul, I had to run somewhere. How it came about I do not know, but before long I found myself at the old-fashioned altar. Later, when I was encouraged to lift up my head, I half expected to see the mighty scepter of the *King* come crashing down upon me, but instead I saw an uplifted Cross with the Lamb of God upon it. Great crimson drops of blood were dropping from a pentateuch of wounds, and it seemed to me that He bent down to whisper in my ear, "Beloved, it is for thee."

Forty years ago I fell in love with the *Lamb*. And so did you, I dare say, the first time you actually saw Jesus Christ. And now, just out of sweet, sentimental, holy love for us, when Jesus comes to our wedding, He is going to look exactly as He did when we fell in love with Him. Someone will probably say to me, "You are a sentimental old fool!" Very well, then, I *am* a sentimental old fool. But I believe with all my soul that when Jesus says, "Blessed are they which are called to the marriage supper of the *Lamb*," He means exactly that. When my Jesus comes to that holy marriage feast, I shall be perfectly at home with Him. I am going to see the same dear Lamb of God who saved, kept and comforted me all these years, and I shall add my voice to the grand chorus of the redeemed of all ages, singing the song of Moses and of the Lamb. "Hallelujah, What a Saviour!"

18

SHADOWS OF ARMAGEDDON

by THE HON. W. R. WALLACE

The broad subject assigned to me, "Shadows of Armageddon," could very easily be construed as an invitation to launch out upon a discussion of the marvelous, startling, and even frightening developments in the scientific realm; the political, moral and economic climates of the world; the prophecies concerning that historic little land of Palestine; the apostasy afflicting the churches of Christendom; the projected influence of ecumenical groups working for one world church; the doctrine of the Antichrist; the Great Tribulation; the Battle of Armageddon; and everything related to the great event of Christ's Second Coming. But as I have thought of the wealth of Scripture bearing upon this theme; of my limited understanding of the Scriptures generally and my ignorance of its teaching on this particular subject; of the fact that I, a layman, am to appear on the same program with the world's outstanding Bible scholars; I wondered with some degree of panic why I ever accepted a place on this program. The only apology I have for being here is my deep and compelling interest in the program God is carrying out in the earth; a program which, I believe, is clearly outlined step by step in prophecy.

PROPHECY AND THE PROPHETS

There is no better definition of prophecy than the one found in II Peter 1:21 — "For the prophecy came not in old time by the will of man; but holy men of God spake as they were moved by the Holy Ghost." No doubt Peter got his conception of what prophecy is from close association with the Lord Jesus, who was Himself the greatest — incomparably the greatest of the prophets.

Peter was one of three who formed the Saviour's inner circle, and it is reasonable to suppose that he asked the Lord many questions concerning the prophecies of the Old Testament.

The prophets were real men with real earthly relations, ambitions, aspirations and affections. For instance, Isaiah, one of the greatest of the Old Testament prophets, was a husband, a father, a citizen, and a true patriot, deeply interested in the things that concerned his nation. He was a warm friend of the king, and this friendship once helped to stem a great crisis in the midst of which he prophesied to the nation. It is important to keep in mind that these men did not speculate about God and the universe, but that they spake to the people for God. It makes all the difference in the world whether a preacher speaks for God or about God. It is clear from Peter's definition that these men did not originate their messages. The messages were God's, and they were His mouthpieces.

What did these men talk about — men like Abraham, Moses, Elijah, Amos, Isaiah, Jeremiah, John the Baptist? Primarily their messages were to the people of their day about man's responsibility to God, to his neighbor, and by the example of faith to oncoming generations. Then, as the Holy Spirit carried these men along, He gave them a vision of the goal of history and told them what would come to pass in the latter days. This does not mean that the principal design of Bible prophecy is to foretell the future, but prophecy bears witness to God's powerful, determining influence over the world at all times. Bible prophecy is not merely God's prediction of future events over which He has no control. It is not only an evidence of foreknowledge, as an astronomer might foretell an eclipse of the sun without possessing power to hasten or hinder it. In Bible prophecy God reveals His plan regarding the affairs of this world and shows that He, not man, is the sovereign of the universe.

Prophecy and its fulfillment is God's signature to His Word. It requires no unusual mind to see that only God can give men power to predict the future, and only God can control history so that it will fulfill prophecy. In fact, that is God's challenge to all false gods. In Isaiah 41:21-23: "Produce your cause, saith the Lord, bring forth your strong reasons, saith the King of

Jacob. Let them bring them forth, and shew us what will happen: let them shew the former things, what they may be, that we may consider them, and know the latter end of them. Shew the things that are to come hereafter, that we may know that ye are gods." That challenge was issued more than 2500 years ago, and it has never been accepted by any school of philosophy or religion.

THE GOAL OF PROPHECY

All prophecy culminates in the Second Coming of Jesus Christ and events related to it. The plainness of the prophetic Scriptures concerning the Second Coming of Christ is such that even skeptics cannot deny it. They are compelled to admit that the subject dominates the New Testament, and their only escape is to deny the veracity of the Scriptures and charge the authors with ignorance or superstition. The events connected with the end of this age are entirely clear in Scripture. The present dispensation closes with the Rapture of the Church. The Great Tribulation, following, leads up to and includes Armageddon. The Scriptures are also quite clear on events which are to take place between the Rapture and the actual coming of the Lord.

The vicious character active on earth during that intervening period is clearly portrayed and will bear careful study. Everyone with even a smattering knowledge of history will recognize that a conflict of forces runs through the whole course of human history. But unless one knows his Bible, he can only watch the progress of this conflict without knowing anything about its origin, its issues, or its termination. In Genesis 3:15 the Bible gives a record of the first declaration of war in all history. God Himself declared war upon Satan. There has never been a truce, an armistice, or a cessation of hostilities in this war from that day till now. While this conflict has raged for 6000 years, there has never been a doubt as to the final outcome. The same Bible that reveals the declaration of this war in Genesis 3:15, also reveals the end and outcome of it in Revelation 20:10: "And the devil that deceived them was cast into the lake of fire and brimstone, where the beast and the false prophet are, and shall be tormented day and night for ever and ever." Between these two verses of Scripture, we have the record of the age-old conflict running through the 66 books of the Bible. God and Satan are in mortal combat. All the wars of history are but skirmishes in this awful warfare. Sometimes it breaks out in the open, at other times it rages behind the scenes, but it is always the same conflict between a righteous and omnipotent God, and Satan and his destructive forces.

THE INVISIBLE BATTLE FRONT

I am not a scientist, but if I understand what I read, material science is coming more and more to recognize the absolute reality of the invisible spirit realm, and that all creative processes originate in that realm. There may be an outer mask of material things, but the life sources are in the unseen spirit realm. For instance, we were taught in my college days that the atom was the ultimate particle of solid substance. We were told that it was an infinitesimal, indestructible, immovable, solid substance. But with the coming of radioactivity and the electronic microscope, scientists have ripped that little atom to pieces and found 1760 charges of electricity tucked away inside of it.

Now ask the materialist what is matter, and he will tell you it is a mass of correlated atoms. Ask him what atoms are made of, and he will tell you, "electrons." Then ask him what electrons are, and he will answer you, "energy." And if you ask what energy is, he will tell you there is not a scientist under the blue dome of heaven who can answer that question. So then, when you take matter through the atom and electrons into energy, you enter the spirit realm. How true is the statement in Hebrews 11:3, "Through faith we understand that the worlds were framed by the word of God, so that things that are seen were not made of things which do appear!" Although made nearly 2000 years ago, it is now found to be scientifically true — things which are seen are not made of things which are apparent. The late Dr. Milliken, discoverer of the cosmic ray and Nobel prize winner, was asked just before his death, what is the cosmic ray, and his answer was, "It is God." A pastor in Pasadena is reported to have said, "Maybe a better answer would have been, it is the hem of God's garment." The cosmic ray is 100 times more powerful than the strongest X-ray. It is an invisible form of energy that will plow through 3 feet of steel and register through 6 feet of lead. Now this invisible, indescribable spirit realm is for the time being the headquarters from which Satan and his federation of evil spirits operate. This is made clear in Ephesians 6:12 — "For we wrestle not against flesh and blood, but against principalities, against powers, against the rulers of the darkness of this world, against spiritual wickedness in high places." To be sure, the phrase "spiritual wickedness" is impersonal, but the American Standard Version translates that, "wicked spirits in heavenly places." Moffatt translates it thus: "against the spirit-forces of evil in the heavenly sphere."

Do you wonder what this has to do with "Shadows of Armageddon"? Well, let me say that there is a surprise in store for the man who for the first time sits down with his Bible to learn what it teaches about the personality of Satan. I am aware that in this day of materialism, higher education, and exalted scholarship, the man who dares to speak seriously about the personality of Satan is looked upon as superstitious. We have eliminated Satan from our thinking, but not from the world. A book that was quite a popular seller a few years ago had this statement in it: "Anyone who is foolish enough to believe there is a personal devil is a fit subject for the psychopathic ward." My answer to that is, that if it were not for a personal devil we would not need psychopathic wards. It is a mistake to underestimate the power and wiles of that personal, malignant, fallen being called Satan. He is at the head of a vast, invisible federation of evil spirits working furiously for the defeat of God's program and the utter ruin of the race. Christ recognized him as a real person and declared war on his kingdom. In Revelation 12:9 Satan is branded as the deceiver of the whole world. He is earth's greatest schemer and counterfeiter. His crowning act in the great drama of deception will be to produce the Antichrist.

The title "Antichrist" is found only in John's writings. In a personal sense, in I John 2:18; then the spirit and servants of the Antichrist are referred to in I John 4:3, and II John 7. "Antichrist" simply means "against Christ," and in that sense there has been a long line of antichrists, beginning with Cain before the Flood and resuming again with Nimrod after the Flood. But that does not alter the teaching of Scripture that

Satan, at the end of this age, will personalize his opposition to God in a single individual. The Antichrist in John's writings is the same individual that Paul speaks of in II Thessalonians 2: 3, 8 and 9 as the "man of sin," the "son of perdition," the "lawless one."

Antichrist will be both a person and a system. He will be the personal head of a system, just as Christ is the personal head of the Church. The early Christians expected the ultimate personification of the anti-Christian movement in a man. In John 5:43 we read that Jesus said to the self-righteous Pharisees: "I am come in my Father's name, and ye receive me not; if another comes in his own name, him ye will receive." It is easy to see that this "another," the Antichrist, must be an individual as certainly as Christ, who speaks of Himself as "I," is one.

The hope of true Christianity is the personal appearing of Jesus Christ. By the same token, the goal of nominal Christianity must be the Antichrist. Satan, the god of this world, knows there are two things that all people and nations aspire to have — peace and money. All political parties and many religious bodies are engaged in all-out effort to bring that about and to make the world a better place to live in. According to the prophetic teaching of the Bible, in the end of the age a system of civilization will arise to fulfill all the longings of mankind built up through thousands of years. At its head will stand a mighty ruler, a genius for organization, a world benefactor (Dan. 11:21, 24, 36). As the acme of human greatness he will inflame and inspire men with the utmost enthusiasm; as the supreme leader in all undertakings he will call forth a consciousness of rest and security. For the world of science it will be the time of great progress and brilliance. But all this will be done without God, in self-confidence and for self-glory, to deify man and belittle God. God's answer to this kind of civilization is found in Jeremiah 17:5: "Thus saith the Lord; Cursed be the man that trusteth in man, and maketh flesh his arm, and whose heart departeth from the Lord."

PRELUDE OF ARMAGEDDON

In our time Russia and her communism have infiltrated many governments. It is attempting to infiltrate our government, and it is aiming for world domination. Things could hardly be in better shape for the Antichrist to appear on the scene. But he will not appear until "the many" Jews referred to in Daniel 9:27 have returned to their homeland. Large numbers are already there and the population of Israel is increasing every day. For more than fifty years the Zionist movement has been under way, and the Jews have been going back to Palestine — sometimes entire shiploads at one time, and they are rebuilding that land today.

Two invasions, two wars are predicted for the land of Israel: One by a Northern empire and its satellites; the other by "all nations." Ezekiel 38:11, 12 gives a partial background for the first invasion:

> And thou shalt say, I will go up to the land of unwalled villages; I will go to them that are at rest, that dwell safely, all of them dwelling without walls, and having neither bars nor gates, To take a spoil, and to take a prey; to turn thine hand upon the desolate places that are now inhabited, and upon the people that are gathered out of the nations, which have gotten cattle and goods, that dwell in the midst of the land.

It is no longer news to say that Israel is becoming one of the richest lands on earth. The oil supply of the land is phenomenal when you take the whole of the Near East into consideration. If we go back to Moses' words in Deuteronomy 33: 24, we get our first reference to oil in Palestine: "And of Asher he said, let Asher be blessed with children; let him be acceptable to his brethren, and let him dip his foot in oil." It was never known that Israel was a land of oil, until one day a Jew read that verse in Deuteronomy, took it as a revelation from God, and another prophecy became history. Oil has been discovered in the Negev.

However, oil is not Israel's only wealth. There is the Dead Sea, over 1000 feet below sea level, with mineral deposits worth, according to a government report, 1 trillion 270 billion dollars. Until 50 years ago, when the Arabs and Turks had complete control of the land, it was a desolate waste. Now it is said that enough wheat may be grown there in the future to feed almost the entire world. We are accustomed to thinking of Palestine as a little strip of land between the Jordan River and the Mediterranean Sea. However, look at Genesis 15:18 and see what God included in his gift to Abraham: "In the same day the Lord made a covenant with Abram, saying, Unto thy seed have I given this land, from the river of Egypt unto the great river, the river Euphrates." Much of this land was once occupied by Israel during the reign of Solomon, and all of it God has preserved for His people against the day when He gathers them back to their homeland. How marvelous to behold His doings!

CHRIST IS VICTOR

The invasion of the Land of Promise predicted by Ezekiel can be only a prelude to Armageddon. The participants in this invasion are Gog and his satellite nations (Ezek. 38:2-6). The battle of Armageddon spoken of in Revelation 16:16, Satan's final attempt to defeat the Son of God by destroying the city where His throne is to be established and the people over whom He is to reign, is the subject of Zechariah's prediction (14:1-3). In this war "all nations" go up against Jerusalem under the leadership of Satan's incarnation — Antichrist.

Revelation 14:14-20 gives us some idea of the fierceness of that combat. Blood will flow up to the horses' bridles, and the people of Israel will be right in the midst of the sea of blood, about to be engulfed in it. All the fury of hell will be poured out upon them. Satan has never forgiven them the fact that the Christ who bested him in the wilderness and defeated him at Calvary is of Judah's seed, and the Antichrist will be consumed with indignation against them because of their refusal to pay him divine homage. But the Lord will save them in the nick of time when He comes back from heaven with clouds of His saints. Zechariah 14:3 and 12 gives a composite description of the Lord's intervention in behalf of His people: "Then shall the Lord go forth, and fight against those nations, as when he fought in the day of battle. . . . And this shall be the plague wherewith the Lord shall smite all the people that have fought against Jerusalem; their flesh shall consume away while they stand upon their feet, and their eyes shall consume away in their holes, and their tongue shall consume away in their mouth." Did you ever read that and wonder how it could be fulfilled? Well, the atomic bomb, the hydrogen bomb and the cobalt bomb have made real this passage of Scripture. Of course, God, who holds the secret of all the elements, could do this without a bomb of any kind.

These are indeed frightening shadows, but they are harbingers of the dawn, destined to disappear when the Sun of Righteousness arises with healing in His wings. The most important event that will climax this age is not the battle of Armageddon, but the return in glory of our Lord Jesus Christ and the establishment of His kingdom. Israel, the one-third of the nation surviving the sword of the great destroyer, will see Jesus coming back to fight in their behalf, and their reactions to the wondrous sight will find expression in acts and words that have been dormant in the Bible for millenniums, awaiting the hour of their fulfillment: "And I will pour upon the house of David, and upon the inhabitants of Jerusalem, the spirit of grace and of supplications: and they shall look upon me whom they have pierced, and they shall mourn for him, as one mourneth for *his* only son, and shall be in bitterness for him, as one that is in bitterness for *his* firstborn" (Zech. 12:10). "And it shall be said in that day, Lo, this is our God; we have waited for him, and he will save us: this is the Lord; we have waited for him, we will be glad and rejoice in his salvation" (Isa. 25:9). And Ezekiel 39:25-29 tells how God will bless the remnant of the Jews, and describes the future glory of the land of Israel:

> Therefore thus saith the Lord God; Now will I bring again the captivity of Jacob, and have mercy upon the whole house of Israel, and will be jealous for my holy name; after that they have borne their shame, and all their trespasses whereby they have trespassed against me, when they dwelt safely in their land, and none made them afraid. When I have brought them again from the people, and gathered them out of their enemies' lands, and am sanctified in them in the sight of many nations; then shall they know that I am the Lord their God, which caused them to be led into captivity among the heathen: but I have gathered them unto their own land, and have left none of them any more there. Neither will I hide my face any more from them: for I have poured out my spirit upon the house of Israel, saith the Lord God.

In the meantime the world continues to reject the Lord Jesus Christ. It is customary today to omit the name of Jesus from public prayers and invocations. However, God is shaping the course of history to His own righteous and benevolent ends. The armament race among the nations is the training camp for Armageddon. At the same time Israel is returning to the land of the Fathers in preparation for a divinely appointed destiny. Ahead of them is the night of weeping, but also the joy of the morning. When the last battle of history is over, the Lord Jesus will take the throne of David and reign over the nations, enforcing perfect righteousness on this earth for 1000 years.

I am inwardly compelled to hold the premillennial view of the Lord's return because I know that human wisdom is incapable of ushering in that glorious period of peace and equity for which humanity is yearning. I deny that the present religious and ethical program of Christendom is capable of adjusting all the world's wrongs and injustices. I believe it requires the personal presence of Jesus Christ, God's Saviour and King.

19

ECUMENICITY, THE TRUE AND THE FALSE

by HARRY J. HAGER, PH.D.

The discussion of a subject so broad will allow only the brief est treatment of its following phases:

1. The origin, nature and mission of the true Church.
2. The inception of the counterfeit church.
3. The emergence of heresies in modern theology.
4. The rise of the ecumenical movement.
5. The separating ministry of the Holy Spirit.
6. The faith of the true Church.

When we turn to the Scriptures, we find that the Word of God gives us the norm of the true Church as the *body* of Christ as the *Bride* of Christ, and finally as a *building* — the habita tion of God through the Spirit.

Some conceive of a church in Old Testament times, dating it back either to the altars of Adam and Eve or to the in stitution of organized worship at Sinai. Stephen in Acts 7:38 speaks of "the church in the wilderness." However, though the Septuagint uses the Greek word *ecclesia* in translating the Old Testament terms, actually it is in the broader sense of a congregation or assemblage of the people of the Old Covenant These, even though gathered in worship, were so gathered within the structure of the "Kingdom-Nation" concept, and no as an "ecclesia" or church bringing to manifestation the invisible body of the Messiah.

That body can only be properly represented as taken from the side of her Saviour, as was Eve from the side of Adam, that she might be a helpmeet and companion unto him. Christ spoke anticipatively when He said: "I will build my church." First of all He laid the ground-work of it. Then, in a little more than

hree busy, crowded years, this Apostle and High Priest of our
rofession, from the multitudes to whom He preached, had
athered about Himself a called-out fellowship of approximately
ve hundred who were to become witnesses of the Resurrection.
Ie shunned the perils of a "mixed multitude," fully confident
hat a small group, when baptized with the Holy Spirit at Pen-
ecost, would under His orders and instructions penetrate to the
ttermost parts of the earth. You and I belong to that Church
f Jesus Christ and perpetuate its witness in these perilous times.
 have a strong conviction that Christians in this age of "joiners"
ad better concentrate on the one thing that really counts, that
s, being a member of the body of Christ and manifesting that
elationship in the outward expression of the local congregation.

Through most of the Christian centuries since Constantine
nother concept of the Church of Jesus Christ has made itself
elt. It was in fact the prolonged dominance of this ideal and
s concomitant evils that gave rise to the Reformation in the
ear 1517. A single example of this "antiquarian" concept of
he mission of the Church will suffice. On November 26, in the
ear 1095, Pope Urban II, at the Council of Clairmont, pro-
laimed to tremendous throngs the call of the first Crusade. His
iessage closed with the memorable words: "Deus vult, Deus
ult": God wills it, God wills it. These words spoken with an
ver-mounting tempo of fanaticism had the effect of stirring the
iultitudes to a frenzied enthusiasm. The knights followed the
eudal barons in putting on their armor; the peasant exchanged
is plow for arms; and these were joined by the dissatisfied, the
utcast and the oppressed. Soon the women and children took
p the Crusaders' banner: the red cross emblazoned on a field
f white. Then the great mob moved on to the Holy Land for
ie recapture of Calvary's holy ground and the retrievement of
ie "Holy Grail."

The net result of this, and the six other Crusades that fol-
owed, was that the so-called Holy Church won the everlasting
ontempt of the Saracens, whose countries they invaded. The
pirit of militarism thus awakened within the Church ultimately
ave rise to the Inquisition and its attempt to exterminate the
ue body of Christ represented in such small conventicles as

the Albigenses, the Waldensians, and other faithful witnesses
who in that long wintertime of Christendom's soul were desper
ately attempting to keep the flickering light of evangelical testi
mony aloft. This, then, was the Church of the Dark Ages, and
who does not revolt from such a concept of Christianity?

If today we ask ourselves, What is the mission of the Church?
the shadow of the medieval Crusader church is in the background, warning us that we must think soberly and seek light
from the Word on this question. The mission of the Church
was never complex in the mind of our Lord. But Protestantism,
aping after Roman Catholicism, has become a ponderous com-
plexity, a vast sort of "Kingdom-of-God" business, analogous to
our huge twentieth century international business concerns and
cartels, with lobbies in Washington, London, Geneva and the
principal capitals of the world. This modern Colossus has spread
itself like the parabolic mustard tree, harboring in its branches
all kinds of unclean birds. This ecclesiastical octopus tends to
fasten itself upon all vital Christian life and expression in such
a way that the true witness of the Church of Jesus Christ is
often neutralized thereby.

What then is the actual mission of the Church? It is simply
this: Corporately the Church is the Bride of Christ; individually
Christians are members of His body; but all the redeemed are
to live in continual communion and fellowship with the Lord,
and to draw *all* life and spiritual energy from within the veil,
where He as the forerunner has entered on our behalf. From
His exalted place on high He has bestowed gifts upon men and
made provision "for the perfecting of the saints, for the work
of the ministry, for the edifying of the body of Christ" (Eph.
4:11, 12). He is absolutely adequate for His Church. It is what
Christ is, as well as what He does, at the right hand of the
Father, that continually assures us that all authority in heaven
and in earth is His as He commands us to go forth and make
disciples of all nations. For "there is one body, and one spirit,
even as ye are called in one hope of your calling. One Lord,
one faith, one baptism, one God and Father of all, who is above
all, and through all, and in all" (Eph. 4:4).

The chief occupation of the Bride is, regardless of the many

.venues of outreach in churchly influence and activity open to
ter, to keep in mind that her Lord and Bridegroom is absent,
hat He has gone into a far country to receive a kingdom, and
hat some day He will return. In the meantime His Bride is
xpected to be faithful. That means that she will keep looking
nd behaving like an affianced woman. For the inheritance of
Christ, His reward for the travail of His soul, is *His Church*.
All this, of course, is foreign to the liberal ecclesiology which
provides the major spark behind the modern ecumenical move-
nent.

True, we need to bring Christian conscience to bear on the
ocial ills, such as city slums, capital and labor relations, inter-
ational peace, race relations, etc. But in the midst of all this
he supreme mission of the Church is not that of a cult, or in-
titute, or reforming agency, but her most basic role is simply
) be herself — the Bride of Christ, ultimately the wife of the
amb. Thus alone does she insure for herself the collaboration
f the Holy Spirit. "And we are his witnesses of these things;
nd so is also the Holy Ghost, whom God hath given to them
nat obey him" (Acts 5:32).

THE COUNTERFEIT CHURCH

We can touch only briefly on the inception of the counter-
eit church in New Testament times, and its development
hrough the centuries prior to the Reformation. The Ephesian
etter gives us a picture of the true Church at its best. In
Colossians we sense the foreign climate of Gnosticism rising as
heretical threat to the life of the infant Church. In the Church
t Corinth we see an incipient denial of the resurrection coupled
ith the carnality of a growing Mammonism and secularism. In
ne letters of Timothy and Titus, with their instructions as to
ne ordering of the church and the qualifications of elders and
eacons, we sense the resoluteness with which the denial of
ound doctrine, joined to worldliness of behavior, was exposed
nd disciplined. In II Peter and in the Epistle of John, Mam-
onism of a monstrous and diabolical nature is rebuked. The
arments of the Bride were early spotted and defiled with all
nanner of uncleanness and lasciviousness. Even worse corrup-

tions were to insinuate themselves into the Church after the purifying effect of the ten great persecutions had faded and Constantinian compromise spread within the precincts of Christendom.

It is evident from all this that the first task of the Church of Christ is not simply to expand, to be big and influential. Our first responsibility is to be true in our testimony to the truth as it is in Christ, for the Church is the pillar and ground of truth. Secondly, it is our duty to be pure in the godliness of our conduct before our fellow men.

"The more sure word of prophecy" gives us an outline of the course the Church will follow in the last times, so that from her own ranks cults shall rise that will serve as the antithesis of the testimony of Jesus Christ. This is described in the first three chapters of the Book of Revelation. Looking at the Laodicean situation in the last of the seven messages, we can understand why the Lord finally exclaims: "Because thou art . . . neither cold nor hot, I will spew thee out of my mouth." What disappointment must our Lord feel today when He hears the old cry, "The temple of the Lord, the temple of the Lord are these," from the lips of men who love their ecumenical prospectings and ignore the New Testament ideal of the Church as "the habitation of God through the Spirit."

MODERN ECCLESIOLOGICAL HERESIES

What are some of the modern heresies that have arisen in these latter days? We pass over the old Liberalism as no longer either vital or relevant. However, a remnant of its surviving devotees have found intellectual shelter in a new crop of religious philosophies, principally Neo-Orthodoxy and Realized Eschatology. The first of these is by far the more influential. Its prophet, Karl Barth, has gone up into the theological stratosphere with his "supra-history" view that no prophecy is being fulfilled in the present age because the Church is not moving toward a historical goal. Prophecy will and can only begin to be fulfilled in eternity. Strange it is that, feeling the inescapable pertinency of eschatology, Barth should nevertheless have employed his

pontifical dogmatism to banish God and the Church from the
historical process.

Realized Eschatology is more euphemistic in its pronouncements, but not one bit clearer in its reasoning. Too well aware
of the fact that chronic wars have made the pipe dream of a
constantly improving world altogether untenable, this school is
following the general line of the Amillennialists by maintaining
that little if any of the predictive Word of God remains to be
realized. The Church is close to her zenith, they say, and the
climax of history can be expected at any hour. But whether
this will take place in "time, or existentially from out of eternity,"
who knows? And all of this hodge-podge of philosophical vapor-
ing is called theology!

THE ECUMENICALISM OF THE WORLD COUNCIL

Now for a brief resume of the rise and development of the
present-day ecumenical movement and its espoused ideal of *One
Church*. The first Edinburgh Conference in 1910 was its birth-
place. Bear in mind that in 1908 the Federal Council of
Churches here in America was born. The next advance was
the Church Congress at the Mount of Olives in 1928. The
Conference of Tambaran followed in 1938. Then came the first
formal World Council Assembly at Amsterdam in 1948 and the
screen of "faith and order" was no longer needed. The World
Church van was now rolling. A new spirit of auspiciousness had
come into the grandiloquent phrases of the Council's leaders.
Here is a sample:

> As we come to this inauguration of the World Council of
> Churches, let us give thanks to God for those who discerned this
> day by faith and devoted their lives to a deeper realization of
> unity between the followers of our Lord Jesus Christ. Now faith
> is the assurance of things hoped for, the proving of things not
> seen. By faith Charles Brent, Bishop in the Philippines and
> later of west New York, conceived a movement for seeking the
> unity of the churches in matters of faith and order and pre-
> sided over the Lausanne Conference of 1927. By faith Nathan
> Soderblom, Archbishop of Upsala, led the churches to cooperate
> in all matters of life and work and presided over the Stockholm
> Conference in 1925. We give thanks to God for the faith and
> witness of V. S. Azariah, Bishop of Dornakal; of G. F. Barbour,
> member of the Continuation Committee of the Edinburgh Con-

ference; Sergius Boulgakoff, member of the Oxford Conference on Church Community and State; and William Adams Brown, Chairman of the Universal Christian Council for Life and Work, member of the Continuation Committee of the Edinburgh Conference.

Time is lacking for a more detailed analysis of the ecumenical movement, the staggering proportions it had by 1954 reached at Evanston, the almost super-synodical complexion of its central governing committee, and the implied groping for an ultimate Protestant Vatican and College of Cardinals.

THE SEPARATING MINISTRY OF THE HOLY SPIRIT

In view of the ecumenical trends of our times, evangelical Christians must set forth at least the minimal concepts of church unity, church cooperation, and ecumenicity as these are apprehended from the Scriptures:

1. The Scriptures repudiate the Roman Catholic concept of ecumenicalism under papal vicarage. "For one is your Master, even Christ, and all ye are brethren. And call no man your father upon the earth: for one is your Father, which is in heaven."

2. The Scriptures warn against the traitorous role that a faithless ecclesiastical octopus will in the end-time play in alliance with the Antichrist, that man of sin "who opposeth and exalteth himself above all that is called God, or that is worshipped; so that he as God sitteth in the temple of God, shewing himself that he is God" (II Thess. 2:4).

3. Evangelicals reject also all proposals for a single World Church, since the primary calling of the Churches of Christ, singly or as groups, is not simply to function as a clearing house for world improvement and control, but to witness to *one Lord* and *one precious faith* (Eph. 4:5).

4. Evangelicals reject and decry the ecumenicity of the World Council:

(a) as not based on *the true ecumenical doctrine* of the inspiration of the Scriptures;

(b) as predicated upon a platform of doctrinal minimization and indifferentism, whereas our times call for a clear creedal witness on the part of the confessing Church of Jesus Christ;

(c) because of the light way the doctrine of Christ, His virgin birth, and His resurrection, are treated in its highest councils. "Hereby know ye the Spirit of God: Every spirit that confesseth that Jesus Christ is come in the flesh is of God: And every spirit that confesseth not that Jesus Christ is come in the flesh is not of God" (I John 4:2, 3);

(d) because it compromises the distinctly Protestant and evangelical character of the true Church of Christ by fraternization with the Mariolatry, sacerdotalism and iconolatry of the Eastern Orthdox Churches;

(e) because in its passion for centralization and solidarity it tends to stifle the articulate voice of the lay members and to obscure the priesthood of all believers.

WHAT EVANGELICAL CHRISTIANS PROFESS ECUMENICALLY

First, that true ecumenicity is a spiritual and not an organizational unity. "Endeavoring to keep the unity of the *Spirit* in the bond of peace" (Eph. 4:3).

Second, that denominational development is not necessarily contrary to the Spirit of Christ as the so-called "collective guilt of the churches," but that at its best it is an instrument of the Spirit of God for the recovery of redeemed personality.

Third, that true ecumenicity expresses itself best in a simple evangelical fellowship and in a common witness to the risen, ascended and returning Christ.

Fourth, that our utmost devotion is to be directed not to church or denomination, but to the Lordship of Christ in the Church, and ultimately to the Kingdom of the Triune God, which is first and foremost the Kingdom of *truth*.

Fifth, that all evangelical Christians must beware of the ecumenical faddism of our times, and work prayerfully and patiently in anticipation of that holy reunion of all true Christians at the return from heaven of the Lord and Head of the Church, "who is the blessed and only Potentate, the King of kings and Lord of lords; who only hath immortality . . . to whom be honour and power everlasting. Amen" (I Tim. 6:15, 16).

20

THE PRETRIBULATION RAPTURE AND THE COMMENTATORS

by Alva J. McClain, D.D., LL.D.

The phrasing of my subject may have conveyed a wrong impression. It sounds a bit like the possible title of a book, and a rather large book at that, considering the immense scope of the suggested field of investigation. But those charged with the arrangement and printing of conference programs, believing quite properly that brevity is one of the surest marks of inspiration, generally exhort the speakers to let their words be few.

As a matter of fact, what I have to say during this period will be restricted to a single argument. And this argument is addressed only to those who believe that the Book of the Revelation, however difficult it may be in certain details, at least presents a general program of "last things" which makes sense. But doubtless your very presence here, in attendance upon a conference of this nature, is the surest evidence that you would not accept the dictum of one otherwise great leader who said of this last book of the Bible: "Even if it were a blessed thing to believe what is contained in it, no man knows what that is."

I. A Statement of the Problem

Here it might be well for us to consider for a moment the two familiar terms which appear so often in recent eschatological discussions. I refer to the words "Millennial" and "Tribulation." What is the Biblical background which led to their use?

Throughout the prophetical Scriptures, especially in the Old Testament, there are presented two great periods at the end-time when God will manifest His sovereign presence and power on the earth: First, there will be a period when God will pour out terrible judgments upon the earth; and second, there will be a period when God will rule in a kingdom to be established on the earth. The first has been called the "Tribulation"; the second the "Millennium." As to the time sequence of these two periods there can be no controversy: The judgment period always precedes the kingdom period. The darkness of the night is first, followed by the rising sun and the day. On this point the testimony of the prophets is beyond dispute. When serious disagreements have arisen, they have been connected with the time relation of our Lord's Return to these two great periods.

As to the relation of His Second Coming to the kingdom period, there are three schools of opinion described by the following terms: First, Premillennial; second, Postmillennial; and third, Amillennial. The meaning of the first two is fairly clear. The former means Christ will come *before* the establishment of the kingdom, while the latter means He will come *after* its establishment on earth. But the third term, which is simply Greek for *"no* millennium," is somewhat confusing. For it is doubtful whether there has ever been an amillennialist who did not believe in a divine kingdom of some kind, either existing now on earth or to be realized in the final and eternal state. Actually, what Amillennialism rejects is the idea of any divine millennial kingdom on earth *at the end* but *within* human history.

We turn now to the time relation between our Lord's Return and the divine judgment period. Here the disagreements are within the Premillennial school, now divided into three camps named Pretribulationist, Posttribulationist, and Midtribulationist. Again, the meaning of the first two terms is fairly clear. The word "Pretribulationist" has generally been associated with the view that Christ's coming for His Church takes place in chapter 4 of Revelation *before* the terrible events of chapters 6 through 19. "Posttribulationist" refers to the view that Christ's rapture of the Church will occur in chapter 20 *after* the events of chapters 6 through 19. But the meaning of the third term has been confused. As I understand the matter, those named "Midtribulationists" place the Rapture of the Church generally at the sounding of the seventh trumpet in Chapter 11. Now this is indeed the middle of Daniel's 70th week of seven years. But by the same token this must be the *beginning*, not the middle, of that last half of the 70th week, 42 months or 1260 days in length, which technically is designated as "the great tribulation" (see Rev. 13:4-7). Thus some of the *Mid*tribulationists claim they are really *Pre*tribulationists! And so, with reference to the prefix "Mid," it always becomes necessary to ask, "The middle of what?"

However, since the settlement of this question is not essential to the purpose of my subject today, and it is only necessary for us to understand clearly what we are talking about, I propose to use the popular term "Tribulation" to indicate the entire period of wrath and judgment covered by chapters 6 through 19 of the Book of Revelation.

Now the basic facts of divine revelation are much simpler than all this sounds. As the English philosopher Berkeley once acutely observed, "We first raise a dust, and then complain that we cannot see." I realize that we cannot, and probably should not, try to stop that natural bent of the human intellect in striving to formulate in theological system and terminology the great truths of the Word of God. But all such attempts must never lose sight of the basic simplicity of the original facts of revelation. This danger is always present in the process of intellectual formulation. Take, for example, the doctrine of the Person of Christ, about which earnest and well meaning men struggled for several centuries, until finally some all but lost their way in the dust of battle and actually fought against their own side. Yet the original facts of revelation were very simple: First, the historical Jesus was true Man in all respects; and second, the same Person was also true God. Men went astray theologically only when they lost sight of either one or both of these two facts.

Likewise, I fear, there is danger today that even well meaning Christian men may become confused in the battle over eschatological terms and distinctions. A colleague of mine reports the case of an able and learned Christian layman who, after listening for several hours to such discussion, said, "Gentlemen, I don't even know what you are talking about!" Here again, I would remind you, the facts of divine revelation are quite simple, not at all dependent upon a few carefully selected and arranged proof-texts. Here are these facts:

1. It is a fact that the Lord Jesus Christ will surely come again personally and visibly to take His Church from the earth to be forever with Him.

2. It is a fact that Christian believers are exhorted to be ever watching and waiting for the Lord's coming as a constant "blessed hope."

3. It is a fact that the time of our Lord's return is not given us to know, and therefore all attempts to fix the date either forward or backward are both vain and dangerous.

These simple facts of divine revelation must never be forgotten in any and all attempts to formulate a systematic doctrine of the events of the end-time. Such an attitude may not solve all the problems, but at least we shall be kept from going very far astray as we grapple with them.

As for my own position in relation to this eschatological problem, let me say that, after some 40 years of study and teaching in this field, I find myself at this very hour believing more firmly than ever that our Lord will come for His Church not only before the Millennial Kingdom, but also before that great judgment period which precedes the Kingdom. I cannot forget that, while the Word of God gives no chronology at all of the present age, it does give a definite chronology of both the coming judgment period and the kingdom period which follows it. The Kingdom will last a "thousand" years, and the Judgment which precedes it will last seven years. Therefore, to set the Lord's coming somewhere after the beginning of either of these periods is certain to get us into the nefarious business of date-setting.

It has been recently charged, however, that practically all the great commentators are against the Pretribulation view of the Lord's Coming. Now if those who make this charge mean that most of the commentators do not teach the full prophetic program of Pretribulationism, then there is truth to what they claim. But if, on the other hand, they mean that no support for Pretribulationism can be found in the ablest of the commentators, we must reply that this is definitely not true.

II. The Testimony of the Commentators

A large majority of the ablest and well known commentators agree on the identification of an important symbol in the Book of Revelation upon which a most powerful argument for the Pretribulation view can be based. I refer to the "four and twenty elders" of Revelation 4 and 5. Who are they? Or what do they represent? Let us read the passages in part:

Revelation 4:1-4 — After this I looked, and, behold, a door was opened in heaven: and the first voice which I heard was as it were of a trumpet talking with me; which said, Come up hither, and I will shew thee things which must be hereafter. And immediately I was in the spirit, and, behold, a throne was set in heaven, and one sat on the throne. And he that sat was to look upon like a jasper and a sardine stone: and there was a rainbow round about the throne, in sight like unto an emerald. And round about the throne were four and twenty seats: and upon the seats I saw four and twenty elders sitting, clothed in white raiment; and they had on their heads crowns of gold.

Revelation 4:10, 11 — The four and twenty elders fall down before him that sat on the throne, and worship him that liveth for ever and ever, and cast their crowns before the throne, saying, Thou art worthy, O Lord, to receive glory and honour and power; for thou hast created all things, and for thy pleasure they are and were created.

Revelation 5:1-10 — And I saw in the right hand of him that sat on the throne a book written within and on the backside, sealed with seven seals. And I saw a strong angel proclaiming with a loud voice, Who is worthy to open the book, and to loose the seals thereof? And no man in heaven, nor in earth, neither under the earth, was able to open the book, neither to look thereon. And I wept much, because no man was found worthy to open and to read the book, neither to look thereon. And one of the elders saith unto me, Weep not: behold the Lion of the tribe of Judah, the Root of David, hath prevailed to open the book, and to loose the seven seals thereof. And I beheld, and lo, in the midst of the throne and of the four beasts, and in the midst of the elders, stood a Lamb as it had been slain, having seven horns and seven eyes, which are the Seven Spirits of God sent forth into all the earth. And he came and took the book out of the right hand of him that sat upon the throne. And when he had taken the book, the four beasts and four and twenty elders fell down before the Lamb, having every one of them harps, and golden vials full of odours, which are the prayers of the saints. And they sung a new song, saying, Thou art worthy to take the book, and to open the seals thereof: for thou wast slain, and hast redeemed us to God by thy blood out of every kindred, and tongue, and people, and nation; and hast made us unto our God kings and priests: and we shall reign on the earth.

I shall not attempt here to reproduce the long and convincing exegetical evidence presented in the commentaries as to the symbolism of these 24 elders, but will only briefly quote their conclusions. The list which follows is of course not exhaustive. The selections were made almost at random, and arranged alphabetically. For obvious reasons, I have excluded modern writers known to have a strong bias either for or against the viewpoint under discussion, and also writers like Moffat who try to find the origin of the symbolism of the 24 elders in "Babylonian astro-theology" and "Egyptian mythology."

Alford says, "These twenty-four elders are not *angels,* as maintained by some, as is shewn . . . by their white robes and crowns, the rewards of *endurance,* ch. 3:5, 2:10 — *but representatives of the Church,* as generally understood" (New Testament for English Readers).

Barnes says of the 24 elders, "They are designed in some way to be symbolic of the church of the redeemed" (Notes on Revelation, p. 117).

Benson says, the 24 elders signify ". . . the most wise, holy and useful of all the former ages, whether of the patriarchal, Jewish, or Christian Church" (New Testament, Vol. II, p. 718).

Binney says, the 24 elders are "the representatives of the entire church of God" (People's Commentary, p. 679).

Carpenter says, the 24 elders "are the representatives of Christ's church and people" (Ellicott's Commentary, Vol. VIII, p. 552).

Clarke says, the 24 elders are "the Christian church in all nations" (Commentary, Vol. VI, p. 992).

Clemance says, "The four and twenty elders . . . represent the whole Church of the Firstborn, the blessed and holy ones whom God hath made kings and priests unto Himself" (Pulpit Commentary, Vol. on Rev., p. 154).

Cook says, "The four and twenty elders . . . are the representatives of the universal church of God" (Speaker's Commentary, Vol. X, p. 554).

Crafer says, the "four and twenty elders . . . represent the church in its perfection, as suggested by the doubling of twelve" (New Commentary on Holy Scripture, p. 689).

Crosby says, "The twenty-four elders represent the glorified church . . . to fulfil the promise of Rev. 3:21" (Homiletical Review, New Series, Vol. XIX, p. 364).

Dusterdieck says, "These 24 elders are *human*, and not . . . angels . . . [they are] either the representatives of the Old and New Testament church . . . or of the church gathered not only of the Jews, but also from the Gentiles" (Meyer's Commentary, Revelation, pp. 193, 194).

Fausset says, "They are not angels, for they have *white robes* and *crowns of victory*, implying a conflict and endurance . . . they represent the heads of the Old and New Testament churches respectively" (Commentary on the Whole Bible, by Jamieson, Fausset and Brown, p. 564).

Girdlestone says of the 24 elders, "In them we see a symbol of Christ's church, elsewhere called 'a royal priesthood'" (New Testament, Part IV, p. 691).

Godet says, "The 24 elders represent the Judaeo-Christian and the Gentile church" (Preacher's Homiletical Commentary on Revelation, p. 494).

Gray says, the 24 elders are "representatives of the church, sitting as kings" (Bible Encyclopedia and Museum, Vol. XV, p. 259).

Hengstenberg says, "That the elders are representatives of the church, there can be no question" (Revelation of St. John, Vol. I, p. 204).

Henry says, the ". . . four and twenty elders [are] presbyters, representing, very probably, the whole church of God . . . not the ministers of the church, but rather the representatives of the people" (Commentary, Vol. VI, p. 1388).

Holden says, "The 'four and twenty' elders . . . seem to represent the true church of God" (Christian Expositor, p. 672).

Kuyper says, ". . . of all creatures that were assembled in the throne room of God, the sainted host of believers is naturally accorded the place of highest eminence" (Revelation of St. John, p. 61).

Milligan says, "The 'four and twenty elders' occupying thrones (not seats) around the throne are to be regarded as representatives of the glorified church" (Expositor's Bible).

Plummer says, ". . . the elders represent the saints of both Old and New Testaments" (Pulpit Commentary on Revelation, p. 145).

Robertson says, the 24 elders are "the representatives of the redeemed" (Word Pictures in the New Testament, Vol. VI, p. 338).

Scott says of the 24 elders, "These are generally allowed to be the emblematic representatives of the whole church of God" (Commentary, Vol. VI, p. 713).

Sheppard says, ". . . these elders represent the church triumphant . . . these crowns mark them as the church triumphant, since Christ promises these to the church militant as its final reward" (Devotional Commentary, Vol. on Rev., p. 76).

Simcox says, the 24 elders "are the glorified embodiment and representatives of the people of God" (Cambridge Greek Text for Schools and Colleges, Revelation of St. John, p. 75).

Slight says, the 24 elders ". . . seem to represent the universal church of God, in all ages" (Apocalypse Explained, pp. 228, 229).

Smith says, the 24 elders ". . . are those which represent the church, or kingdom of Jesus Christ" (American Commentary on the New Testament, Vol. VII, p. 78).

Swete says, "Thus the 24 elders are the church in its totality . . . seen as already clad in white, crowned, and enthroned in the Divine Presence — a state yet future, but already potentially realized in the Resurrection and Ascension of the Head . . ." (Apocalypse of St. John, p. 69).

Vincent says, "The twenty-four elders are usually taken to represent the one church of Christ" (Word Studies in the New Testament, Vol. II, p. 478).

Weidner says, "These elders are the triumphant church in heaven, including the Old and the New Testament saints" (Lutheran Commentary, Vol. XII, p. 68).

III. THE IMPRESSIVE NATURE OF THIS TESTIMONY

1. The commentators cited represent many eschatological viewpoints. They certainly are not all even Premillennialists. Neither were they avowed supporters of Pretribulationism, a term which probably never occurs anywhere in their writings. They were not writing to construct any detailed prophetic program which would uphold the Pretribulationist school of Premillennialism.

2. These commentators are in vast disagreement with one another about much of the Book of Revelation. You would grow weary even trying to follow the various ramifications of all their systems of interpretation of this and that. Some almost despair of reaching any safe conclusions about many things in the Book of Revelation.

3. Furthermore, these scholars do not all agree as to the precise nature and scope of the Church, nor as to its place and purpose in the divine plan for the ages.

4. Yet in spite of all their disagreements about other matters, they are united in their opinion that the 24 elders of Revelation 4 and 5, enthroned in heaven, do represent the true Church of God. Certainly we cannot fail to be impressed profoundly by the fact that so many scholars have come together with regard to the meaning of this particular symbol of the Apocalypse, which interpretation, if accepted by Premillennialists who believe the book presents an intelligible program, shuts out of court any eschatological scheme which would leave the Church on earth during any part of the great judgments of the end-time described in chapters 6 to 19. Not only so, but this unanimity of the commentators lays an exegetical basis for the view which so many of us warmly embrace. Let me try to show you why this is so:

IV. THE ARGUMENT FOR PRETRIBULATIONISM BASED ON THE COMMENTATORS' TESTIMONY

1. In chapter 4 of Revelation the 24 elders, who according to these commentaries represent the Church, are seen by the Apostle John *"in heaven,"* sitting on thrones, wearing crowns on their heads, and clothed in white raiment.

2. In chapter 5 these 24 elders watch with tremendous in-

terest as the Lamb of God takes the Sealed Book of divine judgments out of the hand of Him who sits on the central throne. In the same chapter the same elders sing a song of praise and adoration to the Lamb who only has a right to hold the Book, and they fall down and worship Him.

3. All this takes place *before* a single seal of the Book is broken by the Lamb, *before* a single trumpet is sounded, *before* a single vial is poured out upon the earth, *before* any one of the terrible judgments described in chapters 6-19 is loosed upon the inhabitants of the earth or the heavens.

4. Now, regardless of the chronological interpretation you may make of the judgments of Revelation 6 to 19; whether you adopt some recapitulation or overlapping scheme; shuffle the seals and trumpets and vials as you will; you cannot push chapters 4 and 5 into the picture which follows in chapters 6 to 19. There is no judgment until the first seal is broken; the first seal is not broken until the Lamb receives the Sealed Book; the Lamb does not take the Book until the 24 elders are in heaven, sitting on thrones and with crowns on their heads. If the scene in heaven described in chapters 4 and 5 does not precede the judgments of 6 to 19, then no one can make any sense whatever out of the order of things in the last book of the Bible. And we may as well complain with Martin Luther, "Even if it were a blessed thing to believe what is in it, no man knows what that is."

This argument may not prove absolutely the correctness of the Pretribulation position, but it should put an end to the notion that this position can find no support in the commentators. For the great majority are in agreement as to that symbol which, to the Pretribulationist, establishes his position beyond dispute.

21

THE PARABLES OF THE KINGDOM

by John F. Walvoord, th.d.

One of the strategic portions of prophetic Scripture is before us. Obviously, it is impossible to cover in one message all the parables of the four Gospels dealing with kingdom truth. Our study will therefore be restricted to the seven parables of Matthew 13. Anyone who has studied these parables from the standpoint of their contribution to the sum total of prophetic truth will agree that we have here an important Scripture which determines the interpretation of many other portions of the Word of God. This chapter has been given a wide variety of treatment. The approach taken here is that the thirteenth chapter of Matthew answers the question of what will happen between the two advents of Christ.

Purpose of the Gospel of Matthew

In the providence of God the Gospel of Matthew has been placed first among the books of the New Testament. Here we have God's answer to the natural question: Why was the King rejected, and what happens to the Kingdom now that the King has been rejected? The entire Gospel of Matthew is the answer. In the Old Testament, where the Kingdom was announced in connection with the coming of the Messiah, the presentation of His two advents was mingled to such an extent that those who studied the Old Testament, even the writers of it, could not always distinguish clearly what belonged to the first coming and what to the second coming. It is quite clear that the disciples believed He would establish His Kingdom on earth in connection with His first coming. They did not understand that He needed to die and be raised from the dead; that God had as His immediate purpose the calling out of a people from Jew and Gentile to form the body of Christ; that the millennial, earthly reign of Christ would not be fulfilled in connection with His first advent, nor in the present age, but rather at His second coming.

In the Gospel of Matthew, first of all, proof is presented that Christ is indeed the King. Here is His genealogy, the account of His birth, and the evidence to substantiate the fact that He is the King predicted in the Old Testament. Here He is revealed as Immanuel — God with us, the One born of a virgin, whose kingdom would have no end.

The Gospel of Matthew continues by presenting, in the Sermon on the Mount, the moral, ethical and governmental principles of that Kingdom, together with their immediate application. Following the Sermon on the Mount, Christ performs a series of miracles which fulfill Old Testament prophecies and prove to intelligent students of the ancient Scriptures that He is the Messiah, the King of Kings, the Son of David. The sad record of rejection follows. The religious leaders as well as many of the people reject Him, whereupon He pronounces the most solemn words of judgment on that generation and turns instead to individuals with the invitation: "Come unto me, all ye that labour and are heavy laden, and I will give you rest." After His rejection it becomes evident that His first advent would result in His becoming a crucified Saviour instead of a crowned King.

In the thirteenth chapter of Matthew the question is faced: If the earthly Kingdom is not to be fulfilled until Christ's second advent, what will happen between the two advents? The parables which answer this question are described as mysteries because they present that aspect of the Kingdom which was not revealed in the Old Testament. The main point of this entire chapter is right here, namely, that the present form of the kingdom is not the millennial form. In other words, the thirteenth chapter of Matthew, properly interpreted, refutes the Amillennial theory that we are now in the Millennium and that the millennial promises are being fulfilled in this present age. To this Matthew 13 says "No." There is indeed a form of the kingdom in this present age, but it is not the Millennium because the King is absent, not now upon the throne of David. Other Scripture reveals that He is now on the Father's throne, at the right hand of God. This age is not a kingdom of righteousness and peace but a dual development of good and evil, and it will culminate in the return of Christ to establish righteousness and judge evil.

The first two of the seven parables in Matthew 13 are interpreted in the Scripture itself. With this inspired key the rest of the parables fall into line, each contributing another facet of truth to the concept of what God is doing throughout the present age. It should be observed, however, that the Kingdom is not identical with the Church. Kingdom truth presents the rule of God from a governmental standpoint, the relationship of a king to a subject. In the Church the relationship of the believer is that of one who has been saved, who is in Christ, whether he be Jew or Gentile. The Church as the body of Christ is not in view here, even though the Kingdom period of which this chapter speaks includes the Church Age.

PARABLE OF THE SOWER

The first parable is that of the sower. The historical context is given in the opening verses. Christ sat in a ship a short distance out from shore and the multitude stood on the shore to hear His message.

> Behold, a sower went forth to sow; and when he sowed, some seeds fell by the way side, and the fowls came and devoured them up: some fell upon stony places, where they had not much earth: and forthwith they sprung up, because they had no deepness of earth: and when the sun was up, they were scorched; and because they had no root, they withered away. And some fell among thorns; and the thorns sprung up, and choked them: but other fell into good ground, and brought forth fruit, some an hundredfold, some sixtyfold, some thirtyfold. Who hath ears to hear, let him hear (Matt. 13:3-9).

The interpretation of this parable is given the disciples in the same chapter:

> Hear ye therefore the parable of the sower. When any one heareth the word of the kingdom, and understandeth it not, then cometh the wicked one, and catcheth away that which

was sown in his heart. This is he which received seed by the way side. But he that received the seed into stony places, the same is he that heareth the word, and anon with joy receiveth it; yet hath he not root in himself, but dureth for a while: for when tribulation or persecution ariseth because of the word, by and by he is offended. He also that received seed among the thorns is he that heareth the word; and the care of this world, and the deceitfulness of riches, choke the word, and he becometh unfruitful. But he that received seed into the good ground is he that heareth the word, and understandeth it; which also beareth fruit, and bringeth forth, some an hundredfold, some sixty, some thirty (Matt. 13:18-23).

This parable makes it clear that the word of the Kingdom, instead of enjoying universal acceptance, is mostly like seed fallen into unfavorable kinds of soil, having only one chance in four to produce fruit. Obviously the present age is not the Millennium, since the word of the Kingdom is rejected by most of the hearers and there is no universal recognition of the King. By contrast, in the Millennium all will be forced to submit to the King. No rejection will be allowed until the end of the Millennium. Now, however, hearers are free to reject, free to be hardhearted, free to turn away. This spells the tragedy of the present hour. There are many today who have heard the Word, but have not received it. The Word of God can do nothing for us until it is received and appropriated by faith; only so can we enter into its riches and bear fruit in our lives.

PARABLE OF THE WHEAT AND THE TARES

The second parable is similar to the first, having to do with the sowing of seed. This time, however, the parable is about wheat and tares, and the focal point is the two kinds of seed rather than how the seed is received.

Another parable put he forth unto them, saying, The kingdom of heaven is likened unto a man which sowed good seed in his field: but while men slept, his enemy came and sowed tares among the wheat, and went his way. But when the blade was sprung up, and brought forth fruit, then appeared the tares also. So the servants of the householder came and said unto him, Sir, didst not thou sow good seed in thy field? from whence then hath it tares? He said unto them, An enemy hath done this. The servants said unto him, Wilt thou then that we go

and gather them up? But he said, Nay; lest while ye gather
up the tares, ye root up also the wheat with them. Let both
grow together until the harvest: and in the time of harvest
I will say to the reapers, Gather ye together first the tares, and
bind them in bundles to burn them: but gather the wheat into
my barn (Matt. 13:24-30).

As in the first parable, so here an inspired commentary is given.
The disciples came to Christ and asked Him to explain this
parable. Matthew 13:37-43 records Christ's answer to their
question:

He that soweth the good seed is the Son of man; the field
is the world; the good seed are the children of the kingdom;
but the tares are the children of the wicked one; the enemy
that sowed them is the devil; the harvest is the end of the
world; and the reapers are the angels. As therefore the tares
are gathered and burned in the fire; so shall it be in the end
of this world. The Son of man shall send forth his angels, and
they shall gather out of his kingdom all things that offend, and
them which do iniquity; and shall cast them into a furnace of
fire: there shall be wailing and gnashing of teeth. Then shall
the righteous shine forth as the sun in the kingdom of their
Father. Who hath ears to hear, let him hear.

In this parable Christ makes clear that in the whole of the
present age between His first and second advents there will be
a dual line of development: A development of good in the
righteous described as children of the kingdom, and the development of the children of the evil one right alongside of it. He
further declares that it is impossible to pull up the tares — the
false wheat, representing unsaved but professing individuals,
without uprooting the children — the good wheat, also. His
choice is to let both grow on until the harvest. When the end
of the age comes, the separation will take place. Again it is
clear that the age spoken of here is the present age, not the
Millennium. Satan will be bound in the Millennium and therefore will not be able to sow the tares.

There has been a difference of opinion among respected Bible
teachers as to the actual termination of the period in view. It
is often taught that the end of the age in Matthew 13 should
be identified with the end of the Church Age, which many of
us believe is going to occur some seven years before Christ comes

to establish His Kingdom. There are good reasons, however, for believing the period is not limited to the Church Age, but covers the entire interadvent age — the whole time during which the King is absent from the earth. When Christ comes for His Church, and while He takes His Church home to glory, the tares, those who have not trusted in Christ, are left unjudged and unchanged. There is no real separation as far as final judgment is concerned until Christ comes back to set up His Kingdom. At that time those who have believed in Christ during the tribulation period will be separated from the sheer professors. In this connection it is stated in verse 30, "Gather ye together first the tares, and bind them in bundles to burn them: but gather the wheat into my barn." That is precisely what Christ will do when He comes to establish His Kingdom. There will be judgment upon the wicked, and blessing upon the righteous, who will enter into the millennial form of the Kingdom.

PARABLE OF THE MUSTARD SEED

Following the parable of the wheat and the tares, there are five other brief parables, all without any explanation. Having given us the basic parables and their interpretation, Christ leaves the explanation of the next five to the reader. The third parable is that of the mustard seed: "Another parable put he forth unto them, saying, The kingdom of heaven is like to a grain of mustard seed, which a man took, and sowed in his field, which indeed is the least of all seeds: but when it is grown, it is the greatest among herbs, and becometh a tree, so that the birds of the air come and lodge in the branches thereof" (Matt. 13: 31, 32). This parable is designed to teach one truth, that the kingdom will grow from a small beginning and become a large plant called here a tree.

History has recorded the amazing development of Christendom from a little band of twelve disciples to a tremendous organization of wealth and power, carrying on its work in the name of Christ even though it is at times far from the purposes of its founder. The mustard seed has become a tree in whose branches roost the birds of the air, representing Satan and those whom he controls. To be sure, there is a difference between the branch and the bird. The branch represents those who at least have some outer profession of faith. Certainly in our day everything that is called Christian is not Christian in fact, or even remotely Christian by the standard of Holy Scripture.

PARABLE OF THE LEAVEN

The next in order is the parable of the leaven. "Another parable spake he unto them; The kingdom of heaven is like unto leaven, which a woman took, and hid in three measures of meal, till the whole was leavened" (Matt. 13:33). The illustration is derived from a practice common in the Orient of taking a lump of dough which the fermenting process had puffed up and mixing it in a new batch of dough. In our day we use yeast to accomplish the same purpose. The question is: What does the leaven represent? It has been the common teaching of those holding the Postmillennial viewpoint that the leaven represents the Gospel which has permeated or will permeate the whole world until it is Christianized. This point of view is not nearly as popular as it once was because almost any realistic analyst of modern times recognizes that, while the Gospel has gone out in large measure to the whole world, there are millions of people who are utterly impervious to it, living as if there were no Gospel, no Cross, no Bible. Granting that Christianity has been a force for good in the world far beyond the borders of the Church, it is still highly questionable that this is the teaching of Matthew 13:33.

In the Bible leaven normally represents evil. In Old Testament times unleavened bread was used in connection with the Passover. Leaven was prohibited because it was a symbol of that which puffs up, develops great outer form, but actually has little substance. In the New Testament it is often synonymous with hypocrisy, worldliness, bad doctrine, externalism. Certainly in the Kingdom of Heaven, which includes professing Christendom, there are all of these elements. Thoughtful students of modern Christendom recognize that all is not well within its borders. Large segments of Christendom are not of the true seed, are in the Kingdom only outwardly, and are therefore destined to be eternally separated from the elect people of God.

PARABLES OF THE TREASURE AND THE PEARL

The fifth and the sixth parables recorded in Matthew 13:44-46 are often taken together because they are so similar. "Again, the kingdom of heaven is like unto treasure hid in a field; the which when a man hath found, he hideth, and for joy thereof goeth and selleth all that he hath, and buyeth that field. Again, the kingdom of heaven is like unto a merchant man, seeking goodly pearls: who, when he had found one pearl of great price, went and sold all that he had, and bought it."

A favorite interpretation of this portion of Scripture, found in Trench's book on the parables, is that the man who finds the treasure, and the merchant who finds the pearl, both represent the believer, and that the treasure and the pearl are none other than the Lord Jesus Christ. This view seems plausible until the parable is analyzed. All recognize that Christ is a treasure; but, after all, is Christ hidden in a field? Do we have to buy the field in order to have Christ? To the contrary, is it not a fact that we have nothing with which to come before God for salvation, and that all we can do is accept Christ's work for us on the Cross? This interpretation breaks down because Christ is not for sale. In both of these parables the man and the merchant man represent not the believer, but rather the Lord Jesus Christ. Speaking reverently, He *had* something to sell, and so He was able to buy the field and secure the treasure. That is precisely what Christ did when He died for the sins of the whole world.

But what is the treasure? Many Bible scholars hold that it represents Israel, and Scripture passages like Exodus 19:5 and Psalm 135:4 certainly support this interpretation. There is also a sense in which Israel is hidden, the nation's place in the plan of God receiving no recognition either in the world or in Christendom. As a matter of fact, there was a time when Bible teachers who expressed the belief that Israel was a nation were often laughed out of court. Even today some still deny all the Scriptures that speak of Israel as a nation or a race. Yet there can be no doubt that Christ died for Israel, God's peculiar treasure, even as He died for all the elect. In any case, it is clear that the treasure in the parable is Israel.

The merchant man who found a pearl of great price and sold all that he had in order to buy it represents Christ and redemption, and the pearl is the Church, the body of Christ. The death of Christ has a twofold application. The whole purpose of God with respect to mercy and grace toward Israel, not only in this present age but also in the future Millennium, is based upon His Son's death on the Cross. The same thing is true in the case of the Church. The pearl seems to be a marvelously fitting illustration of what the Church actually is. In the natural world the pearl is the only gem of its character formed organically. Most jewels are mineral in substance. A pearl, however, is an organic formation caused by an irritation of the tender flesh in the side of an oyster. The pearl develops at the point of the irritation. The symbolism is, as many Bible expositors have pointed out, that the Church was begotten in the wounds of Christ, through His death and shed blood. The Church is an organic body, composed of living stones, added one by one. The parable, then, teaches Christ's great love for the Church, and that He gave Himself to redeem it.

PARABLE OF THE DRAGNET

In the concluding parable of the dragnet it is again made clear how utterly different this interadvent form of the Kingdom is from the concept of the millennial Kingdom. The millennial Kingdom is ushered in by the returning Christ and it starts out with a righteous generation. Satan is bound in the Millennium and not permitted to sow his evil seed until he is loosed at its close. By contrast, he is very active in the present age.

In this final parable we are given a picture of modern Christendom. "Again, the kingdom of heaven is like unto a net, that was cast into the sea, and gathered of every kind" (Matt. 13:47). Christendom has gathered all kinds of creatures into its net. According to the parable, when the net is full it will be brought to shore and the process of separation will take place, when the good will be gathered into vessels, but the bad will be cast away. According to verses 49-52 this will occur at the Second Coming of Christ to establish His Kingdom: "So shall it be at the end of the world: the angels shall come forth, and sever the wicked from among the just, and shall cast them into the furnace of fire: there shall be wailing and gnashing of teeth. Jesus saith unto them, Have ye understood all these things? They say unto him, Yea, Lord. Then said he unto them, Therefore every scribe which is instructed unto the kingdom of heaven is like unto a man that is an householder, which bringeth forth out of his treasure things new and old."

The main theme of the seventh parable is the dual line of development running through the present interadvent age and culminating in the final judgment when men are separated, the good from the bad, at the time Christ returns to establish His Kingdom. It should be obvious that here is no Millennium, no righteous reign of the King on earth, but a picture of the present age with its evil and good developing side by side.

The seven parables of Matthew 13 make it abundantly plain that it is not enough to have an outer profession; not enough to be a member of a local church; not enough to have the sacraments administered to us. There must be an experience of inner reality. The tares never become wheat, and the wheat never becomes tares. They are two different kinds of life. Natural life is not enough. Reformation will not suffice. We must be true believers, genuinely born again by faith in the Lord Jesus. While outwardly it may be difficult for us to distinguish the wheat from the tares, God's vision is perfect and the day of separation is inevitable.

Matthew 13 is not designed as a text for the Gospel of grace. There is nothing of the Cross here, except the implication that Christ bought us as contained in the figures of the treasure and the pearl. There is no declaration here of how to be saved. But when this Scripture is placed alongside of others in the New Testament, it becomes perfectly plain that we have an obligation to trust in the Lord Jesus Christ as our personal Saviour, and that it is utterly futile to try qualifying before God on any other basis. Only so can we be born again, receive eternal life, and be joined to the body of Christ. In this way we become, if you please, the good seed, identified as those who belong to God forever.

May God speak to our hearts and cause us to see the absolute necessity of a personal, vital trust in Jesus Christ as Saviour and Lord, so that we may find in Him salvation for time and eternity.

22

THE THREEFOLD MINISTRY OF CHRIST
AS PROPHET, PRIEST, KING

by Peter Hoogendam, th.d.

The text chosen for this address, my contribution in part to the curriculum of this Congress on Prophecy, is found in Revelation 19:10: "For the testimony of Jesus is the spirit of prophecy."

This text has been variously interpreted. It has been taken to mean "the testimony which proceeds from Jesus," that is, Jesus, by imparting this testimony to His servants also imparts to them the spirit of prophecy. This would make the testimony of Jesus entirely subjective. But a more satisfying, and more correct, interpretation is suggested by Dean Alford, who held that the testimony of Jesus is "the testimony borne to Jesus," which means that the manner of bearing this testimony, and the very substance and essence of it, is the spirit of prophecy. To prophesy is to "have the testimony of Jesus," and to understand and proclaim it, especially in the face of prevailing ignorance or opposition (Rev. 12:17).

Prophecy, as the predictive element of Scripture, *has a spirit,* a peculiar nature and urge, giving it purpose and scope. This driving element has but one objective, to give testimony concerning the Lord Jesus Christ. He is the sole theme and burden of it.

The Testimony Borne to Jesus as Prophet

The Word of God in the Old Testament is pervaded by prophecies concerning the Lord Jesus Christ. There are numerous indirect predictions about Him, but we desire to fix our attention on one direct forecast. Perhaps this will encourage others to dig further and deeper in this mine of wealth.

Genesis 3:15, which has been called "the primal prophecy of the Seed of the Woman," is the germ of all Messianic prophecy. "As the oak is germinally in the acorn, and the eagle in the egg, all subsequent Messianic prophecy of the Old Testament is here in germ. In the whole aftercourse of such prophecy there is scarcely added one idea that is absolutely new. Other predictions grow out of and expand this germinal prediction."

All Scripture is the history of two men: "The first man is of the earth, earthy; the second man is the Lord from heaven" (I Cor. 15:47). From these two fountainheads, the fallen Adam and the Woman's Seed, flow two streams, the one dark as death, the other rich with the promise of blessing, ever broadening and deepening into fuller glory. "This history of ruined man, the first stream, rolls on in gathering gloom till it issues in the rejection of the Christ and the reception of the Antichrist. The unfolding of God's purposes in His Son, the second stream, also moves on without interruption, each accession of human guilt only adding to its volume, bringing out the glory of God and His chosen One with more striking beauty."

The promised Seed of the Woman is the one great subject found in the entire Word of God. Genesis 3:15 marks the depths of the ruin into which man fell when he first sinned against God, and it thus becomes the point of departure for all subsequent revelation. This means that all hope of restoration, either for man or for creation, is centered in Christ. Christ is therefore the key to the Word of God, and apart from Him it cannot be understood. The subject matter of the Bible must be arranged with this in view, so that we shall understand that all the counsels and purposes of God are centered in Him, and that He is the circumference of all as well.

I. Concerning the Creation and Position of Adam taught in the New Testament, let us observe the following important facts:

A. ADAM WAS THE FIRST MAN (cf. I Cor. 15:45).

There was no "prehistoric man"! Before Adam there never was another man! Adam was "first formed" (I Tim. 2:13). If the "First Adam" had a predecessor, then the "Last Adam" might have a successor. But both are impossible!

B. ADAM WAS THE FATHER MAN (cf. Acts 17:26).

The race of mankind, with all its divisions, had its human fatherhood in the first man. "He hath made of one blood all nations of men" (the blood of one man, Adam). (See Genesis 5:1; I Chron. 1:1).

C. ADAM WAS THE FEDERAL MAN (cf. Rom. 5:12; 3:23).

The first man held governmental headship for all men; in Adam the whole human race was on probation; the organic union was thus complete, for the "one" included the "all."

D. ADAM WAS THE FIGURE MAN (cf. Rom. 5:14).

Adam, the head of the first creation, prefigures Him who is the head of the New Creation (cf. II Cor. 5:17). So then, the first type in the Word of God, expressly so called in the New Testament, is a prophecy of Jesus. The "Spirit of Prophecy," in a sense, has its beginning here!

II. Concerning the Privileges and Failure of the "first man, Adam," the following is to be noted:

A. ADAM'S STANDING BEFORE THE LORD.

1. Adam was created a *Prophet*. By immediate intuition and direct revelation he knew the mind and will of God.

2. Adam was created a *Priest*. Because of his sinless state, he had the right to stand before God in an intimate relationship.

3. Adam was created a *King*. God "made him a little lower than the angels, crowning him with glory and honour, and gave him to have dominion over the works of His hands." Thus we see that Adam had embodied in himself, by a divine grant, these three parallel functions.

B. ADAM'S SIN AND FALL

1. When Adam sinned, he fell, and in his fall he ceased to be a prophet. In fact, from that moment he needed someone to teach him the content of the mind and will of God.

2. When Adam fell, he ceased to be a priest before God. In fact, from that moment he needed a mediator to stand between

himself and an offended God, someone who would intercede
in his behalf.

3. When Adam fell, he ceased to be a king. By one act of
disobedience he lost the crown of dominion and needed someone to reign over his life and regain for him his lost sceptre.

III. Concerning the Successor of Adam, we must note the
following:

A. THE SEED OF THE WOMAN WAS NOW PROMISED.

"The first man is driven from the garden, excluded from the
tree of life, left helpless in the grasp of his conqueror. Disease
and death, a groaning creation and moral alienation from God
still subsist, the badges of his servitude and the witness of his
fall. But complete triumph is promised to the Second Man. By
Him alone can the enemy of God and the destroyer of man
be stripped of his dominion and trampled in the dust."

At this point God begins to prepare the hearts of men for the
advent of the Seed of the Woman into the world, using for this
three methods:

1. He raised up a *succession of Prophets.* Men who, because
of their special gifts, were God's mouthpieces to speak to the
sons of men.

2. He raised up a *family of Priests.* Men who, because of
their special sanctification, were God's representatives to the
people, and at the same time the representatives of the people
before God.

3. He raised up a *race of Kings.* Men who, because of their
special choice, were God's viceroys over the people.

The old Testament is a record of how these classes of men,
chosen by the Lord, performed their respective offices. However,
though these prophets and priests and kings were used of God
to instruct the people, make atonement for their sins, and
regulate their lives in relation to the rule of Jehovah; yet, through
all of the Old Testament period, not one prophet or priest or
king had been found upon whom the Spirit of God could rest
and remain!

It is most instructive to read in the last book of the Old Testament, "He sought a godly seed" (Mal. 2:15). The Holy Spirit
came upon man after man, anointing a prophet, consecrating

a priest, inaugurating a king; yet it was all in vain, for God could not find a godly seed (Hebrew, the seed of Elohim)! The promised Seed of the Woman had not yet appeared! The one thing that the Spirit of God looked for through all the years of brooding over the waters of humanity could not be found. And so the Old Testament ends with prophecies unfulfilled, ceremonies unexplained, longings unsatisfied.

Yet, and this is the point of our text in Revelation 19:10, throughout the Old Testament the Spirit of Prophecy was bearing witness to the fact that One would come — One who would be the Seed of the Woman: who as *Prophet* would fulfill in His life and work all the prophecies, who as a *Priest* would explain in His death and atonement all the ceremonies, who as a *King* would satisfy in His resurrection and coming again all human longings!

Through Moses God gave to Israel the promise that a great prophet would arise. "Jehovah thy God will raise up unto thee a prophet from the midst of thee, of thy brethren, like unto me; unto him ye shall hearken" (Deut. 18:15, ASV). Here a beautiful line of thought suggests itself. God's revelation of Himself hitherto had been progressive. From the beginning He was known as *Elohim,* the triune, the omnipotent Creator. In this character God's attributes of power, and might, and force, were revealed. To the patriarchs God was known as *El Shaddai,* the all-sufficient God who supplies the wants of every living creature. But to Moses He was manifested as *Jehovah,* the self-existing, unchangeable, eternal; the God in covenant relationship with His people (see Ex. 6:1-4). All the revelations of God under the Old Covenant were additions to this title, such as Jehovah Jireh, Jehovah Ropheka, Jehovah Nissi, Jehovah Mekaddeshkem, Jehovah Shalom, Jehovah Tsebaoth, Jehovah Rohi, Jehovah Elyon, Jehovah Tsidkenu, and Jehovah Shammah (see Gen. 22:14; Ex. 15:26; 17:15; 31:13; Judg. 6:24; I Sam. 1:3; Ps. 23:1; 7:17; Jer. 23:6; and Ezek. 48:35).

Though Moses was preeminent as a prophet, no other man ever being admitted to the same familiar and intimate relationship with Jehovah (cf. Num. 12:6-8 and Deut. 34:10-11), yet it was not until Christ came in the flesh that man received a full revelation of God. All the other revelations of God were fragmentary and partial; not until Christ became incarnate was God made known in that highest and dearest of all relationships — that of Father!

Favored as Moses was, he could only see Jehovah's "back-parts" (Ex. 33:18-33), that is, the less glorious parts of His character. But when the Greater Prophet came, we received the last and highest revelation of God. Henceforth all that we can ever know of God is to be seen in the Lord Jesus Christ, for in Him God has shone forth, giving us "the light of the knowledge of the glory of [himself] in the face of Jesus Christ" (II Cor. 4:6).

Someone has said that "Moses and the prophets were like the moon and the stars in the night, their testimony was infinitely better than total darkness, yet it was night only; but now, in Christ, we have the sun at noon-day." God, having of old time spoken unto the fathers in the prophets by divers portions and in divers manners, hath at the end of these days spoken unto us in His Son!

THE TESTIMONY BORNE TO JESUS AS PRIEST

The Spirit of Prophecy of old indicated that Aaron, the High Priest of Israel, was the type of Christ as the great High Priest of His people. There are points of resemblance and also of contrast between Aaron and Christ. Even as Aaron was chosen from among men to be Israel's priest, so was Christ (cf. Heb. 5:1-3; 2:16-18); and as the priest must be appointed by God (Num. 16), we are told that Christ was thus appointed (cf. Heb. 5:4-10). In contrast to Aaron and his ministry, it is distinctly stated that Christ is a priest by an oath (Heb. 7:20-22); priests in the Aaronic line needed to atone for their own sins, but not so the Lord Jesus (Heb. 7:26-28); neither Aaron nor his successors could ever actually put sin away, but Christ did (Heb. 10:14); Aaron's priesthood was of the earth, but Christ's is carried on in Heaven (Heb. 8:1-5); Aaron entered into the holiest of all alone; no one dared follow him there; but Christ is our forerunner, having entered in before us and leaving the way open so that we might follow Him (Heb. 6:20).

Even as God has spoken unto us in the Son who was greater than all the prophets, so He has also spoken unto us in the

Son who has fulfilled the purpose of the true priest. Christ did this because God's law was in His heart, and He alone of all mankind was willing to do the complete will of God. His sacrifice alone could atone for humanity, and therefore He is now the only High Priest of the universe!

So, throughout the Old Testament, the Spirit of Prophecy bears constant testimony to Jesus — the Seed of the Woman; the Second Man; the Last Adam, the Lord from Heaven; who would, by His death and suffering and resurrection, become *a priest after the pattern of Aaron* (cf. Lev. 8, 9 — an appointed priesthood); *a priest after the nature of Phinehas* (cf. Num. 25 — an acquired priesthood); and *a priest after the order of Melchisedec* (cf. Heb. 7 — an attested priesthood). Thus He forever set fallen man free from the curse of sin and judgment!

THE TESTIMONY TO JESUS AS KING

The Spirit of Prophecy constantly pointed forward also to the advent of the true King! When God spake in times past unto the fathers, there were many implications that He was preparing them for a more perfect and a more enduring revelation. The prophets were but types of Christ, the greater Prophet. The priests were but adumbrations of the eternal Priest, His own Son. The many kings were but foreshadowings of the King of Kings!

In the Epistle to the Hebrews, Moses is spoken of as the great prophet of Israel, but he is mentioned there only to show that Christ was worthy of more glory than Moses, for He is *that prophet* of whom Moses prophesied in Deuteronomy 18:15. Aaron is also mentioned, and no doubt for the same reason, to show that Christ is far greater as the priest of God and the representative of the people. But who is the king mentioned in the Epistle to the Hebrews? Is it David? Is it Solomon? Is it Hezekiah? No, it is none of these, but rather *Melchisedec, the king of Salem!* And when he is described as *king*, it is immediately added that he was also *priest of the Most High God!* Here, incidentally, we have the central truth of that wonderful epistle: "A Priest on His Throne as King!"

In three passages of Scripture, Genesis 14:18-20, Psalm 110, and Hebrews 5, 6 and 7, the Spirit of Prophecy testifies that Jesus will actually be *a priest on His throne* (cf. Zech. 6:12,13); for He is the true *King of Righteousness,* and after that the *King of Peace* (cf. Gen. 14:18; Heb. 7:1-3). Thus throughout His millennial reign on this earth He will fulfill God's order — *righteousness first, and then peace!*

We have endeavored to outline briefly the three offices of Christ, who, by virtue of His incarnation, is the anointed Mediator between God and man. His advent in the fullness of time is the supreme verbal and typical prophecy of the Scriptures, and throughout He is marked as being the Lord's Anointed, or Christ. This title was first given to our Lord in an indirect and anticipatory manner by those who in the theocracy were anointed to office. Bringing this study to a close, we wish to recall the remarkable passages of Scripture in which our Lord was preannounced as the Anointed One in relation to the three offices of Prophet, Priest and King.

To Him All the Prophets Bear Witness

I. In Isaiah 61:1, ASV, our Lord speaks of Himself through the mouth of the prophet: "The Spirit of the Lord Jehovah is upon me, because Jehovah hath *anointed me* to preach good tidings" (see also Luke 4:18; Acts 10:38). Here, by our Lord's own interpretation, is the *charisma* of the prophetic office. While this is the only passage of its kind that He quoted, His apostles used many others with which the prophetic Scriptures abounded.

II. Daniel closes his prophecy proper by giving the name Messiah to the future redeemer. While Daniel included Christ's other offices, he specifically designates Him as High Priest. Three times he uses the word Messiah as a noun or a verb: "Seventy weeks are decreed upon thy people and upon the holy city to . . . *anoint* the most holy." "Know therefore and discern, that from the going forth of the commandment to restore . . . unto the *anointed one,* the prince." "After threescore and two weeks shall the *anointed one* be cut off" (cf. Dan. 9:24-26, ASV).

III. The Psalms commence with *the great name* of the future: "The rulers take counsel together, against Jehovah, and against *his anointed.*" This is the office of king. It is strongly repeated later in the Psalm, "Yet have I set *my king* upon my holy hill of Zion" (cf. Ps. 2:2,6, ASV). Psalm 45 more fully sets forth the regal office of Christ.

Return with me to our text for a moment before we conclude. The testimony of Jesus in the Book of the Revelation is of a prophetic character, "referring to His public assumption of governmental power to be displayed in the kingdom." This testimony we believe to be of a threefold character, reiterating that He is Prophet, Priest and King. Of this there are no less than three indications:

A. The salutation in the first chapter: "Grace unto you and peace, from him *who is* and *who was* and *who is to come*" (v. 4, ASV). As a prophet Christ *was;* as a priest Christ *is;* as a king Christ is yet *to come!*

B. Again in the first chapter, three titles are ascribed to our Lord: *"The Faithful Witness, the Firstborn of the Dead, and the Ruler [Prince] of the Kings of the Earth"* (v. 5, ASV). The title "faithful witness" is no doubt His as the true *prophet* of Jehovah. The name "firstborn of the dead" certainly speaks of Him as *priest,* living in the power of an endless life, walking in the midst of the lampstands (1:13). The title "prince of the kings of the earth" looks into the glorious future when Israel shall be under her *Messiah King!*

C. In the passage where our text is found — Revelation 19:1-16 — the declaration of the angel that "the testimony of Jesus is the spirit of prophecy" does not mean that all predictions found in the prophetic word apply to the Lord Jesus Christ, but it does mean that the whole plan and program of redemption is moving toward the one goal of bringing to its fullness the honor and glory of God's beloved Son. Here *four hallelujahs* are sounded, and John sees the conquering Christ's triumphal procession as *The Prophet* (faithful and true, v. 11), as *The Priest* (a garment sprinkled with blood, v. 13), and as *The King* (King of kings and Lord of lords, v. 16).

May God grant this to us all, that as we look upon the glories of His wonderful Son, we shall be changed into the same likeness, from one degree of glory to another, by the effectual working in us of His Spirit.

23

THE TESTIMONY OF JESUS IN THE BOOK OF THE REVELATION

by Peter Hoogendam, th.d.

The Holy Spirit who inspired all the prophets (II Pet. 1:21), bore testimony verbally through them, and is now continuing to bear testimony in every part of the written revelation, to the Christ of God. "Wherefore when he cometh into the world, he saith . . . in the volume of the book it is written of me" (Heb. 10:5,7). "The testimony of Jesus is the spirit of prophecy." But there is a sense in which this definition of prophecy can be made particularly applicable to the book of the Revelation, the one wholly prophetic book in the New Testament, so that one would be justified in saying, "the testimony of Jesus" is the spirit of [this] prophecy (cf. Rev. 1:2).

The book of the Revelation is preeminently the testimony concerning Christ the King, not in prospect, but in fulfillment. Here we see Him as the Lord of history, and it is no longer correct to say that "we see not yet all things put under him" (Heb. 2:8), for now "the kingdoms of this world are become the kingdoms of our Lord, and of his Christ" (Rev. 11:15).

Since this is the book of the unveiling of Jesus Christ, we naturally expect to find here final summaries of all the great truths related to our Lord. In this we are not disappointed. In the successive scenes of this divine panorama, and in the foreground of each, the most prominent and commanding figure is the Lord Jesus Christ as the Lamb. The name "Lamb," as applied to the Lord Jesus, occurs some twenty-eight times in this book. The only explanation for the constant reference in the

Apocalypse to Christ as the Lamb is that "the spirit of prophecy," which throughout the former parts of Scripture has been bearing witness to the Saviour, here gathers to a point all the typical teaching concerning Him who appeared at the end of the age to put sin away by the sacrifice of Himself. Inspired by the Holy Spirit, John skillfully draws four portraits of the Lamb in this closing book of the Bible.

CHRIST PORTRAYED AS THE WOUNDED LAMB

And I saw in the midst of the throne and of the four living creatures, and in the midst of the elders, a Lamb standing, as though it had been slain (Rev. 5:6, ASV).

In the original the words are extremely expressive: "A Lamb, standing, as if he had been that very instant slaughtered a sacrificial victim." This is the greatest wonder of heaven! A wounded man is there! This means that the Cross appears amid all the splendors of the crown. "Calvary only stands out in sharper and more glorious relief beside Mount Zion, and every one of the redeemed in Heaven, every one of those that cast their crowns before the Lamb, looks back to the Cross, and to One, as if He had been that moment slain, by whose blood they were redeemed, and through whose intercession they have been elevated to the heights of eternal joy."

The *Wounded Lamb* is a title of *function*. It is a truth often taught, that there must be four elements in a sacrifice before God can accept it. These four elements can be illustrated from four sources:

There is the *Lamb of History* in Genesis 22. In the beautiful story of Abraham's offering up of Isaac there is the idea of *substitution*: "And Abraham went and took the ram, and offered him up for a burnt-offering *in the stead* of his son" (Gen. 22:13). It is in this chapter of Genesis that the word "lamb" and "love" are used for the first time in the Bible.

There is the *Lamb of Ritual* in Exodus 12. In this perfect picture of the Cross of Christ the prominent idea is that of *representation*. It has been estimated that about 200,000 lambs were slain on the first Passover; yet in the records of that event the sacrifice is always mentioned in the singular, "a lamb," "the lamb," "your lamb."

There is the *Lamb of Prophecy* in Isaiah 53. It is impossible to escape the inference that "the Spirit of Prophecy" is here indicating that this Lamb is the Son of God, the Lamb now upon the throne; and all through the great prophecy of Isaiah there is strong emphasis on the idea of *identification*.

There is the *Lamb of Reality* in John 1. When John says, "Behold the Lamb of God, which taketh away the sin of the world," he is manifestly pointing back to the sacrificial system which pervades the Bible from the beginning to the end. He is thinking of the great process which led up to Christ. He remembers how from the beginning lambs were slain continually; how they were offered up by Abel, Noah and Abraham; how the altar of God was ever red with blood; and he sees Jesus Christ as coming to complete these sacrifices and terminate them by the offering of Himself. Here, then, is the element of *satisfaction*.

When these elements of substitution, representation, identification and satisfaction are applied to the sacrifice of Christ, it is clearly understood that the atonement made by the Lamb of God was at once vicarious, expiatory and efficacious.

The "spirit of prophecy" reminds us four times in the Apocalypse of "the blood of the Lamb." In this way there is a summing up of the great benefits the believer derives from the "Wounded Lamb":

The Blood of the Lamb gives Pardon (1:5).
The Blood of the Lamb gives Peace (5:9).
The Blood of the Lamb gives Purity (7:14).
The Blood of the Lamb gives Power (12:11).

To this "Wounded Lamb" the preacher of the Gospel directs the weary sinner. His sacrifice is still efficacious as a "substitution." In the pathetic story of Abraham and Isaac man provided *a knife*, and *the wood*, and *the fire*; but the *lamb* was of God's own providing. In a lost eternity there will be plenty of wood and plenty of fire; but alas, there will be no *Lamb!* But Christ's blood still avails to turn away the wrath and judgment of God. On that terrible night in Egypt there was safety *only* under the blood of the Passover lamb; and today there is safety *only* in the blood of Jesus Christ, God's Son. Neither is there salvation in any other!

Christ's mediatorship is still one of close identification with the sinner. Between the one God and sinful man there still stands the one Mediator, Himself man, and thus identified with each one of us. This thought of perfect identification is fittingly expressed by the Rev. John Cumming, D.D.: "Our sins *on Him* brought Him to an accursed death; but by a beautiful transfer His righteousness *upon us* lifts us to everlasting glory. When Jesus died upon the Cross, there was nothing *in Him* worthy of death; and when I shall be admitted into heaven there will be nothing *in me* worthy of heaven."

Christ is still the Lamb of God! God's satisfaction in Him is as great as it ever was, and the condition of salvation is still the same, "Behold!" This is nothing less than faith, for since salvation is vitally and essentially a gift that God is willing to give to man, it is clear that everything must depend upon man's willingness to receive the gift, that is, upon his faith. The connection between faith and salvation is simply inevitable. It is the resting place of the soul.

Christ Portrayed as the Worshiped Lamb

And when he had taken the book, the four living creatures and the four and twenty elders fell down before the Lamb, having each one a harp, and golden bowls full of incense, which are the prayers of the saints (Rev. 5:8, ASV).

Here the Lamb is presented as the object of universal worship, and one of the basic truths of the book of the Revelation is brought to light, namely, that Jesus Christ, who died upon the Cross of Calvary, now sits upon the throne of the universe. This thought is repeated in varying forms.

The *Worshiped Lamb* is a title of *exaltation*. Christ is in the "midst of the throne," and as John withdraws the curtain and lets the light of the heavenly vision filter down to earth, he shows us that the whole redeemed company in heaven worship, adore and give the highest homage to the Lamb that is enthroned and was slain. As the "Worshiped Lamb," seated upon the throne, Christ is also the recorder of the redeemed. In Revelation 13:8, ASV, we read that names have been "written from the foundation of the world in the Book of Life of the Lamb that hath been slain." Chosen in Christ from before the foundation of the world, the believer's name was *then* written in this Book of Life! And He who wrote it there will never erase it!

The *Enthroned Lamb* is the Lord of *benevolent government.* From Him proceed the Seven Spirits of God into all the earth. "Here the mystic number 'seven,' denoting perfection, is thrice repeated. Strength and intelligence are denoted by the 'horns' and 'eyes,' and the fullness of administration of the Holy Spirit in government in the 'Seven Spirits of God.' All are perfect, and all connected with the government of the earth which is about to be assumed by the Lamb in His redemption character 'as slain.'"

Christ is now the *Lord of History.* The seven-sealed Book is in His hands, and He alone can open it. When He takes over this Book — the "Title Deeds to His Purchased Possession," He becomes the Executor of the Divine Administration. God has a definite purpose for the world; it is written in a Book. It will surely come to pass; God has put it in black and white! God's purposes are perfect. When He opens the seals, Christ will set in motion the successional judgments that, driving the enemy from the field, will put Him in possession of the habitable earth, and Revelation 6 through 19 reveals how all this will be done!

CHRIST PORTRAYED AS THE WEDDED LAMB

And I heard as it were the voice of a great multitude, and as the voice of many waters, and as the voice of mighty thunders, saying, Hallelujah: for the Lord our God, the Almighty, reigneth. Let us rejoice and be exceeding glad, and let us give the glory unto him; for the marriage of the Lamb is come, and his wife hath made herself ready. And it was given unto her that she should array herself in fine linen, bright and pure; for the fine linen is the righteous acts of the saints. And he saith unto me, Write, Blessed are they that are bidden to the marriage supper of the Lamb. And he saith unto me, These are true words of God (Rev. 19:6-9, ASV).

The *Wedded Lamb* is a title of *relationship to the Church.* We believe that the central idea found in the Song of Solomon is the same as that in the Book of the Revelation. Ewald has stated it to our full satisfaction:

On the one hand, a king in all the splendors of his glory, transported with admiration, overflowing with passion; on the other, the poor simple shepherd to whom the Shulamite has plighted her faith; the former present, the latter absent; the maiden called to decide freely between these two rivals. Such is the conflict in all its moral grandeur.

So it is in the Apocalypse: Christ is absent, He is in heaven, and His espoused Bride is here on the earth. He is ever sending her messages (Behold, I come quickly); but the Bride to be, in her long hours of waiting, is constantly solicited and wooed by royal suitors. Purple and gold and precious stones are offered her to withdraw her heart from her Heavenly Lover and to accept a throne with the kings of the earth. But, as in the Song of Solomon the Shulamite is true to her absent lover, so the Church is true to her absent Lover, and her noble answer is, "Many waters cannot quench love, neither can the floods drown it; if a man would give all the substance of his house for love it would utterly be contemned" (Song of Sol. 8:7).

Dr. A. B. Simpson says, "In the story of redemption and the history of heaven, the supreme event for which the ages are waiting, is the marriage of the Lamb. The Bible is one long love story, and redemption a divine romance of the love of God." The consummation of it all is reached in this apocalyptic vision. The last of the obstacles have been removed; the great false church has been destroyed; the counterfeit bride has been put away, and now the true Bride is to receive the crown of glory and her place at the side of her Lord. And all of heaven is waiting with suppressed and intense sympathy, while from the grand organ of the skies the mighty notes already begin to swell the wedding march of glory — Hallelujah! The marriage of the Lamb has come and his wife hath made herself ready!

The Church, the Lamb's Bride, is *not* the subject of Old Testament prophecy. The truth of the Church was "hid in God" (Eph. 3:9); "hid from ages and from generations" (Col. 1:26); not made known "as it is now revealed" (Eph. 3:5). The only idea we get in the Old Testament concerning the Church is from its typical pictures, and then it is always the picture of a bride! Are we near the truth of our text, "the testimony of Jesus is the spirit of prophecy," when we see that right here this "testimony" is pin-pointed in the dramatic scene of the marriage of the Lamb and His Bride? To those of us who seek to trace in the Bible the glories and graces of our Saviour, it is not at all difficult to accept the teaching that the Lamb's wife is the Church, which is His Body. Let us refresh our minds and hearts, and retrace some of the precious paths we have trodden through the Scriptures of Truth in this connection: We mention the following:

Adam's Bride, given to him to be his companion, pictured the eternal relationship between Christ and the Church. "It is not good for man to be alone"! So, "Christ . . . loved the church, and gave himself for it" (Eph. 5:25).

Joseph's Bride, given to him to share his glory, is a picture of Christ and the Church in that coming day "When Christ, who is our life, shall be manifested, then shall ye also with Him be manifested in glory" (Col. 3:4, ASV).

Boaz's Bride, given to him to share his wealth, typifies the Church as "heirs of God, and joint heirs with Christ," the Kinsman-Redeemer (Rom. 8:17).

David's Bride, given to him to reign with him over all Israel and Judah, foreshadows Christ and the Church reigning over the earth during the glorious days of the Millennium (Rev. 5:8-10).

Moses's Bride, given to him to share his rejection by his own brethren, is a type of the Church going "forth therefore unto him without the camp, bearing his reproach" (Heb. 13:13).

Isaac's Bride, was given to him to share his love and affection: "And Isaac . . . took Rebekah, and she became his wife; and he loved her: and Isaac was comforted . . ." (Gen. 24:67).

CHRIST PORTRAYED AS THE WARRIOR LAMB

The "rider of the white horse" in Revelation 19:11-21 is to be distinguished from the white horse rider in Revelation 6:2. Here it is Christ returning to the earth as King of kings and Lord of lords. The great day of the wrath of the Lamb has come! In that day the wicked shall say to the rocks and the mountains, "Fall on us, and hide us from the face of him that sitteth on the throne, and from the wrath of the Lamb: for the great day of their wrath is come; and who is able to stand?" (Rev. 6:16, 17, ASV). In that day there shall be "war against the Lamb, and the Lamb shall overcome them" (Rev. 17:14, ASV).

It is a difficult and unwelcome thought that wrath is a part of the character of our Saviour. But since it is the purpose of the Spirit of God to give us a life size portrait of the victorious and regnant Christ, then the shadows and highlights must be left where the divine Artist has placed them. Wrath has been defined as "the dark lines on the face of God."

How wonderful it is that we can still proclaim to all, far and near, that there is an escape from this wrath to come. Jesus bore the penalty of our sins upon the Cross, and "There is therefore now no condemnation to them which are in Christ Jesus" (Rom. 8:11). Today Jesus speaks to us from the throne of mercy: "Come unto me, all ye that labour and are heavy laden, and I will give you rest" (Matt. 11:28). It may be tomorrow that He will begin speaking from the throne of judgment, saying, "I never knew you: depart from me, ye that work iniquity" (Matt. 7:23).

The Lamb of God is also the Lion of Judah!

24

ISRAEL AND THE END OF HISTORY
Are the Israel Covenants Still Valid?

by ROY L. LAURIN, D.D.

"Israel and the End of History" is a phrase used by a professor at Harvard University in an article which appeared in *Land Reborn,* the official publication of the American Christian Palestine Committee. It is a new and interesting phenomenon to find an educator of our day discussing the end of history, and still more interesting that Israel should be brought into the discussion. It has been quite some time since modern historians were willing to admit that Israel is an important factor in history. Perhaps this has been due to the fact that the interpretation of history in the light of Israel's experience required that credence be given to Israel's prophetic writings.

There has been considerable discussion of the end of history during the past decade. This discussion has been almost universally in the morbid and pessimistic mood, sometimes predicting the end of human life, and even of the earth itself, by atomic destruction. But, as long as Israel exists, there cannot be an end of history. Israel is God's promise of a continuing history, as the rainbow is God's promise of a continuing earth.

Prophecy tells us that history has a divine purpose. Therefore, history is neither accidental, nor incidental, but intentional. History is something more than a narrative of unrelated events. It is a connected story which has a goal. History is going somewhere, and its terminals are predetermined by a sovereign God.

The goal of history is represented in the coincidence of God's two great historical instruments: His chosen nation, and His only begotten Son. These will emerge, at a time which we hope is not far removed from us, in a great moment of divine inter- position, when God will break through in human affairs to accomplish His purpose. This will mark the end of history as man has shaped it, because it will signalize the fulfillment of God's purpose, which is redemption of all His creation. It will mean neither the end of the world, nor the end of the race, because the greatest prophetic utterance in the Bible, Revelation 21 and 22, predicts an ongoing world and an ongoing race of men.

If God has a purpose in history, and He has, we believe that purpose is expressed in the prophetic Scriptures, and so prophecy becomes the expression of God's intention for mankind. For example, one method of expressing this purpose and intent has been the *creative fiat*. The formula of creation was the divine Word. Over and over again Scripture records, "And God said," and by that Word the universe came into being. According to this example, the entire program of God's relationship with man is expressed in the five methods God used to make His purpose and will known. These are: the divine fiat, divine decrees, divine commandments, divine promises, and divine covenants. The pur- pose of this address is related to the last of the five — divine covenants.

The history of Israel is a history of covenants. These covenants are God-made blueprints, given in successive stages, to set forth His long-range intentions. They are presently in force, although some are in abeyance, awaiting fulfillment at a time we call the end of history.

The Definition of a Covenant

The outlines of prophecy can be traced in the covenants ac- cording to which God has chosen to deal with His people Israel in the various dispensations. The covenant itself is the oldest form of contractual agreement between two parties. As the basis of carrying out His purpose and intent, covenants were usually accompanied by signs and pledges of performance on God's part, requirements of conformity to their provisions on man's part, and clauses stating the sanctions or penalties to be imposed in the event of breach of contract by man. Since God was in every case the grantor, or party of the first part, consent by parties of the second part often became a matter of long delayed action.

The story of the covenants is a thread woven into the fabric of the Scriptures. It began with Adam, continued with Noah, Abraham, Moses, David, and found its conclusion in the New Covenant of which Jesus Christ is the mediator.

Israel's history was dominated by the covenant idea. Their sacred literature speaks of the Book of the Covenant, the code of laws given through Moses (Ex. 24:7); the Tables of the Covenant, referring to the Ten Commandments (Deut. 9:11); the Blood of the Covenant, referring to atonement (Ex. 24:8); the Ark of the Covenant (Num. 10:33); the Mediator of the Covenant, referring to Jesus Christ (Heb. 9:15).

THE COVENANTS THEMSELVES

There are four major covenants affecting Israel:

1. *The Covenant with Abraham* (Gen. 12:1-22:18). This was an unconditional covenant which rested solely in the intention and integrity of Jehovah. The Abrahamic covenant guaranteed three things to Israel: a Seed (Gen. 12); a Sphere (Gen. 13); a Son (Gen. 15).

2. *The Covenant with Moses* (Ex. 20:1-31:18). This was a conditional covenant, the benefits of which depended upon keeping the Mosaic law (Ex. 19:5, 6). It promised national blessing and prosperity, and set forth laws of life to govern relationship to Jehovah. Needless to say, this covenant has been broken, and national apostasies have resulted in the captivities and the scattering of the nation throughout the world.

3. *The Covenant with David* (II Sam. 7:11-16). This was an unconditional, perpetual, everlasting covenant. It also guaranteed three things to Israel: a king (II Sam. 7:12); a throne (II Sam. 7:16); a kingdom (Luke 1:31-33).

4. *The New Covenant* (Jer. 31:31-34). This was unconditional in that it was not predicated upon man's ability to perform it (Rom. 4:1-5). Its guarantees were three: a New Man through regeneration (II Cor. 5:17); a New Body through resur-

rection (I Cor. 15:20-22); a New World through renovation (II Pet. 3:1-13).

THE PROVISIONS OF THE COVENANTS

There are five irrevocable provisions in the covenants given to Israel, and through Israel to the world. These provisions constitute prophecy's great expectations.

1. *A Nation Forever* (Gen. 17:7, 8; Jer. 31:35-37). As long as national identities exist, Israel will continue to be a nation. Israel's national origin is unique. The Gentile nations came into being out of the clashing linguistic problems at Babel. Israel was conceived in a man's faith and nurtured and preserved by the decrees of a sovereign God.

2. *A Land Forever* (Gen. 15:18). The title-deed to this land was granted by Jehovah, and it is irrevocable. It is one of the most significant land-grants of all time; it guarantees Israel an abode from which the nation cannot be permanently dispossessed. Although Israel has been scattered for centuries, the people's return to their land is one of the miracles of contemporary history.

This land has furnished the stage for the enactment of the great drama of redemption. Over this land-bridge between the continents has flowed the commerce of the nations, and its strategic location has furnished an unparalleled sounding board for communicating the Gospel to the world. None but God could have chosen so wisely.

3. *A King Forever* (II Sam. 7:16). In the dynastic successions of the divided kingdom after the death of Solomon, the Davidic line remained intact. Providentially the royal line of succession was perpetuated in Judah. There is not even a shadow of suggestion that our Lord's descent from David was ever questioned.

4. *A Throne Forever* (II Sam. 7:16; Ps. 89:34-37). Although Israel has for millenniums passed through successive captivities and scatterings, this covenant remains in force. It was renewed in the message of Annunciation when the angel said to Mary, "He [Jesus] shall be great and shall be called the Son of the Highest: and the Lord God shall give unto him the throne of his father David: and he shall reign over the house of Jacob

forever; and of his kingdom there shall be no end" (Luke 1: 32, 33).

5. *A Kingdom Forever* (II Sam. 7:16). This kingdom will be established on earth by the returning Christ. It will be the kingdom restored again to Israel (Acts 1:6), upon the land God promised to their fathers. As a pilot-kingdom it will demonstrate the glories and blessings of the new heavens and the new earth.

THE VALIDITY OF THE COVENANTS

The covenants, which are at the foundation of all prophecy, possess a validity which is irrevocable and unchangeable. They cannot be set aside either by human defections or historical changes because they constitute the purposes of a sovereign God. For instance, the covenants of God are valid so long as redemption is in process, and God's redemption will not be accomplished until there are three new things: namely, a new man, a new body, and a new earth. The new man is now a reality in the Christian, but the new body and the new earth are still a part of the blessed hope. Their fulfillment waits for the coming again of Christ, the resurrection of the Just, and the reconciliation of Israel.

The immutability of the Abrahamic covenant rests in the unchangeableness of God. When this covenant was given to Abraham, it was ratified by a formality which consisted of the cutting asunder of a sacrificial animal. In ordinary covenants between man and man, both of the contracting parties would pass between the sundered pieces, the act being equal to an oath. But in this case God alone passed between the parts of the divided sacrifice, thus indicating that the covenant was established by Him and its performance guaranteed by His integrity (cf. Gen. 15:5-16).

Jeremiah's promise of a nation forever is another example of the irrevocable nature of the covenants. "Thus saith the Lord, which giveth the sun for a light by day, and the ordinances of the moon and of the stars for a light by night, which divideth the sea when the waves thereof roar; The Lord of hosts is his name: If those ordinances depart from before me, saith the Lord, then the seed of Israel also shall cease from being a nation before me for ever. Thus saith the Lord; If heaven above can be measured, and the foundations of the earth searched out beneath, I will also cast off all the seed of Israel for all that they have done, saith the Lord" (Jer. 31:35-37). The physical universe would cease to be if God did not keep His covenant with Israel.

The covenants, promising the restoration of Israel to her land; the placement of a king upon David's throne; the establishment of an earthly kingdom of peace, prosperity, and righteousness; are in every instance irrevocable, unchangeable, and without repentance (Rom. 11:29; Jer. 31:35-37; 32:40; 33:20,21).

We live in days of great importance. They are important to the world; they are also important to us; for the knowledge of these truths puts upon each of us a binding moral compulsion: "Seeing then that all these things shall be dissolved, what manner of persons ought ye to be in all holy conversation [manner of life] and godliness" (II Pet. 3:11).

25

THE DOCTRINE OF THE LORD'S RETURN IN THE SCRIPTURES

by WILLIAM F. KERR, TH.D. *

The importance of the doctrine of the Lord's return in the Scriptures cannot be overemphasized, for we are told that one out of every twenty-six verses in the New Testament is devoted to this subject. Since this subject has been woven into the very warp and woof of Scripture by the Holy Spirit, its importance for the Christian believer becomes rather obvious. The Christian who loves the Word of God must of necessity love the Lord's appearing.

But even apart from this very fundamental consideration the Christian believer of our day cannot but be aware of the fact that he is living in an eschatological age, in which the thinking of all men — statesmen, historians, scientists, educators, theologians — is agitated by the possibility of the rapid consummation of history. What form this consummation will take, men of the secular world are not prepared to say. Some think it may prove cataclysmic through the uncontrolled use of atomic and hydrogen bombs. It certainly cannot result from the utopian dreams of a decadent liberalism, others affirm. However, the thought of awful possibilities fills men's hearts with fear and they are thinking as never before in terms of the last times.

Conditions of modern life have made the doctrine of the Lord's return relevant for our times, and every preacher of the Gospel, as well as every lay member of the Church, if they are properly oriented in the Word of God, are circumstantially placed under the high moral obligation to declare the truth of the Lord's impending return. To do less is to shirk a sacred duty in a time of crisis.

Let us then turn to the Word of God and look at the doctrine of the Lord's return from four vantage points:

I. THE PRINCIPLE OF ITS INTERPRETATION

Any approach to the Scriptures must be governed by some principle of interpretation. And there are a number of principles of interpretation from which to choose. For instance, the adherents of the postmillennial and amillennial eschatological systems rely mostly upon what we term the *spiritual* principle of interpretation, and its use is quite frequently called spiritualization. In contrast, the principle of interpretation utilized by the premillennial system is that which is termed *literal*, which, from the practical standpoint, means taking the Bible at face value.

It is by this latter principle of interpretation that we shall be guided in our study of the doctrine of the Lord's return in the Scriptures. We believe this to be the Golden Rule of interpretation, that one should always interpret Scripture literally unless the context demands that it be treated otherwise. Writing about the interpretation of prophecy, Dr. Bernard Ramm, in his *The Protestant Biblical Interpretation*, page 172, states: "Therefore, interpret prophecy literally, unless the evidence is such that a spiritual interpretation is mandatory." Then Dr. Ramm further quotes from Craven in *Lange's Commentary on Revelation*, page 98, to this effect: "The literalist . . . is not one who denies that figurative language, that symbols are used in prophecy, nor does he deny that great spiritual truths are set forth therein; his position is, simply, that the prophecies are to be normally interpreted (i.e., according to the received laws of language) as any other utterances are interpreted — that which is manifestly literal being regarded as literal, and that which is manifestly figurative being so regarded." It can be seen from the above quotations that the literal method is a necessary and vitally important one in interpreting Scripture.

In addition another dictum of significance is that of Augustine, who said, in effect, that the Old Testament was in the New Testament revealed, and that the New Testament was in the

Old Testament concealed. And this dictum, most assuredly, applies to the doctrine of the Lord's return. Many facets of it can be seen from the standpoint of the New Testament. For instance, the concept of the twofoldness of the coming of the Messiah is clearly made manifest through the New Testament. The two strands of prophecy concerning the coming of the Messiah — His coming to suffer, and His coming in power and glory — are made clear through the New Testament (cf. I Pet. 1:10, 11). And conversely, there are facets of the prophetic teaching of the New Testament upon which added light is shed by the Old Testament. For instance, the teaching of Christ concerning the Kingdom of God can only be fully understood in the light of the Old Testament presentation of the Messianic Kingdom.

Because of this interdependence and interrelationship between the two Testaments, we might characterize the teaching of both as follows:

a. In the Old Testament there is *Prediction* that the Messiah will come.

b. In the Gospels there is *Revelation*. Here the Messiah is revealed as having come, and at the same time there is given the revelation of His Second Coming.

c. In the Epistles there is *Interpretation*. In the letters of the New Testament the Second Coming of Christ is interpreted by the Spirit of God as having two main phases: the Rapture of the Church, and the return of Christ to set up His earthly Kingdom.

d. In the Book of Revelation there is *Consummation*. The two main phases of the Second Coming of Christ are set forth in detailed fulfillment.

Turning from this analysis, we note in the second place:

II. THE PROGRESSIVENESS OF ITS REVELATION

In the early sections of the Word of God, the return of the Lord is not clearly defined. In Genesis 3:15 we read:

> And I will put enmity between thee and the woman, and between thy seed and her seed; it shall bruise thy head, and thou shalt bruise his heel.

Here a brief gleam of the coming of a Messiah is given, but nothing is clearly delineated. Not even a definition of the

nature of His coming is given. The same is quite characteristic
of Genesis 12:1-3:

> Now the Lord had said unto Abram, Get thee out of thy
> country, and from thy kindred, and from thy father's house, unto
> a land that I will show thee: And I will make of thee a great
> nation, and I will bless thee, and make thy name great; and thou
> shalt be a blessing: And I will bless them that bless thee, and
> curse him that curseth thee: and in thee shall all families of the
> earth be blessed.

But as the revelation of the coming Messiah progresses, we see
it developing into a twofold concept. In the Prophets two seemingly conflicting lines of prediction are noted. In Jeremiah 23:
5,6 we have the coming of a glorious, majestic King prophesied:

> Behold, the days come, saith the Lord, that I will raise unto
> David a righteous Branch, and a King shall reign and prosper, and
> shall execute judgment and justice in the earth. In his days Judah
> shall be saved, and Israel shall dwell safely: and this is his name
> whereby he shall be called, THE LORD OUR RIGHTEOUSNESS.

But in Isaiah 53:4,5 the picture of a lowly, suffering Servant
is presented:

> Surely he hath borne our griefs, and carried our sorrows: yet
> we did esteem him stricken, smitten of God, and afflicted. But
> he was wounded for our transgressions, he was bruised for our
> iniquities: the chastisement of our peace was upon him; and with
> his stripes we are healed.

Such paradoxical prediction confused the prophets themselves,
so that the apostle Peter could express their dismay and un-
certainty when he wrote the following words in I Peter 1:11 —

> Searching what, or what manner of time the Spirit of Christ
> which was in them did signify, when it testified beforehand the
> sufferings of Christ, and the glory that should follow.

However, the paradox so concisely expressed by Peter was for
him and also for us resolved through Christ's first advent. For
it then became evident by a more detailed delineation in the
Gospels that the coming of the Messiah actually had two important phases. The Incarnation of God in Christ was the first
phase, or first advent, which culminated in His suffering on
the Cross, as is declared in Luke 24:20, 21, 25-27:

> And how the chief priests and our rulers delivered him to be condemned to death, and have crucified him. But we trusted that it had been he which should have redeemed Israel. . . . Then said he unto them, O fools and slow of heart to believe all that the prophets have spoken: Ought not Christ to have suffered these things, and to enter into his glory? And beginning at Moses and all the prophets, he expounded unto them in all the scriptures the things concerning himself.

So Christ reveals what the meaning of the Old Testament prophecies concerning His suffering is, and also predicts the fulfillment of yet unfulfilled Old Testament prophecies by declaring that He is to come again in power and majestic glory. Notice His prophecy in Matthew 24:30:

> And then shall appear the sign of the Son of man in heaven: and then shall all the tribes of the earth mourn, and they shall see the Son of man coming in the clouds of heaven with power and great glory.

The Gospels, therefore, give us the key to the doctrine of the Lord's return in the Old Testament. They open up to view the real meaning of such predictions as found in Genesis 3:15, for they insist that forgiveness of man's sins depends upon faith in the Crucified Messiah. At the same time they affirm that the Jews, having rejected Christ as Messiah, must now look to His Second Coming as the time when the prophecies relating to an earthly kingdom shall be fulfilled. Two strands of prophecy found intertwined in the Old Testament now give their clear and distinct meanings under the light of Gospel revelation.

Following hard upon the teaching given in the Gospels, come now the predictions contained in the Book of Acts. At the Ascension of Christ, we have this prophecy recorded in Acts 1:11—

> Ye men of Galilee, why stand ye gazing up into heaven? This same Jesus, which is taken up from you into heaven, shall so come in like manner as ye have seen him go into heaven.

This verse asserts that Christ will return personally and visibly, and that it will be "this same Jesus." The Acts of the Apostles dogmatically denies that the second coming of Christ can be spiritualized. He must come personally and visibly.

When we come to the Epistles of the New Testament, a

striking similarity to the situation in Old Testament prophecy begins to make itself known. For, if there were two strands of prophecy in the Old Testament relating to Christ's first coming, we find here two events associated with His Second Coming. In I Thessalonians 4:16, 17 we read that He is to come *for* His saints:

> For the Lord himself shall descend from heaven with a shout, with the voice of the archangel, and with the trump of God: and the dead in Christ shall rise first: Then we which are alive and remain shall be caught up together with them in the clouds, to meet the Lord in the air: and so shall we ever be with the Lord.

But in Jude 14 there comes that rather interesting declaration that when Christ comes back again, His saints shall come with Him: "And Enoch also, the seventh from Adam, prophesied of these, saying, Behold, the Lord cometh *with* ten thousands of his saints." And with this declaration compare Zechariah 14:5: "And ye shall flee to the valley of the mountains; for the valley of the mountains shall reach unto Azal: yea, ye shall flee, like as ye fled from before the earthquake in the days of Uzziah king of Judah: and the Lord my God shall come, and all the saints with thee."

The two aspects seem to be confusing, and not a few have found it hard to understand these two seemingly paradoxical statements of Scripture. However, a careful perusal of the Scriptural teaching on the Lord's return shows them to be two aspects of the one Second Coming. At the beginning of the period of the Tribulation, Christ shall come *for* His saints; after the Tribulation is over and the kingdom on earth is to be set up, Christ will come *with* His saints. The seeming contradiction thus becomes clear and a unity of prediction in both Testaments is established.

As we come to the final book of the Bible and note the climactic chapter in the progressive revelation of the Lord's return, we see set out before us the program of the consummation which our Lord's return will bring about. We therefore turn now to:

III. THE PROGRAM OF ITS CONSUMMATION

The program of the Lord's return, detailed against its Old and New Testament background, may be briefly stated in the following ways:

It is *imminent* as to the time of His return. No one knows the day nor the hour. It may occur at any moment. All prophetic details relating to the first aspect of His coming have been fulfilled, and so we live in constant expectancy that He may appear at any time. When He comes, we know it will be *Rapture* for the Church. Paul tells us so in I Thessalonians 4:16, 17.

Following this event, according to II Thessalonians 2:7, 8, the *revelation* of the Antichrist will take place:

> For the mystery of iniquity doth already work: only he who now letteth will let, until he be taken out of the way. And then shall that Wicked be revealed, whom the Lord shall consume with the spirit of his mouth, and shall destroy with the brightness of his coming.

In conjunction with this there will be the outpouring of the wrath of God, and Antichrist also will have great wrath, so that *Tribulation* for Israel and for the world will result. This is predicted in Matthew 24:15, 21 and in Revelation 6:17—

> When ye therefore shall see the abomination of desolation, spoken of by Daniel the prophet, stand in the holy place. . . . For then shall be great tribulation, such as was not since the beginning of the world to this time, no, nor ever shall be. . . . For the great day of his wrath is come; and who shall be able to stand?

The end of the period of Tribulation will see the return of Christ in power and great glory to set up His Kingdom. Thus His Second Coming will be *premillennial*. Revelation 20:4, 5 reads:

> And I saw thrones, and they sat upon them, and judgment was given unto them: and I saw the souls of them that were beheaded for the witness of Jesus, and for the word of God, and which had not worshipped the beast, neither his image, neither had received his mark upon their foreheads, or in their hands; and they lived and reigned with Christ a thousand years. But the rest of the dead lived not again until the thousand years were finished.

After the thousand years a scene of judgment is painted in Revelation 20:12-15. History has been consummated. The Lord has gloriously returned and His kingdom has been established for a thousand years. The time for the judgment of the wicked has arrived and their eternal doom is to be settled:

> And I saw the dead, small and great, stand before God; and the books were opened: and another book was opened, which is the book of life: and the dead were judged out of those things which were written in the books, according to their works. . . . And whosoever was not found written in the book of life was cast into the lake of fire.

The doctrine of the Lord's return with its program of consummation at the last days of history is a blessed hope. It imbues us with confidence that God is the Lord of history and that He will bring it to a successful conclusion by His glorious victory over all evil.

This is the doctrine we preach, and we believe that it has practical values for Christian living. Let us, as we close, summarize some of these values.

IV. THE PRACTICALITY OF ITS TEACHING

Here are some of the ways in which the truth of the Lord's return influences by practical application the lives of men:

1. It is a *rebuke* to the scoffer.

In the days of the Early Church many men scoffed at the promises concerning our Lord's blessed return. To them life seemed to grind out nothing but a hum-drum existence, and eventually the promise of His return came to be viewed with scorn and abject unconcern. Peter saw, felt this, and wrote about its recurrence in II Peter 3:3, 4 —

> Knowing this first, that there shall come in the last days scoffers, walking after their own lusts, and saying, Where is the promise of his coming? for since the fathers fell asleep, all things continue as they were from the beginning of the creation.

But Peter rebukes such scoffers by asserting the long-suffering of God and His faithfulness to His promises (vv. 8, 9):

> But, beloved, be not ignorant of this one thing, that one day is with the Lord as a thousand years, and a thousand years as one

day. The Lord is not slack concerning his promises, as some men count slackness.

2. It is a *warning* to the unsaved.

Any who are living in wickedness, ungodliness, and unbelief, should heed the warning of Jude. For the return of our Lord will bring judgment from which there is no escape. This warning is found in Jude 14, 15:

> Behold, the Lord cometh with ten thousands of his saints to execute judgment upon all, and to convince all that are ungodly among them of all their ungodly deeds which they have ungodly committed, and of all their hard speeches which ungodly sinners have spoken against him.

3. It is a *comfort* to the saints.

When death has snatched away a loved one and the pangs of sorrow have engulfed our hearts, we look with blessed confidence to the certain comfort that when He returns we will see our loved ones again and be with them eternally. Paul, in writing to the Thessalonians, who had suffered much in the terrible persecutions of that day and the death of many loved ones, voiced the hope of the Second Coming of Christ as a blessed confidence, and concluded his words of comfort with this exhortation in I Thessalonians 4:18 – "Wherefore comfort one another with these words."

4. It is a *motivation* toward holy living.

The Early Church lived in the very center of an eschatological day. The soon return of Christ, with all its impending judgments, made an impact upon their lives. They knew they were eking out a temporal existence, but they had eternity in their hearts, and the reality of this was made all the more significant for them in the light of the Lord's return. He might come within their time, and it was imperative that their lives should be found pleasing to Him. The exhortation of John, the beloved apostle, was taken seriously by them, when he wrote in I John 3:3 – "And every man that hath this hope in him purifieth himself, even as he is pure."

This important truth, so inextricably intertwined in the pages of God's Book, should be heartily believed, passionately preached, confidently taught, and diligently practiced in our lives.

26

ARNOLD TOYNBEE AND THE JEWS

by FRANK E. GAEBELEIN, LITT.D.

Arnold Toynbee is unquestionably one of the major figures in the intellectual life of our time. The leading historian of the day, he has recently completed his gigantic work entitled *A Study of History*. It is doubtful whether any other historian, not even Gibbon excepted, has ever approached the dimensions of this achievement. In sheer scope it is staggering. Toynbee identifies, surveys, compares and analyzes twenty-six civilizations that have arisen since the dawn of history, and seeks to understand their origin, growth and decay. With awe-inspiring learning, such as few, if any, other living scholars possess, he ranges over the whole history of mankind in practically all the nations of the earth — from the Eskimos in the north to the Polynesians in the south. All this, and much more, is put down in ten massive volumes, totalling 6,289 pages of closely knit argument and exposition.

Toynbee writes with endless embellishment, and is partial to obscure polysyllabic adjectives. Witness the following sentence: "However, the most popular of the racial theories of civilization is that which sets upon a pedestal the xanthotrichous, glaucopian, dolichocephalic variety of *homo leucodermaticus,* called by some the Nordic man and by Nietzsche 'the blond beast'; and it is worth while inquiring into the credentials of this idol of the Teutonic market-place." At this point, his editor, D. C. Somervell, comments in a footnote: "'Is't not possible to understand in another tongue?' asks Horatio. It is: to wit, 'yellow-haired, grey-eyed, long-headed variety of white-skinned man.'"[1] It is

[1]*A Study of History,* Abridgment of Volumes I-VI by D. C. Somervell, 1947, p. 52.

only fair to say that at other times Toynbee writes beautifully and with moving power.

This tremendous work is, of course, thoroughly indexed. Moreover, there is D. C. Somervell's one-volume abridgment of Toynbee's first six volumes, this in itself being a volume of some six hundred closely printed pages. But there is as yet no abridgment of the last four volumes. It would hardly be just to a writer of Toynbee's stature simply to look up references in an index and to draw conclusions from passages taken out of context. The only valid procedure is to make some honest attempt to see what he says about a particular subject in relation to his general system of thought. This I shall hope to do in the time before us.

I

But before I come to this part of my discussion, let me pause to answer a few questions, especially those which came immediately to mind when I was asked to speak on this subject: "Why take time to talk about Arnold Toynbee and the Jews?" "What is the relevance of such a topic to a conference like this?"

Already these questions have been answered in part. Toynbee is one of the key thinkers of our age. As such, his work is bound to have an effect upon many minds. And when he deals with a subject of such Biblical and current interest as the Jews, we should know what he says. A good many years ago the late Dr. Samuel M. Zwemer, the distinguished missionary to the Moslems, while speaking in the school chapel at Stony Brook, pointed out that the great currents of world events can be classified under these four heads: Nationalism, Communism, Mohammedanism and Judaism. The analysis is an acute one, and today the last of the four (Judaism) is close to the center of contemporary history.

Again, a discussion of Toynbee's thought belongs on the program of a conference like this, because he is to a considerable extent a religious writer and thus a religious thinker. Certainly he is more than an historian, recording events of the past with cold objectivity. Actually he is a philosopher of history, seeking to know why things happened and how they happened, searching to discern, as it were, the pattern behind the enormously com-

plex loom of human events and even to find out its relationship
to God.

It is hardly possible for any thoughtful person to read even
fifty pages of *A Study of History* without realizing that Toynbee
is a scholar whose roots go very deeply in two directions: first,
into the Bible; and secondly, into the classics, particularly those
of Greece. Of the two, it is Toynbee's Biblical background that
concerns us most. For one thing, it is a major influence upon
his style. Over and over, he draws upon Scripture for his figures
of speech; many times, and often with great power, he quotes
the Bible, especially the New Testament. In his tenth volume,
he pays this tribute to the Bible: "The Authorized Version of
the Bible, made in the reign of King James I, gives me . . .
an intimation of the divine presence in forming our fragment
of a mysterious universe. The effect of a diction that is archaic
yet at the same time familiar is more like that of music than
like that of ordinary speech. It pierces through the Intellect and
plays directly upon the Heart." [2]

Especially in his final volume, Toynbee speaks in religious
terms. It is here that he defines history as "a vision dim and
partial, yet . . . true to reality as far as it went of God revealing
Himself in action to souls that were sincerely seeking Him." [3]
And it is here also that he says that he is an historian, because
he has found his vocation in a call from God to "feel after Him
and find Him." [4]

Elsewhere (at the end of Volume VI), after passing in review
the various would-be saviour-gods, as he calls them, who sought
to deliver man, he comes to Christ and, after quoting John 3:16,
writes this: "When the Gospel thus answers . . . it delivers
an oracle. The one remains, the many change and pass. And
this is in truth the final result of our survey of saviours. When
we set out on this quest we found ourselves moving in the
midst of a mighty host, but, as we have pressed forward, the
marchers, company by company, have fallen out of the race. . . .
At the final ordeal of death, few, even of these would-be saviour

[2] *A Study of History,* Volume X, p. 235.
[3] *Ibid.,* Vol. X, p. 1.
[4] *Ibid.,* Vol. X, p. 1.

gods, have dared to put their title to the test by plunging into the icy river. And now, as we stand and gaze with our eyes fixed upon the farther shore, a single figure rises from the flood and straightway fills the whole horizon. There is the Saviour; 'and the pleasure of the Lord shall prosper in his hand; he shall see of the travail of his soul and shall be satisfied.'" [5]

II

It is this very matter of Biblical allusion, however, that is misleading in Toynbee. When it comes to confession of the historical, supernatural Christianity of the Bible, the great doctrines of God and Christ, of sin and redemption, that rest not upon religious myth, but upon the fact of what God actually did in history through His chosen people down through the ages, and especially in Jesus Christ — the things that we may call the grand particularities of faith — it is clear that Toynbee himself does not claim to be a Christian. In plain fact, his outlook upon Christianity, as upon other religions, is thoroughly naturalistic, though also strongly mystical. Let us follow this clue further, because it forms the frame or context of what he has to say about the Jews.

In the first six volumes of his work, the last of which was published in 1939, Toynbee identifies twenty-six civilizations in history, including five arrested civilizations. Of these twenty-six, he says, sixteen are dead; the ten that remain include two "in their last agonies," and seven others "are all, in different degrees, under the threat of annihilation or assimilation by the eighth, namely our own civilization of the West." [6] It is in these volumes that he formulates his famous explanation of the genesis, growth, breakdown and disintegration of civilizations. Here we meet the terms that he has added to the vocabulary of modern historical thought, such as "challenge and response," "time of troubles," "withdrawal and return," "creative minorities," and especially of interest to us in this message, "fossil civilization," under which head he includes the Jews.

To put it simply, it is Toynbee's theory that the civilized societies arose from the challenge of difficulties, such as an un-

[5] *A Study of History,* Abridgment of Volumes I-VI by D. C. Somervell, p. 547.
[6] *Ibid.,* p. 244.

favorable physical environment, or from blows from some enemy. For example, he points out that the New England colonists, who landed on a bleak, rocky coast, achieved more than those who landed in the more hospitable Southern climate. The environment acted as a stimulating challenge to which they responded. So also with the remarkable record of Holland, a good part of which was wrested with great difficulty from the sea. In amazing detail he ranges over the world and shuttles back and forth in time to support his thesis. As for the breakdown of a civilization, he has a particular theory related to the "times of troubles" that come upon civilizations. Such "times of troubles," which are set forth, again with a vast amount of illustrative data, tend toward the formation of a universal state, the universal state being the next step to the disintegration of a civilization.

Now the impression given by the first six volumes, despite their constant references to religion, is that of Toynbee's thorough-going naturalism. Though in his latter volumes he speaks in even more religious and specifically Christian terms, he nevertheless continues to refer over and over again to the historical events of both Testaments as "myths" or "legends" on a par with the mythology of Egypt, Babylonia, Syria, Media, Greece, or China. Not only that, but his explanation of the growth of religion as the result of the forces of challenge and reponse and withdrawal and return is in itself essentially naturalistic.

Consider this quotation: "But if we turn our attention again to the doctrine of the Second Coming in its classic Christian exposition, we shall see that it is really a *mythological* [italics supplied] projection into the future, in physical imagery, of the spiritual return in which the Apostles' vanquished Master reasserted His presence in the Apostles' hearts, when the Apostles took heart of grace to execute, in spite of the Master's physical departure, that audacious mission which the Master had once laid upon them. This creative revival of the Apostles' courage and faith, after a moment of disillusionment and despair, is described in the Acts — again in *mythological* [italics supplied] language — in the image of the descent of the Holy Ghost on the Day of Pentecost."[7] Similar to this relegating of the Second

Coming to the realm of myth is his characterization of Paul's great resurrection chapter (I Cor. 15) as "human speculation on death and immortality." [8]

Along with this insistent naturalism, there is in Toynbee a pervasive syncretism. He simply cannot see the exclusiveness of Christianity. For him, it is just not true, as Peter said of the Lord Jesus Christ before the priests and rulers in Jerusalem, that "there is none other Name under heaven given among men whereby we must be saved." As he said in a recent lecture at Union Theological Seminary, Christianity must be purged of its self-centeredness and the egotistical idea that it has an exclusive revelation from God. And in his seventh volume, in speaking of the four higher religions (Christianity, Judaism, Mohammedanism, and Buddhism), he quotes Paul's figure, "one star differeth from another star in glory," and asks, "and does the last word lie with a living God or with a brooding Brahma?"[9]

This syncretism, or confusion of religions, and this denial of the very heart of Christianity, comes out dramatically in the strange prayer with which this great scholar concludes the more than 6,000 pages of his *Study of History*. It reads in part as follows: "Christ Tammuz, Christ Adonis, Christ Osiris, Christ Balder, hear us, by whatsoever name we bless thee, for suffering death for our salvation . . . Buddha Gautama, show us the path that will lead us out of our afflictions . . . Mother Mary, Mother Isis, Mother Cybele, Mother Ishtar, Mother Kwanyin, have compassion on us. . . ." Then he invokes Lucretius and Zarathustra and "tender-hearted Muhommad" and "Blessed Francis Xavier and Blessed John Wesley." Whereupon he calls upon Zeno, the Stoic philosopher, to "help us to find God by playing the man" and Socrates to "show us, like Stephen, how to suffer death in perfect charity towards those that despitefully use us." And he closes with this ascription — "Blessed Francis, who for Christ's sake didst renounce the pride of life, help us to follow Christ by following thee . . . to Him return ye everyone." [10]

[7] *Ibid.*, p. 224.
[8] *Ibid.*, p. 221.
[9] *A Study of History*, Volume VII, p. 735.
[10] *A Study of History*, Volume X, pp. 143, 144.

III

So much for Toynbee and his thought. Now let us look in some detail at what he has to say about the Jews. The many references to the Jews throughout his ten volumes may be summed up under four main heads: Their origin and history; their present status in the context of civilized societies; their relation to Zionism; and their future. In considering these four, we shall let Toynbee himself speak as much as possible by direct quotation.

First, the origin and history of the chosen people. It is obvious that Toynbee does not, to put it mildly, care for the idea of Israel's being God's chosen people. In his first volume, he says: "The Jews suffered from the illusion that they were not *a* but *the* chosen people." [11] And in Volume VIII he speaks of "that fanatical Judaic hallucination of being 'a chosen people.'" [12]

Now it is interesting to see how Toynbee accounts for the chosen people idea. Among the many important insights in *A Study of History* is the clear diagnosis of man's persistent and sinful tendency to idolize himself to the extent of setting self in the place of God. Taking this very useful insight, Toynbee proceeds to read it into the history of the Jews. "The most notorious historical example of this idolization of an ephemeral self," he says, "is the error of the Jews which is exposed in the New Testament. In a period of their history which began in the infancy of the Syriac civilization and which culminated in the Age of the Prophets, the people of Israel and Judah raised themselves head and shoulders above the Syriac peoples round about by rising to a monotheistic conception of religion. [Observe the author's naturalism!] Keenly conscious and rightly proud of their spiritual treasure," he continues, "they allowed themselves to be betrayed into an idolization of this notable but transitory stage in their spiritual growth. They had indeed been gifted with unparalleled spiritual insight; but after having divined a truth which was absolute and eternal, they allowed themselves to be captivated by a relative and temporary half-truth. They persuaded themselves that Israel's discovery of

[11] *A Study of History*, Abridgment of Volumes I-VI by D. C. Somervell.
[12] *A Study of History*, Volume VIII, p. 729.

the One True God [Note: their *own* discovery] had revealed
Israel itself to be God's Chosen People; and this half-truth
inveigled them into the fatal error of looking upon a momentary
spiritual eminence, which they had attained by labor and travail,
as a privilege conferred upon them by God in an everlasting
covenant." [13] All this, of course, is nothing less than a naturalistic
inversion of what Scripture actually says about monotheism and
the Jew.

Regarding the origin of Jewish religion, Toynbee says: "Judaism was born from a primitive religion of one of the parochial
communities into which the Syriac society had come to be
articulated. This occurred in the eighth century, B.C." [14] Furthermore, their history is for him in good part mythical. For example,
he talks about the "myth of the Exodus from Egypt," and refers
to "the Syriac myth of Moses' solitary ascent of Mt. Sinai." [15]
Again, he calls "a Syriac fable" that tremendous scene when God
said to Solomon at the beginning of his reign, "Ask what I
shall give thee." [16] For him, when Israel "took over" Jehovah,
he was just the tribal god of some volcano. [17] As for the later
stages of Israelitish history that he accepts as factual, he explains
them on the naturalistic grounds of challenge and response,
withdrawal and return, etc.

We come next to Toynbee and the present status of the Jews.
Here he has coined a term especially for them and a few smaller
civilizations, such as certain remnants of Monophysite and Nes-
torian Christianity, and the Parsee remnant of Zoroastrianism.
This term is "fossil." [18] By this not very flattering word Toynbee
means a society that should have died but by some means has
continued to preserve its identity. So he uses it of the Jews in
their present dispersed state. As he explains it, they did not
go ahead with a world-wide mission after the break-up of Babylon, but converted themselves into a "social cement" possessing

[13] *A Study of History*, Abridgment of Volumes I - VI by D. C. Somervell,
p. 310.
[14] *A Study of History*, Volume V, p. 119.
[15] *A Study of History*, Abridgment of Volumes I - VI by D. C. Somervell,
p. 217.
[16] *Ibid.*, p. 94.
[17] *Ibid.*, pp. 501, 502.
[18] *Ibid.*, pp. 135 ff.

the astonishing property of being able to hold together a fossilized community in dispersion. And what made them a fossil civilizaiton was their "backward" spiritual rather than material conception of the Messianic kingdom.

This labelling of the Jews as a social fossil has, of course, aroused a great deal of resentment. For example, a review of *A Study of History* in "Jewish Bookland" by Louis Newman accuses Toynbee of writing as a biased Christian theologian, not an objective historian, and bitterly charges him with adding fuel to the fires of anti-Semitism. Revealing also is the symposium in *Jewish Frontier* (Dec. 1954 - Feb. 1955), entitled "Arnold Toynbee and the Jews" by Marie Syrkin, W. F. Albright, Abba S. Eban, Horace Kallen, Mordecai M. Kaplan, Reinhold Niebuhr, and Arnold Toynbee.[19]

In the third place, we consider what Toynbee says about Zionism. Here again his ideas are resented by much of Judaism. At the beginning of his work (Volume II) his evaluation of Zionism is fairly moderate, as in this quotation: "Though the Zionist movement as a practical undertaking is only half a century old, its social philosophy has already been justified by results. In the Jewish agricultural settlements in Palestine the children of the ghetto have been transformed out of all recognition into a pioneering peasantry which displays many of the characteristics of the Gentile colonial type. The tragic misfortune of the experiment is its failure to conciliate the pre-existent Arab population of the country."[20]

But in his later volumes Toynbee modifies this estimate. Writing mostly before the inception of the state of Israel, he sees clearly that Zionism is primarily a nationalistic movement. According to him, the Jews all along had confidently expected to return to Palestine, but they had consistently left it to God to carry out the consummation of this return on His own and *not* on His chosen people's initiative. In other words, the future restoration was to be one which all schools of orthodox Judaism held to be an act of God's own prerogative. But, he

[19] This Symposium is available from *Jewish Frontier* in brochure form.

[20] *A Study of History*, Abridgment of Volumes I - VI by D. C. Somervell, p. 139.

points out, the Zionists were in conflict with this orthodox position that God would restore Israel to Palestine in His own time. So he gives us this indictment of Zionism: "In pursuit of this inveterate Gentile idolatry in the particularly sinister form of man's self worship of a human herd, the Zionist Jewish addict to a pagan cult of blood and soil had abandoned his father's faith that the Jews were a chosen people in virtue of God's grace in having condescended to make a covenant with Abraham and his seed, in which the Lord's choice of Israel was conditional upon Israel's continuing to obey the Lord's commandments." Here Toynbee is speaking seriously of Scripture concepts, though on the other hand, as has already been pointed out, his whole view of the Bible is largely naturalistic. But we go on with the quotation: "In thus leaving God's will and Israel's conduct out of his reckoning, the Zionist was parting with the spiritual ground which was the only sure basis for the Jew's title to the soil of the Holy Land." [21]

Again, he says at the end of Volume VIII: "The Zionist state had its core in the land of the Philistines in the Shephelah which had never before been colonized by an Israelite or Jewish population, and which, during the 13 centuries through which Philistines and Israelites had lived in Palestine side by side had not even been united politically with Ephraim or Judah."[22]

In respect to the British mandate of Palestine as "administered blindly with no regard for the Arab history or the Zionist movement," Toynbee is highly critical. Plainly he is very much on the side of the Arab. "The British promises to Arabs and Jews," he declares, "were incompatible and led to the 1948 Zionist movement in that the Jews were promised a national home in Palestine but not discouraged from considering it a national State. At the same time the British simply ignored the fact that the Arabs were the majority by far and had held tenancy for 1700 years." [23]

Moreover, he charges that Zionism had been aided by the attempts of various Western nations to win Jewish support and

[21] *A Study of History*, Volume VIII, p. 601.
[22] *Ibid.*, Volume VIII, p. 309.
[23] *Ibid.*, Volume VIII, p. 304; cf. also pp. 307 ff.

avert Jewish hostility. In World War I the Jews were an appreciable force in the domestic political life of the European powers and of the United States, and the United States would have the last word to speak in a European conflict, and this American last word might be affected appreciably by its Jewish citizens.

But Toynbee's most scathing denunciation is reserved for the attitude of Israel toward the Arabs. Consider, for instance, this passage: "If the heinousness of sin is to be measured by the degree to which the sinner is sinning against the light that God has vouchsafed to him, the Jews had even less excuse in A.D. 1948 for evicting Palestinian Arabs from their homes than Nebuchadnezzar and Titus and Hadrian and the Spanish and Portuguese Inquisition had had for uprooting, persecuting and exterminating Jews in Palestine and elsewhere at divers times in the past. In A.D. 1948 the Jews knew from personal experience what they were doing and it was their supreme tragedy that the lesson learnt by them from their encounter with the Nazi German Gentiles should have been not to eschew but to imitate some of the evil deeds that the Nazis had committed against the Jews. On the day of judgment," Toynbee charges, "the gravest crimes standing to the German National Socialists' account might be, not that they had exterminated a majority of the Western Jews but that they had caused the surviving remnant of Jewry to stumble." [24]

When it comes to the future of the Jews, or eschatology in relation to Israel, Toynbee's position is plain. Since the Jews are for him nothing more than a fossil civilization, they can hardly have much of a future. Of the Biblical doctrine of the believing remnant in Israel that continues through the ages, he seems to know nothing. For a remnant, a believing, living remnant, is a very different thing from a fossil. He does, however, deal with eschatology respecting the Jew in accord with his idea of what he calls "futurism." His thought is that when people are up against a stone wall of frustration, they seek escape. They may either go back into "archaism," as he calls it, and try to live in the past, or they may go forward to "futurism."

[24] *Ibid.,* Volume VIII, pp. 290, 291.

Both ways of escape usually fail. After the exile, according to Toynbee, Judah could not find solace in going back to archaism, so they were driven to look forward to the future. Thus they got the idea of the establishment of a Davidic kingdom in totally new form. Consequently they took up the Messianic hope, involving the millennial idea of the future kingdom that the Jews felt was promised them. But this was simply a naturalistic response to their adversity. Be that as it may, this idea became transfigured, as Jewish futurism was transmuted into the Kingdom of God.[25]

IV

Finally, let us step aside from the learned theories of this scholar who, with all his mysticism and high religious sensibility, has somehow missed "the way, the truth, and the life." Let us move for our closing moments into the clear light of revelation. For the Bible speaks in no uncertain terms concerning the Jews. From Genesis to Revelation their history and their future is written in God's Book, and what it says prophetically has in large part been authenticated by events. The covenants of God with Israel were not dreamed up as a response to some challenge in the history of an obscure, parochial group of Semites in ancient Syria; they were given by the living God through His sovereign election of this nation to be His own people. As Moses put it so grandly: "For thou art an holy people unto the Lord thy God; the Lord thy God hath chosen thee to be a special people unto himself, above all people that are on the face of the earth. The Lord did not set his love upon you, nor choose you, because ye were more in number than any people; for ye were the fewest of all people: but because the Lord loved you, and because he would keep the oath which he had sworn unto your fathers, hath the Lord brought you out with mighty hand, and redeemed you out of the house of bondmen, from the hand of Pharaoh king of Egypt." [26]

How different this is from Toynbee's idea that Israel, having discovered monotheism, invented the idea that they were the

[25] *A Study of History,* Abridgment of Volumes I - VI by D. C. Somervell, pp. 521 f.
[26] Deuteronomy 7:6-8.

chosen people! Even a glance at the Abrahamic covenant reminds us of the fact that with Israel is inextricably bound up the salvation and blessing and hope of all men. For in Abraham, said God, "shall all nations of the earth be blessed." [27] This can never come about through any fossil, imbedded in the stream of history.

It is refreshing, then, to turn from Toynbee to such a passage as the great eleventh chapter of Romans, where the Apostle Paul answers with masterly logic the rhetorical question, "Hath God cast away his people?" [28] by setting forth the sovereignty of God, shown in His gracious exercise of the power of His election, and manifest even now in the remnant according to grace, the believing Israel. This chapter, facing so plainly the present blindness of Israel as a nation, warning the Gentiles so pointedly, and looking forward to the future conversion of the nation Israel when the fullness of the Gentiles is come in and their King and our Lord returns — this chapter presents a picture vastly different from the one Toynbee gives.

The difference may be summed up in the great doxology with which Paul closes this profound section of Romans: "O the depth of the riches both of the wisdom and knowledge of God! How unsearchable are his judgments, and his ways past finding out! For who hath known the mind of the Lord? or who hath been his counsellor? Or who hath first given to him, and it shall be recompensed unto him again? For of him, and through him, and to him, are all things: to whom be glory for ever. Amen." [29]

[27] Genesis 12:3.
[28] Romans 11:1.
[29] Romans 11:33-36.

THE SPIRITUALITY OF THE MILLENNIAL KINGDOM

by Alva J. McClain, d.d., ll.d.

In the field of inductive logic there is a class of fallacies which arise through the careless use of language. Bacon named them "Idols of the Marketplace." Nothing could be more profitless than discussion without some prior agreement as to the meaning of important terms. To try to win an argument where terms are not mutually understood is like trying, as Locke has reminded us, "to dispossess a vagrant of his habitation who has no settled abode" (*Essay Concerning Human Understanding,* Book III, Chap. x).

Current discussions of the Kingdom of God involve the use of certain terms which often carry different meanings when used by different writers. Sometimes a single writer will use the same term in more than one sense, or use different terms to convey the same idea. Among such terms are *establish, earthly, heavenly, carnal, force, conditional, certainty, postponement, abeyance,* etc. All these deserve attention, but I shall discuss only one.

False Platonic Influence

This is the term *spiritual.* No other word in the vocabulary of the doctrine of the Kingdom has been the occasion of more misunderstanding and useless argument. A great deal of this confusion, in my opinion, has been due to the influence of Platonic philosophy in the field of Christian theology. Many a preacher, who may have never read a single sentence from Plato, has been perhaps unconsciously more or less under the sway of the rigid metaphysical dualism of this philosopher. To such men the premillennial doctrine of a divine kingdom established on earth, having political and physical aspects, seems to be sheer materialism. Yet their own theological views on this matter may involve some serious practical inconsistencies. It has been said, with some justification, that a man's life and actions are the surest guide to his actual beliefs.

Let me illustrate this with a parable: During a church banquet a group of preachers were discussing the nature of the Kingdom of God. One expressed his adherence to the premillennial view of a literal kingdom established on earth among men. To this a rather belligerent two hundred pound preacher snorted, "Ridiculous! Such an idea is nothing but materialism." When asked to state his own view, he replied, "The Kingdom is a spiritual matter. The Kingdom of God has already been established, and is within you. Don't you gentlemen know that the Kingdom is not eating and drinking, but righteousness and peace and joy in the Holy Ghost?" And then this preacher reached hungrily across the table and speared another enormous piece of fried chicken! Nobody tried to answer him. As a matter of fact, no answer was necessary; he answered his own argument. As the French would say, he was hoist with his own petard. At the risk of being thought tiresome, let me recite the obvious conclusion: If the Kingdom of God can exist now on earth in a two hundred pound preacher full of fried chicken without any reprehensible materialistic connotations, perhaps it could also exist in the same way among men on earth who will at times be eating and drinking under more perfect conditions in a future millennial kingdom. Personally I have always had a very high opinion of the value of fried chicken, but this was the first time I had ever seen its apologetical value as an argument against the inconsistencies of that view of the Kingdom based on a Platonic notion of spirituality!

But let us get back to a more serious side of the argument. Of course, the Kingdom of God is primarily a spiritual kingdom, always, and wherever it exists. But a spiritual kingdom, in Biblical parlance, can manifest itself and produce tangible effects in a physical world, or, to be more precise, in the world of sense experience. If it cannot, I would see no practical value in having it here and now. But strangely enough, some of the very men who are so scornful of the alleged materialism of a millennial kingdom, are the most insistent that the Church today must make effective in society what they call the social and moral ideals of the present Kingdom of God. Thus, it is our duty to vote the right ticket politically, give to the Red Cross, help the Boy Scouts, support the United Nations, endow hospitals, etc. But if a spiritual kingdom can and should produce such effects at the present time through the very imperfect agency of sinful men, why cannot the same thing be true in larger measure in the coming age when the rule of God will be mediated more perfectly and powerfully through the eternal Son personally present among men as the mediatorial King? In other words, if there can be a divine kingdom functioning here and now in the realm of sense experience without the taint of materialism, what is wrong with the same thing in the future? Any denial of such a possibility, on alleged rational grounds, would at last plunge us back philosophically into the hopeless dilemma of Platonic dualism, which is still the curse of much that is called Christian thinking in the field of Eschatology. The conventional sneer at what has been called the "materialistic and carnal kingdom" of premillennialism, in my judgment, has lost much of its force. What the opponents of the premillennial view of the kingdom must now do to win the argument is to show that our Lord will never return to earth in glory personally and visibly.

It should hardly be necessary to point out that in the Word of God it is nothing new to find a spiritual cause producing tangible effects in the area of sense experience. On this point the personal testimony of the late Ananias and his wife Sapphira would be very impressive. These two people lived in the very beginning of that historical era when, as it is claimed by some, God established a spiritual kingdom among men. But they learned by bitter experience that a spiritual force can operate in a physical world. Berkhof, in criticizing the idea that God will use force in the establishing of His Kingdom, seems to feel that there is something utterly incongruous between spiritual power and physical effects, and that any such effects in the material world cannot be due to the power of God's Spirit (*The Kingdom of God*, p. 174). But Ananias and his wife certainly died a sudden physical death because they had lied to the Holy Ghost. As to the question of whether a display of force could have any salutary results in the Kingdom of God, which Berkhof seems to doubt, Luke is careful to describe the effect of the death of Ananias and Sapphira thus: "And great fear came upon all the church, and upon as many as heard these things" (Acts 5:11).

The notion that a spiritual kingdom can have no relation to considerations which are the stuff of physical existence, is one of the strangest idols ever constructed in the cave of the human mind. God is spirit and wherever His power breaks supernaturally into the system of nature, the cause may properly be called spiritual, whatever the effect may be, whether the healing of a disease, the raising of a dead body, the regeneration of a sinner, or the setting up of a political state on the earth. The kingdom established at Sinai was not an earthly kingdom, although it was on the earth. It was a spiritual kingdom which came down from heaven historically into the world of physical existence by the supernatural agency of God Himself. If we hold fast this truth, we shall have less difficulty dealing with philosophically inclined theologians who seem to feel that there is something degrading about the idea of a spiritual kingdom established on earth in control of human affairs in the realm of sense experience.

THE THEOLOGICAL CONFUSION

One particular thing in this connection that seems to disturb some theologians is the thought of a kingdom in which the glorified Christ with His risen saints will be mingling with men of flesh and blood on the earth. To illustrate this point, I shall quote from Berkhof's final paragraph in his book *The Kingdom of God*. The author first states the premillennial view as follows: "Jesus Christ, the glorified Lord, will be seated upon the throne at Jerusalem. And the risen and immortal saints will reign with him 'the thousand years.' And besides these there will be also

men in the flesh, both of the Jewish and of other nations, some
converted and others unconverted. They will all share in the
glory of the Kingdom, and all enjoy the open vision of Jesus
Christ." Then with considerable indignation Berkhof exclaims,
"With Brown we too would call out, 'What a mongrel state of
things is this! What an abhorred mixture of things totally incon-
sistent with each other.' This representation is not warranted
by Scripture and grates upon our Christian sensibility. Beet truly
says: 'We cannot conceive mingled together on the same planet
some who have yet to die and others who have passed through
death and will die no more. Such confusion of the present age
with the age to come is in the last degree unlikely'" (p. 176).

Here we have a prime example of the influence of philosophic
dualism in Christian theology. If Plato were living today, giving
a series of lectures on the millennial question, he might very
well employ the exact language of Berkhof, Beet, et al. Certainly
in his philosophically sensitive soul he would regard with abhorrence the idea of a spiritual kingdom having any genuine
and worth-while relation to the world of sense experience. But
the writers of Holy Scripture are not bound by any such philosophical prejudices. While they recognized the reality of both
mind and matter, of both spirit and body, to them there was not
only one God but also one world. And in this universe of God
there is no unbridgeable chasm between that which is physical
and that which is spiritual. In the Garden of Eden, God who
is spirit walks and talks with man made of the dust of the
ground (Gen. 3:8-10). The Lord Himself with two angels is
entertained in the tent of Abraham (Gen. 18). To Moses the
Lord spoke face to face "as a man speaketh unto his friend"
(Ex. 33:11). But the incarnation of the eternal Son in a body
of flesh and blood is the supreme demonstration that there is
no inherent or necessary antagonism between matter and spirit.
This is to say nothing of the risen Christ appearing over and
over to men and women in the flesh, mingling with them, eating
with them, and teaching them for the space of forty days.

The entire history of divine revelation bears no uncertain witness that the penetration of spirit into the physical realm of
nature is never regarded as something strange, abnormal or in-

congruous. It is true that human sin has introduced a limiting factor into the situation. Man did lose his personal fellowship with God. But sin itself at bottom is a spiritual problem. While its effects are most apparent in the physical realm, matter is not an evil in itself. The ancient error of Gnosticism has been universally rejected by orthodox theologians, yet its baneful shadow still hangs over certain areas of Eschatology. This alleged abhorrence at the thought of any intermingling of the spiritual and the material in a future millennial kingdom is not necessarily a normal reaction of the human reason. It is rather what the psychologists have called a "learned reaction." The Apostle Paul, well schooled in the philosophies of his day, solemnly warned against this danger: "Beware lest any man spoil you through [his] philosophy and vain deceit, after the tradition of men . . . and not after Christ" (Col. 2:8). And the next verse makes it clear that the warning had to do with a false dualism which would later develop into the historic school of Gnosticism, but which already was present in Paul's day: "For in him [Christ] dwelleth all the fulness of the Godhead bodily [*somatikos*]." The incarnate Son of God, in whose body both deity and humanity dwelt together in perfect union, is still the most complete answer to all Gnostic tendencies, whether ancient or modern.

It is only fair to say that Berkhof, from whose scholarly book I have quoted above, recognizes that spiritual and material blessings can dwell together in the final stage of the Kingdom without any necessary incongruity or discord. In fact, in generous vein he concedes that the premillennial view of the Kingdom has done some service as an antidote to the "one-sided spiritual conception of the Kingdom." He says, "It reminds us of the fact that the Kingdom of God is something more than the purely spiritual invisible reign of God in the hearts of men; and that in the future it will find expression also in a visible external organization. It corrects the mistaken idea that the Kingdom consists only in spiritual gifts and spiritual graces, and teaches us to look with confidence for a material creation of resplendent beauty. In view of the prophetic utterances to which it directs our attention, the erroneous impression that the future Kingdom will offer enjoyments only to the soul, is swept away by the glad

assurances that it will afford rich and varied material blessings
as well" (p. 158). I doubt whether even the late C. I. Scofield
could have written any finer words on the point at issue. They
prove that Berkhof is not basically a Platonist in his philosophy.
If I understand him rightly, Berkhof has no serious objection to
the mingling of spiritual and material blessings in the final
and eternal state. But he just does not like the idea of such
a mingling of things in a millennial kingdom this side of the
eternal state.

THE BIBLICAL USAGE OF "SPIRITUAL"

While time does not permit any adequate discussion of the
Biblical usage of the Greek adjective *pneumatikos,* at least something should be said about it. It occurs twenty-six times in the
New Testament, twice in adverbial form. In itself the term does
not necessarily connote something morally good: in Ephesians 6:
12 the demonic hosts are called *pueumatika.* Nor does the term
necessarily exclude the idea of physical substance; in I Corinthians 15:44 the resurrection body of the Christian is named a
soma pneumatikon. With reference to the things of God, which
is its general connection, the meaning of *pneumatikos* is something *"emanating from the Divine Spirit,* or *exhibiting its effects
and so its character:"* that is, something *"produced by the sole
power of God himself without natural instrumentality, supernatural"* (Thayer, *Lexicon of the New Testament,* p. 523, 3.a).
Therefore, the term may be used to designate a divine origin
or cause, and also to describe the effects produced by such a
cause in any realm whatsoever, whether physical or metaphysical.
If we hold fast to this general idea we cannot slip into un-
necessarily narrow definitions.

Without pursuing this point any further, I close by observing
that if, in the Word of God, a spiritual food can breed worms,
we should not be afraid to speak of the coming millennial
kingdom on earth as a spiritual kingdom; and we need not be
too much disturbed by the taunt of some opponents to the effect
that the kingdom of premillennialism is a "mongrel" mixture of
things which are abhorrent one to the other.

28

AS IT WAS IN THE DAYS OF NOAH

by M. R. DeHaan, m.d.

> And as He sat upon the mount of Olives, the disciples came
> unto Him privately, saying, Tell us, when shall these things be?
> and what shall be the sign of thy coming, and of the end of the
> world (age)? (Matt. 24:3).

The twenty-fourth chapter of Matthew is the answer of our
Lord Jesus Christ to His disciples' question concerning His
return and the end of this age. The question is definite and
unmistakable: "What shall be the sign of thy coming, and of
the end of the world?" And Jesus immediately and directly
plunges into a recitation of the signs by which we may know that
His coming is near. In the beginning of the chapter He speaks
about deception, wars, rumors of wars, famines, pestilences, apostasy, earthquakes, anti-Semitism, false teachers and a number of
other signs. Then He warns them of the coming of the great
Tribulation, gives them a picture of His glorious Second Coming,
gives them the sign of the fig tree, and finally caps it all by a recapitulation of the foregoing signs when He says:

> For as in the days that were before the flood . . . so shall also
> the coming of the Son of man be (Matt. 24:38, 39).

These verses are the heart of the entire chapter. Jesus says,
when the conditions which existed before the flood are repeated
in our time, then we may know that it is near at hand, even
at our doors. All we need to do, therefore, is to find out what
the conditions were in those antediluvian days and compare
them with events as they are today, and the results may bring

271

us the assurance we seek of His near return. The statement is positive and admits of no juggling or tampering.

As it was in the pre-flood days, so shall it be in the days just before the Lord's return. No one, therefore, can have any excuse for being in darkness, because he can find out in less than half an hour just exactly what Jesus referred to. The entire record of the "days before the flood" is contained in three brief chapters of the Word of God, Genesis 4, 5 and 6. The whole section can be read in ten minutes. There is no other authentic record of the days to which Jesus refers in Matthew 24; no secular history goes back to the days of the flood, let alone before the flood. All that is written concerning those days is therefore in these three brief chapters which anyone can read at will.

The fourth chapter of Genesis gives us a picture of the economic and industrial conditions which existed before the flood. Genesis 5 gives us a dispensational picture of those same days, and Genesis 6 is a picture of the moral conditions before the flood which caused God to send the deluge upon the earth.

THE ECONOMIC PICTURE

The economic picture as related in Genesis 4:17-24 is very pointed and brief:

> And Cain knew his wife; and she conceived, and bare Enoch: and he builded a city, and called the name of the city, after the name of his son, Enoch.
>
> And unto Enoch was born Irad: and Irad begat Mehujael: and Mehujael begat Methusael: and Methusael begat Lamech.
>
> And Lamech took unto him two wives: the name of the one was Adah, and the name of the other Zillah.
>
> And Adah bare Jabal: he was the father of such as dwell in tents, and of such as have cattle.
>
> And his brother's name was Jubal: he was the father of all such as handle the harp and organ.
>
> And Zillah, she also bare Tubal-cain, an instructor of every artificer in brass and iron: and the sister of Tubal-cain was Naamah.
>
> And Lamech said unto his wives, Adah and Zillah, Hear my voice; ye wives of Lamech, hearken unto my speech: for I have slain a man to my wounding, and a young man to my hurt.
>
> If Cain shall be avenged sevenfold, truly Lamech seventy and sevenfold.

Now in studying this brief section we find six striking things stated in it about the age of Noah which stand out above all others. These, when recounted, will constitute together a sign of the coming of the Lord in the end of the present age.

1. It was an age of city building.
2. It was an age of polygamy.
3. It was an age of great agriculture.
4. It was an age of music.
5. It was an age of the metallic arts.
6. It was an age of unprecedented violence.

Note each of these carefully, and see what Jesus meant when He referred to the days of His coming again as being a repetition of the days which immediately preceded the flood. The first one of these signs is city building, and we have the record in Genesis 4:17,

> And Cain builded a city, and called the name of the city, after the name of his son, Enoch.

This is the first mention of cities in the Word of God. When God created man, He did not place him in a city, but in a garden. Cities were first invented and built by wicked man, and ever since they have been the symbol and concentration point of wickedness and corruption. In the crowded life of our large cities sin develops at an alarming rate. It all began before the flood, in the days of Cain. It was the first great city-building boom in history, and it was followed by all the evils which are peculiar to urban life. In the past generation or two there has been a literal repetition of the days of Noah. A little over fifty years ago, we are told, almost 75 per cent of the population of the world lived on farms and in small rural communities. Then came the industrial revolution of the nineteenth century, with its machinery and labor-saving implements and devices, as a result of which millions previously employed on farms were no longer needed. But as the opportunities for labor closed in the country, factories springing up everywhere called for the services of rural young people and the great exodus from the country to the city began. New and better machinery was built, throwing more and more men out of work on the farms, at the same time demanding more and more help for the city factories, to build more labor-saving machines, and so ad infinitum, until today the ratio has been completely reversed. More than 75 per cent of the entire population of the nation now live in cities, with a corresponding increase of wickedness and crime. The simple rural life has vanished and the mad scramble and screech of city life has broken down the composure and contentment our forefathers knew. But God still lives in the country, and Jesus knew what He was talking about when He said: "As it was in the days of Noah, so shall it be in the days of the coming of the Son of man."

THE SCOURGE OF POLYGAMY

And Cain knew his wife, and she conceived, and bare Enoch: and he builded a city (Gen. 4:17).

As a direct result of this concentration of the population in cities, we have the second characteristic of the age mentioned in this passage, namely, the breakdown of the home. Lamech was the first man in human history to break God's rule of creation by committing a sin which culminated in the flood: "And Lamech took unto him two wives."

In the wake of city life came the evils of divorce and polygamy. Crowded slum conditions led to the closer association of the sexes, and when women began leaving their homes and children to enter factories and shops and offices, these evils broke all restraints. There can be no question that the Lord Jesus Christ had this kind of condition in mind when in Matthew 24 He told us that the days of Noah would be re-enacted in respect to "marrying and giving in marriage." Certainly He was not condemning marriage, for that is a God-given institution. God Himself brought the first man and woman together in the Garden. The evil therefore is in the abuse of marriage rather than its legitimate use. God made one man, Adam, to be the husband of one wife, Eve, and said: "Therefore shall a man leave his father and his mother and cleave unto his wife [not wives], and they shall be one flesh." But today we have a repetition of the days of Noah. Some years ago a divorce was the height of shame. The parties concerned were often so ashamed that they left

the community to begin life anew where they were unknown.
Divorces were hard to obtain, and better still, seldom sought.
Churches refused fellowship to the guilty parties and emphatically
discouraged divorce. Today, thanks to our modern enlighten-
ment, all of this has changed. Divorce has been glorified and
made a means of lucrative popularity in certain quarters. The
divorce rate in the last fifty years has doubled, trebled, quad-
rupled, and then doubled again, while our land is raising a
generation of children who have never known the blessings of
a happy home. This alone is considered by many authorities the
greatest single contributing factor to juvenile delinquency. Statis-
tics show that by far the greater majority of juvenile crime cases
come from broken homes. Divorce is a cancer, social and spiritual,
and should never even be mentioned among those who name the
name of Christ. Yet today in many states there are as many as
four divorces annually to every ten marriages, and the number
is on the increase. Never before has this condition existed so
generally. This, among other things, is undoubtedly what the
Lord referred to when He said, "As it was in the days before
the flood, so shall it also be in the days of the coming of the
Son of Man."

Agricultural Development

And Adah bare Jabel: he was the father of such as dwell in
tents, and of such as have cattle (Gen. 4:20).

We come now to the third subsidiary sign mentioned in our
passage. The age before the flood was one of great development
in farming and animal culture. It is significant that we should
have in Genesis the record of the beginning of the cattle industry, and the first mention of cattle being used for man's
profit.

Today also, closely associated as a result of city growth, is
the development in agriculture and in animal husbandry. The
depletion of labor on the farms has called for more efficient
production methods; and so, helped by the machinery produced
in the city and by scientific research, the whole business of
farming has been revolutionized. Are the Lord's comparisons of
the end-time with the days of Noah suggesting that it is time

we looked to the foundations of our boasted civilization? Are we as modern as we think? How far have we come in true progress from the days of Jabel in Genesis 4:20? All along the way the words of our Lord are proving true: "As it was . . . so shall it be."

THE MUSICAL AGE

And his brother's name was Jubal: he was the father of all such as handle the harp and organ (Gen. 4:21).

The first mention in the Bible of musical instruments and music is another significant characteristic of the antediluvian days when we remember the words of our Lord, "As it was in the days before the flood." The ancients were not without a sense of the aesthetic. "Music hath charms," you know. In our own civilization there has never been more music in the air than today, and much of it is very good. But the inner quality of our way of life is exposed by the fact that this is predominantly the age of jazz, swing and pagan syncopations. Music, music everywhere! Squeaks and squawks, baby talk and monkey talk, until we read of people going berserk under the spell of the repetitious off-beat sounds. The world has called them "jitter bugs," probably because they are "bugs" and give everyone the "jitters." It seems that nothing can be done any more without the accompaniment of music. We sell our wares and hawk our products by music, but the sad thing is that the habit has invaded our churches, the precincts of the holy place. Music has been substituted for the preaching of the Word of God. Corny choruses and spooky spirituals are supposed to prepare men's hearts for the Gospel. Empty phrases are repeated over and over again to the tune of religious syncopation, until the emotionally unstable break beneath the strain and imagine that they have heard a voice from heaven. "As it was . . . so shall it be."

THE STEEL AGE

And Zillah, she also bare Tubal-cain, an instructer of every artificer in brass and iron (Gen. 4:22).

It was the metallurgical age. This, too, is one of the "firsts" in the Bible. It was the infancy period of civilization when man began to utilize the heavy metals. And how tremendously striking is the similarity of that day to the age in which we live. This may indeed be called the metal or steel age. The steel industry today ranks at the top of all industries. Its failure would mean industrial collapse. As the supplies of wood decreased, man developed the products of metal to an amazing degree. New alloys and compounds of unbelievable strength and durability have been developed. Rust-proof and corrosion-resisting metals have revolutionized industry, agriculture, domestic life and even warfare. Steel products and by-products have been shaped into servants for modern man until our locomotives and cars can thunder along upon two thin strips of steel in almost perfect safety. Warships, airplanes, tanks and all the destructive tools of war shriek out the truth of Jesus' prediction. Tubal-cain, the instructor of every artificer in brass and iron, has been resurrected in the lives of tens of thousands today. The modern Moloch has come upon us in perfect, chronological order according to the pattern laid down in Genesis. "As it was . . . so shall it be."

The Age of Violence

And Lamech said unto his wives, Adah and Zillah . . . hearken unto my speech: for I have slain a man to my wounding, and a young man to my hurt. If Cain shall be avenged sevenfold, truly Lamech seventy and sevenfold (Gen. 4:23).

Here we have a picture of the first real "big shot" in history, a man who not only committed violence, but was boastful and proud enough to brag about it. As further developed in the sixth chapter of Genesis, this was an age of violence, murder and unprovoked atrocious crimes. Has ever an age in history recorded more brutal, unprovoked atrocities than ours today? It is a sadistic age. Every newspaper tells the sad story. People have to live behind bolted doors for fear of being attacked in many areas.

These, then, are the six collective signs in Genesis 4 to which our Lord must have referred in Matthew 24. Five of them — city building, divorce, agriculture, music, steel — have developed in chronological order during the past few decades. Now with the tremendous expansion of our great and modern cities, the last one is also here: unprecedented violence and destruction on every hand. Thus, with all our apparent progress, morally we are still living in the days of Noah.

This we believe to be the sign of the Lord's return. And now follows the dispensational setting of the Rapture. In Genesis 5 we have the record of six successive generations of death, and then Enoch is raptured into heaven. The monotonous, droning story in this chapter is, "and he died." This is said of Adam, Seth, Enos, Cainan, Mahalaleel and Jared. Then, suddenly, we come to a breath-taking interruption in the obituary column, and we read:

> And Enoch walked with God: and he was not; for God took him (Gen. 5:24).

Remember, Jesus said, "As it was . . . so shall it be." This leads me to say that having all these signs before us, I cannot but believe that the next event in the program of God will be the catching away of the Church of the Lord Jesus Christ.

In closing we would call your attention to one significant statement of the Lord Jesus in the chapter with which we began. Matthew 24:14 reads:

> And this gospel of the kingdom shall be preached in all the world for a witness unto all nations; and then shall the end come.

Notice carefully the closing phrase of this verse: "and then shall the end come." The end will be signaled by the preaching of the Gospel across the world. While I believe that this will have its complete fulfillment in the Tribulation period, we are nevertheless seeing a token fulfillment of this prophecy today. Great events cast their shadows before them, sometimes far in advance. For the first time in six thousand years of human history it is now possible to send the Gospel to every square foot on the surface of the earth. By means of radio we are now able to reach every human being in hearing distance with the message of salvation. If every man in the world had a radio, and was able to understand what was being said, the possibility is here right now to preach the Gospel to every creature. We believe that we are seeing at least the beginning of the fulfillment of our Lord's words.

29

THE TRUMP OF GOD

by HERMAN A. HOYT, TH.D.

Recent pronouncements by students in the field of eschatology, bearing especially on the coming of Christ for His Church, have spread consternation among the saints.

This is not a new phenomenon. A comparable situation was created at a point in the first century. To alleviate a resulting state of unrest bordering on panic, Paul found it necessary to write his Second Epistle to the Thessalonians. Then, as now, the peace of the household of faith was threatened by some who thought they could predict the exact moment when Christ would return to catch away the Church. It is not surprising therefore that, the coming of the Lord being so close at hand, brethren of our time, given to speculative thinking, should fall into a similar pattern and produce the same effect upon the saints of the present generation.

The pronouncements referred to seem to be calculated to establish the idea that the time of the catching away of the Church is not a matter of secret. They declare that this event, generally known to the Church as the Rapture, will indeed take place at the last trump; but that this trump, being synonymous with the seventh trumpet of Revelation 11:15, will occur in the middle of the seven-year span known as the Tribulation period.

Now these eschatological assertions lead to some inescapable conclusions. First, the very mention of the possibility of a Midtribulation Rapture, seeing the Tribulation has definite time delineations, is tantamount to setting a date for the coming of the Lord. Second, as a result of placing the Rapture of the Church in the middle of the period, or at the end of it, as the Posttribulation advocates do, the Church is immediately deprived of the blessed hope. The prospect then becomes Antichrist, tribulation and wrath before the coming of the Lord. Third, the imminency of the Lord's return ceases to be a sanctifying and motivating factor in the lives of believers.

Small wonder, therefore, that such pronouncements have stimulated children of God to re-examine the foundations of the faith concerning this event so vital to the Church. But, as always, a re-examination of the foundations of our faith has only served to deepen the convictions of God's people and to establish them more firmly in the truth. I can say this with new fervor after examining 115 passages in the Bible relative to the subject of trumpets. In these passages three kinds of trumpets appear: divine, angelic and human.

The human trumpets are largely those used in the past by the nation of Israel to make announcements, to mobilize for war, to inaugurate a king, to assemble for worship or festive occasions. Angelic trumpets announce judgment or victory. Divine trumpets follow the same pattern. This study will center attention upon the latter in six movements of thought.

I. THE TRUMP OF GOD AND THE LAST TRUMP ARE ONE AND THE SAME

Two passages of Scripture demonstrate this beyond the shadow of a doubt:

> For this we say unto you by the word of the Lord, that we which are alive, and remain unto the coming of the Lord, shall not prevent them which are asleep. For the Lord himself shall descend from heaven with a shout, with the voice of the archangel, and with the trump of God: and the dead in Christ shall rise first: then we which are alive and remain, shall be caught up together with them in the clouds, to meet the Lord in the air: and so shall we ever be with the Lord. Wherefore comfort one another with these words. (I Thess. 4:15-18).

> Behold, I shew you a mystery: We shall not all sleep, but we shall all be changed, in a moment, in the twinkling of an eye, at the last trump: for the trumpet shall sound, and the dead shall be raised incorruptible, and we shall be changed. (I Cor. 15:51, 52).

At least five things in these two passages identify "the trump of God" with "the last trump." First, the two passages have the same *destination*: they were both written to believers in the

Church. Second, they both discuss the same *subject*: the resurrection of the dead in Christ. Third, they both describe the same *effect* upon the saints: the dead saints will be raised and glorified, and the living saints will be transformed. Fourth, both passages hold forth the same *hope* for the living saints: a hope which was shared by the Christians of that day, including the Apostle Paul himself. Fifth, both passages use this great hope as an *occasion* for comfort and exhortation (I Thess. 4:18; I Cor. 15:58).

Where there is such remarkable agreement, there is but one conclusion. The last trump and the trump of God are the same. The *trump of God* identifies it as to kind: it is a divine trumpet. The *last trump* identifies it as to order: it is the final trump in a series.

II. THE LAST TRUMP OF GOD POINTS TO THE FIRST TRUMP OF GOD

Any fair-minded student of the Bible will agree that the terminology of the Scriptures must be followed if any progress is to be achieved in the realm of Biblical knowledge. Upon this basis our proposition is advanced. The term "last" means the final or end thing in a series. The series may consist of any number, two or more. It may be two, such as the first Adam and the last Adam (I Cor. 15:45). Or it may be more, such as the appearance of Christ to Paul as the last in a series of appearances (I Cor. 15:8). In any case, the series must be characterized by something that makes it uniform. It is therefore right to insist, since this last trumpet is characterized as the trump of God, that it is the last in the series of divine trumpets.

An intensive study of every passage of the Bible that deals with trumpets reveals just two trumpets that may be called divine. In order to understand the last trump of God, it is necessary to know something about the first trump of God. And the first mention of any trumpet in the Bible is the trumpet of God. It was this trumpet that inaugurated God's dealings with Israel upon the basis of the Old Testament law.

Let us turn to Exodus 19:13, 16, 19:

> There shall not an hand touch it, but he shall surely be stoned,
> or shot through; whether it be beast or man, it shall not live:
> when the trumpet soundeth long, they shall come up to the
> mount. . . . And it came to pass on the third day, in the morning,
> that there were thunders and lightnings, and a thick cloud upon
> the mount, and the voice of the trumpet exceeding loud; so that
> all the people that was in the camp trembled. . . . And when the
> voice of the trumpet sounded long, and waxed louder and louder,
> Moses spake, and God answered him by a voice.

Look also at Exodus 20:18, 19:

> And all the people saw the thunderings, and the lightnings, and
> the noise of the trumpet, and the mountain smoking: and when
> the people saw it, they removed, and stood afar off. And they
> said unto Moses, Speak thou with us, and we will hear: but
> let not God speak with us, lest we die.

As if to confirm all that has been written concerning the first
trump of God and the giving of the law, the writer of Hebrews
refers to this very event: "For ye are not come unto the mount
that might be touched, and that burned with fire, nor unto
blackness, and darkness, and tempest, and the sound of a trumpet, and the voice of words; which voice they that heard, in-
treated that the word should not be spoken to them any more"
(Heb. 12:18, 19). That voice then shook the earth, and God
promised that there would be yet one more shaking of the
earth (Heb. 12:26).

III. THE LAST TRUMP OF GOD WILL ANNOUNCE THE RESUMPTION AND COMPLETION OF GOD'S DEALINGS WITH ISRAEL UPON THE BASIS OF THE LAW

No true Jew would ever admit that the enactments of Sinai
have been set aside. He would rather insist that the covenants
and promises still abide and must be fulfilled. And the Bible
provides clear information on this point. It was not until God's
people were in captivity that God unfolded His plan for them
to Daniel in the remarkable prophecy of the seventy weeks
(Dan. 9:24-27). Of those seventy weeks of years 483 were fulfilled, bringing Israel down to that day when her King, meek
and lowly, riding upon an ass, made entrance into the imperial
city of Jerusalem. But the seventieth week of years never followed. Since Israel thrust away her King, God has not been

dealing with the nation as in days of old. To the Early Church the seventieth week was yet future. And since nothing in the history of the past 1900 years quite fulfills this prophecy, faith assumes that it will yet be fulfilled in the experience of Israel.

This final week of years in God's dealings with Israel is known as the "day of the Lord." It is ushered in by the ministry of the two witnesses (Rev. 11:3) and covers a period of three and one-half years. This is followed by three and one-half years known as the "time of Jacob's trouble." It is during this seven-year period that God will plead with His people upon the basis of the Old Testament law. In the final chapter of the Old Testament God speaks to His people of that day. "For, behold, the day cometh that shall burn as an oven. . . . Remember ye the law of Moses my servant. . . . Behold, I will send you Elijah the prophet before the coming of the great and dreadful day of the Lord" (Mal. 4:1-6).

This very day of the Lord is to be characterized by the trumpet of the Lord. It is this trumpet that will announce and mark the passing of that period of years. Zephaniah proclaims this fact: "The great day of the Lord is near, it is near, and hasteth greatly, even the voice of the day of the Lord: the mighty man shall cry there bitterly. That day is a day of wrath, a day of trouble and distress, a day of wasteness and desolation, a day of darkness and gloominess, a day of clouds and thick darkness, a day of the trumpet and alarm against the fenced cities, and against the high towers" (Zeph. 1:14-16). All this has special application to Israel (Zeph. 1:12, 13). It is during this period that God carries to completion His program for Israel under the old covenant of the law, and He announces it by the blowing of the trumpet as in days of old.

IV. THE LAST TRUMP OF GOD WILL COVER THE PERIOD OF SEVEN YEARS

Following the pattern when the trump of God was blown at Sinai, it seems quite evident from the various references that the blowing of the last trump will continue through the seven years, or at stated intervals during that period. At Sinai the trumpet sounded long and waxed louder and louder (Ex, 19:13,

16, 19). The description in Exodus leads one to believe that this covered an extended interval of time. It seems quite reasonable to conclude that this will be true also of the last trump of God.

The last trump announces the arrival and progress of judgment during the day of wrath. Such is the sense of the passage quoted from the book of Zephaniah (1:14-16). The expression "a day of the trumpet" means the period of the trumpet; and that period is coextensive with the wrath, trouble, distress, wasteness, desolation, darkness, gloominess and clouds of that same period. It also announces the gathering of Israel from among the nations back to the Promised Land. Isaiah states it this way: "And it shall come to pass in that day, that the great trumpet shall be blown, and they shall come which were ready to perish in the land of Assyria, and the outcasts in the land of Egypt, and shall worship the Lord in the holy mount at Jerusalem" (Isa. 27:13). Our blessed Lord re-emphasizes this great prophecy. "And he shall send his angels with a great sound of a trumpet; and they shall gather together his elect from the four winds, from one end of heaven to the other" (Matt. 24:31).

Wrath for the Gentiles (Joel 3:1, 2, 16) as well as tribulation for the Jews (Zeph. 1:4, 12) is in the sound of this trumpet. But at the very moment when Israel is sore pressed by the great adversary, the Antichrist, the trumpet will announce the coming of the King in glory. "And the Lord shall be seen over them, and his arrows shall go forth as the lightning: and the Lord God shall blow the trumpet, and shall go with whirlwinds of the south. The Lord of hosts shall defend them. . . . And the Lord their God shall save them in that day as the flock of his people" (Zech. 9:14-16).

V. THE LAST TRUMP OF GOD AND THE SEVENTH TRUMPET OF REVELATION ARE NOT IDENTICAL

This does not mean that there is no connection between the trump of God and the seventh angelic trumpet. Both will be blown during the same period and, in general, perhaps for the same purpose. But there are certain unmistakable distinguishing characteristics, and these mark the contrast. As to *kind*, the two are sharply differentiated. The one is called the trump of God, while the other is the trump of an angel. As to *accompaniment*, the voice of the archangel goes with the trump of God, while great voices follow the blowing of the angelic trumpet. As to *place*, the trump of God is sounded from the air and heard in the earth, while the trumpet of the angel is blown in heaven and heard in heaven. As to *immediate effect*, the trump of God is followed by the resurrection, transformation, and translation of the saints of the Church (I Thess. 4:15-17; I Cor. 15:51, 52), while a whole series of events yet to take place in the earth are inaugurated by the blowing of the angelic trumpet (Rev. 11:15-18). As to *scope*, the trump of God covers the entire period of Tribulation, while the trumpet of the angel occurs at the middle of the Tribulation and announces only events of the last half of the Tribulation period. As to *message*, the trump of God announces the fulfillment of the mystery of the deliverance of the saints from this world (I Cor. 15:51, 52; I Thess. 4:15-17), while the trumpet of the angel announces the fulfillment of the mystery of the deliverance of the wicked into the winepress of divine wrath (Rev. 10:5-7; 11:15, 18).

There is one other detail that should be mentioned for the sake of clarifying the difference between these two trumpets. Each trumpet can be identified by the voice of the trumpeter. In the case of the seventh angel we read in Revelation 10:7, "But in the days of *the voice* of the seventh angel, when he shall begin to sound . . ." The word "sound," in the original, is substantially the same as the word "trumpet." But concerning the divine trumpet we are told in Revelation 1:10, 11, "I was in the Spirit on the Lord's day, and heard behind me a *great voice*, as of a trumpet, saying, I am Alpha and Omega." This is the voice of none other than the Lord Jesus Christ, with all the power and majesty behind it.

VI. THE LAST TRUMP OF GOD ANNOUNCES THE DELIVERANCE
OF THE SAINTS FROM THE WORLD

It is significant that the apostle Paul uses the sounding of the trumpet of God to signalize the time when the dead in Christ shall rise and the living believers shall be changed (I Cor 15:52). The Old Testament clearly sets forth the trumpets of God.

The first was at Sinai with its tremendous import for Israel. The response of this people to the law and to the long promised King caused God to turn from them to the accomplishment of a great program among the Gentiles. But the sounding again of the final trumpet of God will mark the completion of the Church and the renewal of relations with Israel. At that moment the Lord Jesus will catch away His bride from the earth. And to this agrees the account of events given at the great Jerusalem council: "Simeon hath declared how God at first did visit the Gentiles, to take out of them a people for his name. And to this agree the words of the prophets. . . ." (Acts 15:14-16).

Several details make it clear that the Rapture of the Church takes place as the trump of God begins to sound. The speed of this event is marked by two expressions, "in a moment," "in the twinkling of an eye." The first is a translation of the Greek word *atom.* This refers to a period of time so minute that it is indivisible. The second refers to a flash of the eye, a glint so swift that it can scarcely be detected. In this incomprehensible moment of time, the dead in Christ will be raised and glorified, the living saints will be transformed, and both companies will be caught away into the air.

The trump of God, we believe, gives forth a sound sustained over some period of time, and all of the facts direct our attention to the point when this trumpet begins to sound. The word of God declares, "For the trumpet shall sound, and the dead shall be raised incorruptible, and we shall be changed" (I Cor. 15: 52). The verb "shall sound" is future. But the future here is made upon an aorist stem, which usually points to the single occurrence of an act at a given point of time. This must be an indivisible point of time, as already marked out in the early part of this verse. Therefore the verb must have an inceptive sense, and mean, "For the trumpet shall begin to sound." At this point of time God's administration through the Church Age is finished. The righteous dead are now raised and the living saints are changed and caught away. And at this same moment God resumes with Israel where He left off some nineteen hundred years ago. The seventieth week begins to run its course.

SCRIPTURE INDEX

GENESIS
1-3 ....27, 54, 55
1:2 147
1:31 21
3:8-10 268
3:13 62
3:15 ....27, 53, 54, 57, 70,
182, 220, 244
4-6 273
4:17-24 ....273, 275
4:20 276
4:21 277
4:22 277
4:23 278
5 34
5:1 221
5:24 279
6 147
11 28
12 28
12-17 28
12-22 238
12:1, 2 102
12:1-3 245
12:3 263
13:16 29
14:18 226
14:18-20 225
14:20 60
15 36
15:5, 6 29
15:5-16 240
15:13, 14 29
15:18 ....187, 239
17:1-8 103
17:7, 8 239
18, 19 ....36, 268
22 229
22:14 223
24:67 234
28:14 109

EXODUS
1:22 60
6:1-4 223
12 229
15:26 223
16 271
17:15 223
19:5 215
20-31 238
24:7, 8 238
30, 32, 33 37
33:11 268

LEVITICUS
8, 9 225
26:40-45 30

NUMBERS
10:33 238
11 271
12:6-8 ....37, 38, 223
14:35 163
15:2 163
25 225

DEUTERONOMY
4:6 109
6:4 108
8:20-23 113
9:11 238
18:15 223
18:15-18 29
28-30 29

28:1-10 ....110, 111
28:15-20 111
30:1-10 ....29, 30, 112
33:18-33 224
33:24 186
33:26-29 108
34:10, 11 223

I SAMUEL
1:3 223
20:15 61
26:1-9 11
27:7 11
30:26 61

II SAMUEL
3:17, 18 14
7 47
7:11-16 238
7:12-16 103
7:16 ....239, 240
15:12 13

I KINGS
11:5 166

II KINGS
23:13 166

I CHRONICLES
1:1 221
10 127
12:32 ....9, 11, 12

PSALMS
2 ....44, 47
2:1, 2 17
2:2, 6 227
7:17 223
8:4-6 27
23:1 223
33:11 26
41:9 10
45:6 45
72:1, 7, 17 25
89 48
89:34-37 239
110 ....46, 47, 225
118:22 78
135:4 215
139:8 56

SONG OF SOLOMON
8:7 233

ISAIAH
2:2 144
2:4 110
4:5 38
9:6, 7 114
11:1-9 109
14:14, 26, 27 26
25:9 188
28:18 164
30:26 110
32:17, 18 30
41:21-23 181
43:10, 11 108
46:9-11 26
51:1, 2 28
52:14 40
53 230
53:4, 5 245
53:10-12 51
61:1 226

65:20 ....110, 130
66:22-24 29

JEREMIAH
17:5 185
20 34
22:30 49
23:5 114
23:5, 6 ....15, 245
23:6 223
30:7 ....104, 165
31:31-34 238
31:31-37 113
31:35-37 ....239, 241
32:40 241
33:14-17 103
33:20, 21 241

EZEKIEL
20 30
21:26, 27 15
26:33-38 ....104, 105
38:2-6 187
38:11, 12 186
38, 39 123
39:4 169
39:25-29 188
39:30 169
48:35 223

DANIEL
2 30
2:3, 4 17
2:10, 11 118
2:31-35 118
2:37-40 118
2:45 119
7 96
7:5-8 119
7:8 30
8:20, 21 119
9 30
9:24 ....104, 161, 167
9:24-26 226
9:24-27 166
9:25-27 106
9:26, 27 103
9:27 ....105, 164, 166, 186
11:21, 24, 36 185
12 ....163, 166
12:1, 10, 11 166

HOSEA
5:15 ....30, 42
6:1, 2 30

JOEL
2:11 167

AMOS
5:18 104
8:9 167
9:11-15 29

MICAH
4:4 ....109, 110
5:2 46

HABAKKUK
2:14 17

ZECHARIAH
4:7 16
6:12, 13 226
6:13 15

287

8:4 110
8:5 131
12:10 .... 10, 42, 103, 169, 188
12:10-14 163
12, 13 30
13:8 122
14:1-5 .... 103, 187
14:1-9 42
14:2 17
14:3, 12 187

MALACHI
2:15 222

MATTHEW
1 48
2:1-4 .... 12, 16, 147
3:7 99
4:17 164
4:23 164
7:23 235
10:6, 7 164
11:28 235
12:14 78
12:28 76
13 .... 117, 121, 209
13:3-9 210
13:18-23 211
13:21 99
13:24-30 .... 211, 212
13:24-43 75
13:25, 28, 29 63
13:28, 39 37
13:31, 32 213
13:33 214
13:37-43 212
13:44-46 215
13:47 216
13:49-52 217
13:54-56 138
16:4 167
16:16 79
16:21-23 148
16:22, 23 79
22:41-46 46
23:37-39 .... 30, 42, 102, 103
23:39 .... 103, 163, 165
24:3 .... 162, 272
24:4, 11, 23, 25 62
24:6 .... 15, 166
24:9-14 .... 162, 164
24:9, 21, 26 99
24:13 166
24:14 .... 165, 279
24:15 105
24:15, 21 248
24:15-26 165
24:24 168
24:27-42 .... 168, 169
24:30 246
24:38, 39 272
24:44 151
24, 25 .... 32, 59, 160, 163
25 170
25:31 127
25:32 165
26:1, 2 170
27:20 78

MARK
1:23-26 78
3:6 78
8:31 80
9:26 76
11:18 78
12:7, 8 78
13:7, 22 64
13:37 151

LUKE
1-33 .... 238, 240
1:32 .... 48, 239, 240
2:9 169
3 .... 48, 49
4:6 77
4:18 226
10:17 76
10:19 75
19:47 78
20:34, 35 110
21 .... 32, 162
21:6, 12 160
21:8 64
21:23 99
21:24 .... 17, 116, 121, 122, 161, 162, 163
21:25, 28 169
21:39-41 170
22:53 80
24:20ff 245
24:44 9

JOHN
1 230
1:1, 14 136
1:11 10
1:14 .... 32, 40
1:18 .... 31, 40
1:29 41
1:31, 45 29
2:11 66
3:6-8 102
3:16 27
3:19 66
3:36 100
4-17 31
5-24 104
5:30 9
6:70 80
8:43-46 71
8:44, 45 .... 59, 75
10:10 .... 58, 75
12 50
12:31 .... 50, 81
13:2 80
13:18 10
13:27 80
14:3 151
14:9 39
14:17 71
14:21, 23 .... 37, 38
14:26 32
14:30 74
16:7-14 102
16:12 162
16:13-15 32
16:21 100
16:26 71
17:12 80
17:16 103
18:37 71

ACTS
1 171
1:6 240
1:7 159
1:11 246
2:17 143
2:20 167
3:22 29
4:25-28 79
5:11 267
5:32 193
7:19 60
7:37 29
9:1-20 42
10:38 226

,11:19 100
14:15-17 34
15:6-17 163
15:13-18 42
15:14 .... 16, 32
15:18 26
16:31 165
17:20-29 34
17:26 221
17:30 28

ROMANS
1:18 66
1:20 33
1:24-32 28
1:24, 25 66
3:23 221
4:1-5 238
5:12 .... 55, 221
5:14 221
5:17 9
5:20, 21 83
8:1 104
8:11 235
8:17 234
8:29 32
9:4 42
9-11 42
10:12-15 42
11:1 263
11:1, 18-28 .... 114, 115
11:1, 26, 29 .... 95, 96
11:5, 25, 26 .... 16, 42
11:25 102
11:25-27 103
11:26 105
11:26-29 42
11:29 241
11:33-36 263
12:1 115
13:4, 5 99

I CORINTHIANS
7:28 100
10:3 270
10:11 143
10:32 31
12:13 102
15 256
15:8 42
15:20-22 239
15:23, 24 144
15:25 15
15:45 .... 9, 220
15:46 21
15:47 220
15:51, 52 .... 32, 129
15:52 131

II CORINTHIANS
4:6 224
4:18 21
5:17 .... 221, 238
5:19 140
5:21 140
6:17, 18 155
7:1 155

GALATIANS
3:16 29
4:4 39

EPHESIANS
1:10 .... 15, 39
2:7 32
2:13-18 16
3:5, 9 233
3:8-11 166

3:9 ... 162
3:10, 11 ... 32
4:3 ... 197
4:4, 11, 12 ... 192
4:5 ... 196
4:22 ... 64
4:30-32 ... 155
5:6 ... 64
5:25 ... 234
6:12 ... 81, 184

PHILIPPIANS
1:10 ... 157
2:6, 7 ... 138
2:8-11 ... 51
2:9-11 ... 39
4:5 ... 157

COLOSSIANS
1:6, 23 ... 165
1:26 ... 130, 233
1:26, 27 ... 139
2:8 ... 64, 269
2:9 ... 39
2:15 ... 50, 81
3:4 ... 234
3:4, 5 ... 157, 158

I THESSALONIANS
3:3 ... 100
4:13-17 ... 32, 102, 131
4:16 ... 168
4:16, 17 ... 159, 247, 248
4:16-18 ... 42
4:17 ... 94, 95, 163, 164
4:18 ... 250
5:1-11 ... 132
5:9 ... 101, 104
5:23, 24 ... 156

II THESSALONIANS
2 ... 65
2:3 ... 15, 80
2:3, 8, 9 ... 185
2:4 ... 167, 196
2:6, 7 ... 102
2:7-9 ... 135, 248
2:8-12 ... 66
2:10 ... 64

I TIMOTHY
2:13 ... 62, 220, 221
3:16 ... 135
4:8 ... 21
6:10 ... 64
6:11-14 ... 158
6:15, 16 ... 197
6:20, 21 ... 70

II TIMOTHY
3:8 ... 60
3:13 ... 15
3:16 ... 65
4:1, 2 ... 157
4:8 ... 154

TITUS
2:11-14 ... 156, 157
2:13, 14 ... 157

HEBREWS
1:1, 2 ... 31, 39, 143
1:1-3 ... 33
1:8 ... 45
2:5-9 ... 27
2:8 ... 107
2:14, 15 ... 73, 82
2:16-18 ... 224
3:13 ... 64
5, 6, 7 ... 226
5:1-10 ... 224
6:20 ... 224
7 ... 225
7:1-3 ... 226
7:20-22 ... 224
7:26-28 ... 224
8:1-5 ... 224
9:15 ... 238
9:26 ... 143
10:5-7 ... 40, 228
10:14 ... 224
11 ... 36
11:3 ... 183
11:5, 6 ... 35
12:5-7 ... 104
13:8 ... 136
13:13 ... 234

I PETER
1:3-9 ... 103
1:7 ... 158
1:10, 11 ... 244
1:11 ... 30, 34, 245
1:18-20 ... 42
3:18 ... 10
4:1-3 ... 65
4:7, 8 ... 157
5:8 ... 58

II PETER
1:16-18 ... 32
1:21 ... 180
2:1-3 ... 64
2:5 ... 28
3 ... 152, 153
3:1-13 ... 239
3:3, 4 ... 141, 143, 144, 146, 248, 249
3:5, 6, 7 ... 147
3:8, 9 ... 249, 250
3:11 ... 241
3:12 ... 133
3:13 ... 144

JAMES
1:19 ... 100
5:8 ... 157

I JOHN
1:1-3 ... 40
2:18 ... 144, 184

2:18-23 ... 67
3:2 ... 103
3:3 ... 250
3:8 ... 61, 73
4:1-3 ... 145
4:2 ... 147
4:2, 3 ... 67, 197
4:3 ... 184
4:5 ... 7
4:6, 7 ... 67

II JOHN
7 ... 147, 184

JUDE
11 ... 35
14 ... 27
14, 15 ... 35, 127, 250
16, 17 ... 144

REVELATION
1:2 ... 228
1:4, 5, 13 ... 220, 230
4:1-4 ... 202
4, 5 ... 202, 206
4, 6, 19 ... 200, 206ff
4-18 ... 105
4-19 ... 134
5:1-10 ... 202, 203
5:5-13 ... 51
5:6 ... 229
5:8 ... 231
5:8-10 ... 234
5:9 ... 230
6:2 ... 234
6:16, 17 ... 101, 234
6:17 ... 248
7:1-8 ... 165
7:14 ... 230
9:11 ... 58
11:15 ... 228
12:9 ... 54, 184
12:11 ... 230
12:17 ... 219
13:4-7 ... 200
13:8 ... 231
13:13 ... 168
13:14, 15 ... 166
14:14-20 ... 187
16:16 ... 187
17:14 ... 235
19 ... 127, 168
19:6, 7 ... 45
19:6-9 ... 232
19:10 ... 219, 223
19:11-21 ... 234
19:16 ... 44
20 ... 89, 91, 96, 128
20:2 ... 54
20:4, 5 ... 249
20:10 ... 182
20:12-15 ... 249
21:22, 23 ... 110
21, 22 ... 237
22:20, 21 ... 280

SUBJECT INDEX

Aaron, 224
Abomination of Desolation, 163, 166, 167, 248
Abraham, 28-30, 34, 36, 38, 42, 60, 102, 176, 187, 230, 238, 240
Abrahamic Covenant, 238, 240
Adam, typical of our Lord, 9, 176, 190, 220-222, 234, 238, 275
Ahithophel, defection of, 10
Alford, 219
Amillennial, 22, 149, 150, 195, 199, 209, 243
Anderson, Sir Robert, 120
Antichrist, 59, 72, 80, 94, 122, 135, 184-187, 248, 285
Armageddon, 180
Arnold, Matthew, 157
Asher, 196

Barth, 22, 194
Beast, 165
Beet, 268
Beginning of Sorrows, 160
Bennett, 22

Berkhof, 22, 267, 268
Blessed Hope, 132, 156, 201
Bride, 172, 192, 193
Bridegroom, 171, 173
Brunner, 22

Cain, 59, 184, 273, 274, 275
Christ, see Lord Jesus Christ
Christian realism, 22
Christian Science, 63
Christianity, 20
Church, 98, 101-106, 190-195, 197, 232-234
Church Age, 117, 131
Church fathers, 85, 86, 89, 90
Communism, 68
Coniah, 49
Covenants, 42, 237-241
Cross, 80, 81
Cults, 75, 193

David — prophetic of our Lord, 10
David, King, 13, 46-49, 238
Day of God, 133
Day of Grace, 133
Day of Jehovah, 133
Day of the Lord, 133, 167
Dead Sea, 186
Death, 55
Deception, 59, 65
Decree of God, 45
Deification of man, 122, 185
Democracy, 14
Destruction of Jerusalem, 168
Diaspora, 96
Dictatorship, 14
Divine Revelation, 26

Elijah, 42, 130
Enoch, 34, 35, 42, 127
Eternal state, 59
Everlasting righteousness, 166

Floods, 147
Four Empires and prophecy, 119
Four and twenty elders, 202-205

Gap, 164
Gentiles, 287
Gnosticism, 86, 87, 193, 194
God, government, 114
God, over all program, 116
God, over all purpose, 15, 26, 27
God, program for present hour, 15
God, purpose for man, 26
God, ultimate triumph, 32
Gog, 187
Golden age, 24, 108, 110, 114
Gospel of the kingdom, 164
Great White Throne, 128

Hebrew race, 61

Image of the beast, 166
Incarnation, 136, 137, 245
Isaac, 230
Isaac, prophetic of our Lord, 10
Isaiah, 181
Israel, 42, 101-106, 236-241

Israel, land, 186, 239, 245
Israel, gathering, 285
Israel, restoration, 30, 186, 240, 241
Jechoniah, 49
Jerusalem, 116, 187
Jesus, see Lord Jesus Christ
Jews (see also Israel), oppression, 23
Jews, religion, 258
Jews, restoration, 86
Jews, and Toynbee, 251
Jews, won to Christ, 17
Joseph, 10
Judas Iscariot, 10
Judgment, sheep and goat nations, 130
Judgment, white throne, 128

Kierkegaard, 22
Kingdom of glory, 86
Kingdom of God, 87, 192, 244, 262
Kings, 222
Last Days, 40
Last Things, 282, 283
Lord Jesus Christ—
  advent as king, 225
  coming, 42, 43, 168, 169, 244, 245
  coming as prophet, 29
  coming for the Church, 132, 133, 197, 201
  coming for His own, 129
  coming to establish kingdom, 127, 128, 244, 248
  coming to reign, 31, 114
  executor, 232
  judgment, 86, 249
  judge, 32, 47
  Lamb, 171, 229-235
  return for and to Israel, 29, 30
  return to earth, 31
  right to rule, 31, 47, 51
  Seed of David, 47
  two advents, 212

MacArthur, 136
Man of Sin, 185
Marriage Supper, 171
Melchizedek, 60, 225
Messiah, 103, 226, 244-246
Messianic Kingdom, 244
Millennium, 91, 99, 127, 133, 198, 199, 209, 210, 216
Millennial earth, 130
Millennial kingdom, 25, 47, 88, 89, 117, 125, 126, 128-130, 146, 199, 216, 269
Milliken, 183
Morgan, 155
Moses, 36, 37, 186, 223, 238
Mosaic Covenant, 238
Mullins, 24
Mystery of Iniquity, 248

Near East, 186
Negev, 186
New Covenant, 238
Niebuhr, 22, 259
Nimrod, 184
Noah, 36, 158, 237, 272

Olivet Discourse, 159-162, 168-170
Origen, 89

Parables, 208-217
Partial Rapture, 126
Passover Lamb, 230
Pentecost, 16
Perilous Times, 191
Philosophy, 24
Platonic philosophy, 264
Postmillennialism, 21, 22, 199
Posttribulation, 125, 134, 199, 201
Prehistoric man, 220
Premillennialism, 20-25, 91, 199, 243, 248, 271
Present age, 212
Pretribulation, 125, 131, 198, 199, 200, 201
Priests, 222
Primal prophecy, 220
Primitive revelation, 27
Promised land, 28, 285
Prophets, 222
Purity, 158

Ramm, 243
Rapture, 94, 95, 102, 121, 130, 133, 134, 141, 164, 182, 244, 248, 280
Rapture, partial, 126
Rebellion against God, 122
Rees, 156
Remnant, 263
Resurrection, 128, 131, 146, 186
Robertson, 156
Roman Catholicism, 97
Roman Empire, 87, 88, 121, 123

Satan, 53-72, 185
Sealed Book, 207
Second Coming of Christ (see Lord Jesus Christ), 126, 127, 141, 152-158, 182
Seed of woman, 57
Sermon on the Mount, 209
Seventieth Week, 105, 106, 161, 200, 287
Seventy weeks, 103, 120, 226, 283
Sin, 55
Son of Perdition, 185
Social Gospel, 150
Syncretism of Religions, 256

Temptation, 77
Theocracy, 114
Theology of Crisis, 22
Time of Sorrows, 161
Time of Troubles, 254
Times of the Gentiles, 116-124
Toynbee, 251
Transfiguration, 32
Translation, 131, 133
Tribulation, 41, 68, 86, 94-96, 98-106, 117, 125, 126, 134, 149, 165-168, 182, 199, 200, 228, 280
Trump, last, 129, 131
Trumpets, 131
Twenty-four elders, 202-207

World Church, 64, 195
World council, 195
World government, 64
World war, 22

Zionism, 257, 259